Working with Children and Young People

Open University module:
Working with children, young people and families

This Reader, along with the companion volume *Children and Young People's Spaces: Developing Practice* edited by Pam Foley and Stephen Leverett, forms part of the Open University module Working with children, young people and families (K218), a 60-point, second-level undergraduate module. The Readers are also part of the module K229 Social work with children, young people and families which is a compulsory component of the Open University BA (Hons) Social Work: Scotland.

Details of this and other Open University modules and qualifications can be obtained from the Student Registration and Enquiry Service, The Open University, PO Box 197, Milton Keynes MK7 6BJ, UK: Telephone +44 (0) 845 300 6090, email general-enquiries@open.ac.uk.

Alternatively, you may wish to visit the Open University website at http://www.open.ac.uk, where you can learn more about the wide range of modules and qualifications offered at all levels by The Open University.

Working with Children and Young People

Co-constructing Practice

Edited by

Lindsay O'Dell
Stephen Leverett

First published 2011 by
PALGRAVE MACMILLAN

Palgrave Macmillan in the UK is an imprint of Macmillan Publishers Limited,
registered in England, company number 785998, of Houndmills, Basingstoke,
Hampshire RG21 6XS.

Palgrave Macmillan in the US is a division of St Martin's Press LLC,
175 Fifth Avenue, New York, NY 10010.

Palgrave Macmillan is the global academic imprint of the above companies
and has companies and representatives throughout the world.

Palgrave® and Macmillan® are registered trademarks in the United States,
the United Kingdom, Europe and other countries.

ISBN: 978–0–230–28008–3

This book is printed on paper suitable for recycling and made from fully
managed and sustained forest sources. Logging, pulping and manufacturing
processes are expected to conform to the environmental regulations of the
country of origin.

A catalogue record for this book is available from the British Library.

A catalog record for this book is available from the Library of Congress.

10 9 8 7 6 5 4 3 2 1
20 19 18 17 16 15 14 13 12 11

Printed in China

Contents

Acknowledgements

The authors and publishers wish to thank the following for permission to use copyright material: United Nations Children's Fund (UNICEF) for Figure 1.1, originally Figure 1.0 from UNICEF Innocenti Research Centre (2007) *Child Poverty in Perspective: An Overview of Child Well-being in Rich Countries*, Report Card 7.

The editors would also like to thank Tabatha Torrance, Linda Camborne-Paynter and Gill Gowans from The Open University.

Every effort has been made to trace the copyright-holders, but if any have been inadvertently overlooked the publishers will be pleased to make the necessary arrangements at the first opportunity.

List of contributors

Lisa Arai is a social scientist with a public health background. Her work and research interests are primarily concerned with the health and wellbeing of children and young people, and she has special interests in teenage pregnancy, the design and evaluation of interventions, access to services and methodological innovation. Her most recent publication is *Teenage Pregnancy: The Making and Unmaking of a Problem* (Policy Press, 2009). She has worked for the Medical Research Council and at the Institute of Education, University of London and is currently a Senior Lecturer in the School of Health and Social Care at Teesside University.

Sarah Crafter is a Senior Lecturer in the Psychology of Human Development and Culture at the University of Northampton. Her research interests include home and school mathematics learning in multicultural communities, learner identities, children who work, young caring, language brokering and representations of the build and space in child and adolescent mental health services.

Alison Davies qualified as a counsellor in 2006 from the University of Hertfordshire, where she studied psychodynamic and person-centred models of counselling. She works integratively with adults and children. She spent two years as a counsellor with the Place2Be, a school-based counselling service. Currently, she practises part time from a therapeutic centre in Hertfordshire where she mainly counsels children under 10. She is a member of the British Association for Counselling and Psychotherapy. Alison is a full-time PhD student with the Open University, researching the discursive practices around the medicalisation of behaviour within education, specifically with reference to ADHD.

Pam Foley is a Senior Lecturer at the Open University's Faculty of Health and Social Care, writing and teaching the distance learning courses for students and practitioners working with children, young people and families. Her research interests include social policy affecting children and young people and children's agency. She has co-edited several books for students and practitioners, including *Children and Society: Contemporary Theory, Policy and Practice* (Palgrave Macmillan, 2001) and *Connecting with Children: Developing Working Relationships* (Policy Press, 2008).

Dan Goodley is Professor of Psychology and Disability Studies, the father of two girls, ally to the self-advocacy group Huddersfield People First and a long-suffering Nottingham Forest fan. His research and teaching aims to shake up dominant myths in psychology as well as contributing, in some small way, to the development of critical disability studies theories that understand and eradicate disablism. His most recent publication is *Disability Studies: An Interdisciplinary Introduction* (Sage, 2010).

Wook Hamilton works for Young People in Focus, a national charity support-ing practitioners who work with young people through research, training and publications. Here she manages a project for practitioners working with parents of young people, as well as delivering training courses on young people's mental health. Her background includes training and working as a counsellor for many years in voluntary sector mental health organisations; she has worked in schools with groups of young people and taught adults in many capacities, including teaching social sciences for the Open University.

Amanda Holt is Senior Lecturer in Criminal Psychology at the Institute of Criminal Justice Studies at the University of Portsmouth. Her current research includes exploring anti-violence strategies in schools, adolescent-to-parent violence in the family home and issues around subjectivity in qualitative data analysis. She teaches on a range of criminology, criminal psychology and foren-sics courses at undergraduate and postgraduate levels.

Gail Jackson is a social worker, having previously fostered from 2001 to 2008 for the local authority and the independent sector. Gail's views about the position of sons and daughters within foster care have been particularly informed by the experiences of her own two sons.

Tracy Kelly-Freer qualified as a primary teacher specialising in the early years, and has led practice and worked in early years and primary settings in Worcestershire. During this time, she studied developmentally appropriate curricula in early years and the importance of the outdoor classroom, studying the former as a Masters degree. Since 2000, she has worked as a Senior Lecturer in Education at the University of Worcester undergraduate and postgraduate primary education programmes, Early Childhood Studies course and has become an Early Years Professional Status assessor and a Forest School leader. Forest School is the focus of her current study for a PhD.

Gerison Lansdown was the founder director of the Children's Rights Alliance for England, and is now an international children's rights consultant and advo-cate in children's rights. She was actively involved in drafting the Convention on the Rights of Persons with Disabilities, is an Honorary Fellow of UNICEF UK, an associate of the International Institute for Child Rights and Development in Victoria, Canada, and co-director of CRED-PRO, an international initiative to develop educational programmes on the human rights of children for professionals working with children. Her publications include *The Evolving Capacities of the Child* (UNICEF, 2005) and *See Me, Hear Me: A Guide to the UN Convention on the Rights of Persons with Disabilities to Promote the Rights of Children* (Save the Children, 2009).

Stephen Leverett is a Lecturer in Children and Young People at the Open University's Faculty of Health and Social Care. He has a practice background in social care and social work in the statutory and voluntary sectors. He co-edited *Connecting with Children: Developing Working Relationships* (Policy Press, 2008).

Lindsay O'Dell is a Lecturer and Director of Postgraduate Studies at the Open University's Faculty of Health and Social Care. Her research interests focus on children who are in some way 'different', including sexually abused children, children with a visible difference and children with autism.

Andy Rixon is a Lecturer in Children and Young People at the Open University's Faculty of Health and Social Care. He has a background in social work practice and in education, training and development in children's services. Contributions to publications for students and practitioners include those to *Youth in Context: Frameworks, Settings and Encounters* (Sage/OU, 2007) and *Critical Practice with Children and Young People* (Policy Press, 2010). He also co-edited *Changing Children's Services: Working and Learning Together* (Policy Press/OU, 2008).

Katherine Runswick-Cole is a Research Associate at Manchester Metropolitan University where she works on *Does Every Child Matter, Post Blair? The Interconnections of Disabled Childhoods*, a project funded by the Economic and Social Research Council. A former early years teacher, she has a MA (Hons) in Modern History and Philosophy from the University of St Andrews and a BSc (Hons) in Psychology from the Open University. She completed her PhD in 2007 in the Department of Educational Studies at Sheffield University, since when she has focused her teaching in higher education and research on disability and the family.

Peter Squires is a Professor of Criminology and Public Policy at the University of Brighton. His recent research interests have spanned youth criminalisation and anti-social behaviour management to issues concerning urban violence, weaponisation and 'gangsterisation', and policing responses. His key publications include

Gun Culture or Gun Control? (Routledge, 2000), *Young People and Anti-social Behaviour* (Willan, 2005), *ASBO Nation* (Policy Press, 2008) and *Shooting to Kill?: Policing, Firearms and Armed Response?* (Wiley/Blackwell, 2010).

Peter Unwin is a Senior Lecturer at the University of Worcester who is committed to raising the profile of children who use social care. Together with his wife, he is a foster carer for a local authority. Peter is also a panel member of an independent sector agency and practises as a social work assessor of potential foster families.

Introduction

Lindsay O'Dell and Stephen Leverett

In this book we examine working with children and young people within a changing landscape of practice, policy and public opinion. Many of the profound changes in the organisation and focus of the children's workforce in the UK can be linked to wider political, social, cultural and economic changes. Since the 1970s, globalisation has led to greater mobility of capital and populations between communities and nations, and the process of individualisation, started in the 1960s, has evolved and interrelated with the later emergent emphasis on consumption and choice (Parton, 2006). As a result, in the early twenty-first century, practice with children and young people operates within a context of changing family structures and networks of support, a mixed economy (involving state, private and third sector agencies) of health, social care and education, and intense media scrutiny. There have been political and policy changes including a divergence of practice approaches and frameworks across the four UK nations, greater government regulation of services and the reorganisation of the children's workforce in pursuit of a wide range of economic, health and social goals. There has also been a shift in emphasis in children's services, policy and research towards partnership working with children and young people rather than imposing practice solutions on them. In part this has been the result of the United Nations Convention on the Rights of the Child, which has also been influential in exposing and changing government policy on children's rights (for example in 2008, the UK government finally extended the 'best interest' rule to immigrant children), although criticisms are still levelled at the UK's record on corporal punishment (UN Committee on the Rights of the Child, 2008).

In the book we draw on these developments to discuss, interrogate and generate new approaches to practice. We have framed the book using perspectives from social ecological and social constructionist theorisation to discuss and deconstruct changing childhoods, social policies and practice relationships across time and through geopolitical contexts. In particular, in the book these perspectives have been used to argue that policy and practice approaches are not simply directed at childhood, families and social problems, but are implicated in how these concepts are created or reproduced. In addition, the perspectives also allow us to argue that the difficulties facing children, young people and families are not purely nested within the individual relationships but are 'nested' within many layers of meaning.

The book draws on the broad theoretical move to a critical approach to knowledge and practice. It is informed by a social constructionist theoretical framework, drawing on 'deconstruction' and 'co-construction' as tools with which to question dominant knowledge and practice to enable these to be scrutinised. The emphasis on power in practice relationships is open to scrutiny and ideas about how practice can be co-constructed between practitioners, children, young people and their families are discussed in a number of settings in the book. We also place the discussion within an ecological perspective that keeps the child or young person at the centre. The theoretical underpinnings of the book are described briefly here to provide readers with a backdrop against which the chapters in the book can be viewed.

Social ecology

Bronfenbrenner's (1979) original social ecological model highlighted that the ability of parents to help and support their children could be affected by wider environmental factors including social networks with friends and neighbours, employment responsibilities, availability of childcare, degree of safety in the immediate neighbourhood and the quality of welfare services. Bronfenbrenner's model represented these as a series of four nested environments with the child at the heart.

Others have adapted this model, with the individual child at the centre interacting first with their primary carers and extended family, second with direct (for example schools) and indirect (for example parents' workplace) neighbourhood and social contacts and finally with cultural beliefs, expectations and values at the societal level. The model has been widely and critically adapted in relation to a range of issues, including parenting and child development (Jack, 2000; Aldgate, 2006), child abuse (Sidebottom, 2001), assessment (Jack, 2001), work with families experiencing poverty (Gill and Jack, 2008), and promoting physical activity and health (Cochrane and Davey, 2008). The model has been widely drawn upon in practice guidance and government policy. It is clearly articulated in, for example, *Getting it Right for Every Child* (Scottish Executive, 2008), which draws explicitly on a social ecological model to keep the child at the centre of all practice and planning, and the *Framework for the Assessment of Children in Need and their Families* (DH, 2000), with its three overlapping domains of children's needs, parental capacity and wider family and environmental factors.

Although the social ecological perspective has a strong emphasis in practice, it does have limitations that need to be taken into consideration when applying it. First, it may only be a snapshot in time representing the interrelationships between a child and their surrounding environment, in which case it is necessary to also consider changes to the child in terms of their development (Sidebottom, 2001) and, as highlighted in this book, their evolving capacity (see Gerison Lansdown's discussion in Chapter 11). Second, the model can imply a deterministic view of the world in which certain events or factors predict particular behaviours or events. However, it is possible to use a social ecological perspective as a basis for reflecting on probable rather than absolute consequences; for example in child protection, an observed 'factor may increase or decrease the probability of abuse occurring but cannot determine it' (Sidebottom, 2001, p. 108).

A key tenet of a critical perspective on knowledge is that ideas, experiences and understandings are not easily reducible to an individualised, causal model in which it can be demonstrated that, for example, poor parenting caused a child to perform badly at school. Rather, it is possible to argue that difficulties and issues facing children, young people and families are a complex web of interrelated factors. Research consistently shows, for example, how children and young people's life chances and different areas of development can be negatively affected by a range of family factors, including parental poverty (Duncan and Brookes-Gunn, 2000), disablism (Broomfield, 2004; Mencap, 2007) and poor housing (Rice, 2006; Harker, 2006), which in turn are interrelated to wider community, cultural, societal and global factors. However, resiliency research drawing upon an ecological model also highlights how protective factors, such as consistent relationships, social capital and networks of support, located within the child, their family and the wider social ecology can offset or minimise the impact of negative factors (Masten and Powell, 2003).

Another way of dealing with these critiques is to use the social ecological perspective alongside a social constructionist approach. One of the advantages of an ecological approach in terms of assessing and supporting children is that it can provide a way of organising different, even competing theoretical explanations (Seden, 2006). This enables the possibility of considering multiple meanings (including those of children and young people themselves) of interrelationships between children and their environment and how these change over time. By bringing social constructionist and social ecological perspectives together, it is possible to broaden the scope beyond predetermined behavioural goals to consider the subjective realities and alternative pathways that enable children and young people to survive adversity, even where these behaviours and solutions may be considered 'deviant and disordered' (Ungar, 2004, p. 360). The value of this can be found in Peter Squires' work (Chapter 12), where he discusses a reconstruction of gang culture in relation to young people's agency and social ecology. This is an example of young people constructing their own spatial and relational boundaries in order manage their day-to-day lives, in contrast to formal societal boundaries.

Drawing on a combined social constructionist and social ecological perspective also allows practitioners to connect issues of power, geographical location and agency and their role in practice. In Chapter 6, Alison Davis, a counsellor who works with children and young people, discusses how her practice is impacted by the material circumstances of children's lives such as poverty, absent parents and so on. She reflects upon how, as an individual practitioner, she engages with the wider social ecological issues that impact upon the child (both as a barrier and strength/resource).

Social construction

The notion of 'construction' is drawn on as a central theoretical tool in this book to reflect the view that knowledge is produced through discourse, where the activities of many different stakeholders, such as children and young people, families and practitioners, and the wider socio-cultural discourse found, for example, in everyday media and policy agendas are all implicated in the co-construction of knowledge. Although Hacking (1999, p. vii) argued that the term 'social construction' is often 'obscure and over used', it is evident that a move towards looking at the social world as socially constructed has begun to be incorporated into mainstream thinking. While we recognise that 'we cannot hope to do justice to all parties' (Hacking, 1999, p. 5), there are some key aspects of the theoretical perspective drawn on in this book that we will detail here.

The theoretical approach argues that knowledge is socially produced through discourse, that is, through language and through social practices. As such, all knowledge is produced within particular socio-cultural locations and therefore it is difficult to sustain generalised, universal 'truths' about any phenomena such as children's capabilities and the notion of 'development', for example. Theoretically, social constructionist work does not seek to define issues and suggests that we 'don't ask for the meaning, ask what's the point' (Hacking, 1999, p. 5). An explicit focus of social constructionist work is on challenging 'taken-for-granted' truths and the established order of things (Gergen and Gergen, 2003; Burr, 2003). The theoretical approach therefore argues that we live in a socially constructed world within which multiple meanings coexist and compete for legitimacy.

A key aspect of social construction is the extent to which the focus of practice and the meanings behind it vary across space and time. This is clearly articulated in relation to understandings of family in Lindsay O'Dell's work (Chapter 2) and parenting and parenting support in Amanda Holt's work (Chapter 13). It is also addressed in Dan Goodley and Katherine Runswick-Cole's work (Chapter 5), in which they have compared disablism with ableism to consider how these are constructed and experienced by young children, parents/carers and practitioners. Changes in practice are also discussed by Wook Hamilton in Chapter 7, where she considers how different constructions of mental health and youth are realised within different practice approaches.

The view that childhood is a constructed rather than 'natural' state is a key theme for much research and practice with children, young people and families. In this book, the social construction of childhood is evident through most of the chapters, for example in the contributions by Alison Davies (Chapter 6), Tracy Kelly-Freer (Chapter 14) and Gail Jackson and Peter Unwin (Chapter 9). These authors argue that positioning a child as dependent and vulnerable does not fully address the lived lives of the children and young people who the authors have worked with. In Chapter 8, Lisa Arai argues that viewing children and young people as vulnerable and 'damaged' through exposure to domestic abuse in their family presents a particular set of concerns and issues for practitioners seeking to support children and their parents.

A critical perspective on the notion of 'development', suggesting that there is not one universal path of development that all children and young people follow (or are seen to fail), is addressed within the book. In Chapter 11, Gerison Lansdown draws on the concept of developing capacities in a discussion of children's rights. In their work on parents and disabled babies (Chapter 5), Dan Goodley and Katherine Runswick-Cole argue that the proposition of a single pathway of development is a powerful and oppressive framework with which families with a disabled child are often forced to engage. They suggest alternative ways of conceptualising development and practice to work with families with young disabled children.

A key aspect of a social constructionist approach is to scrutinise, or deconstruct, how current taken-for-granted truths about children, young people and families are produced and maintained, to ask questions such as: 'Whose interest are being met? Who is rendered marginal, invisible or problematic?' For example, the construction of some children, young people and parents as problematic is evident in Gail Jackson and Peter Unwin's work on foster carers (Chapter 9), Peter Squires' work on young people and 'gangs' (Chapter 12) and Amanda Holt's work on parenting support (Chapter 13).

One of our intentions is to encourage readers to critically approach and deconstruct aspects of practice. This can operate at many different levels, for example some chapters examine how, at the macro-level, policy designed to enable good practice with children and young people also serves other ideological causes such as the economic and employment needs of the nation (see Pam Foley's discussion in Chapter 4), or leads to seemingly unintended consequences such as surveillance and suspicion (see Lisa Arai's work in Chapter 3). In contrast, chapters focusing on the micro-level deconstruct practice to reveal that there is no singular way in which children experience the world, for example in terms of experiences at school (see Sarah Crafter's work on multicultural classrooms, Chapter 10) and children's wellbeing (see Andy Rixon's discussion in Chapter 1).

While deconstruction of practice is a worthwhile activity in its own right, our intention is also to consider how practice is productive. Practice is not just something that is done to people, it is a process through which practitioners and service users position and influence themselves and each other. This involves consideration not only of structural forces such as belief systems and institutional power but also the agency of practitioners, parents, carers and children and young people. We have used the term 'co-construction' in the book to denote the shared processes involved in practice with children, young people and families. Ideas about co-construction have been discussed in a variety of arenas in the social sciences and in social research such as linguistics, education and socio-cultural theory. We are drawing on the work of theorists such as Rogoff (2003) and Lave and Wenger (1991) to argue that meanings and understanding are not an individual 'cognition' but arise between people and are linked to wider discourses.

In its broadest sense, co-construction is a process involving a shared version of reality or practice between various people in a practice situation, such as in nursing research where paediatric nurses and families co-construct meanings when working together to care for a sick child (Meiers and Tomlinson, 2003).

Sarah Crafter's work (Chapter 10) draws explicitly on a socio-cultural theoretical position in which the notion of co-construction is central to her work with newly immigrant children and their families. She discusses how the middle classes align their discourses with those of formal schooling, while other families remain marginalised. She argues that learners do not operate without reference to family, wider community and society.

Co-construction operates not just at the level of individuals but also involves institutions, policy and broad socio-cultural influences that are key in co-constructing practice. For example, the different policy and legislative contexts of the four nations of the UK have given rise to different forms of practice. In Chapter 13, Amanda Holt discusses the ways in which this has led to different experiences of parental 'support' in Scotland (where Parenting Orders are not routinely administered) in contrast to England. A further example of how practice is linked to broad levels of influence concerns the ways in which policy initiatives become enacted within particular institutions. For example, initiatives such as resilience training (as discussed by Wook Hamilton in Chapter 7) are successful depending upon the level at which they are 'bought into' by the institution (such as school) that needs to roll out the programme. At an institutional level, policy is instrumental in providing a context through which practice occurs, which is addressed by Pam Foley (Chapter 4), Gerison Lansdown (Chapter 11) and Peter Squires (Chapter 12). In these chapters and others (such as Amanda Holt's work in Chapter 13 and Lisa Arai's work on surveillance in Chapter 3), the authors highlight the role of the media in the co-construction of language and opinion that is often addressed within policy debates.

The structure of the book

In Part I, four chapters outline key theoretical perspectives and conceptual issues. These reflect upon various 'layers' of influence on children, young people, families and practice. In some cases, this involves challenging cultural or societal expectations and norms, and in other cases, it involves practitioners democratically sharing their individual or institutional power with children, young people and families. Part I introduces the theoretical concepts and shows how, together, they shape policy development and practice involving children, young people and families.

In Part II, a range of authors considers what it means to 'co-construct practice', with reference to the theoretical perspectives and conceptual issues discussed in Part I, and highlights the ways in which these perspectives are used to frame the themes and values for practice. Authors challenge existing, or promote alternative, constructions of childhood, families, communities, 'problems', practitioners and practice. These chapters represent a range of contexts and practice approaches from the children's workforce, community/voluntary groups and academics outlining new developments and innovative possibilities. The authors reflect upon their own practice, either as direct practitioners working with children, young people and families or as academic practitioners who have researched the issues in a particular area of practice. In some, the authors consider examples where these practice approaches are built upon, or contribute to, research and evidence-based practice. The topics addressed in Part II are not intended to be a fully comprehensive 'list' of all aspects of work with children, young people and families, but provide an illustration of key themes, concerns and priorities for practice.

References

Aldgate, J. (2006) 'Children, development and ecology', in J. Aldgate, D. Jones, W. Rose and C. Jeffrey (eds) *The Developing World of the Child*, London, Jessica Kingsley, pp. 17–35.

Bronfenbrenner, U. (1979) *The Ecology of Human Development: Experiments by Nature and Design*, Cambridge, MA, Harvard University Press.

Broomfield, A. (ed.) (2004) *Celebrating Diversity: Review 2002–2004*, London, Parents for Inclusion.

Burman, E. (2007) *Deconstructing Developmental Psychology* (2nd edn), New York, Routledge.

Burr, V. (2003) *Social Constructionism*, New York, Routledge.

Cochrane, T. and Davey, R.C. (2008) 'Increasing uptake of physical activity: A social ecological approach', *The Journal of the Royal Society for the Promotion of Health*, 128: 31.

DH (Department of Health) (2000) *Framework for the Assessment of Children in Need and their Families*, London, TSO.

Duncan, G.J. and Brooks-Gunn, J. (2000) 'Family poverty, welfare reform, and child development', *Child Development*, **71**(1): 188–96.

Gergen, M. and Gergen, K.J. (2003) *Social Construction: A Reader*, London, Sage.

Gill, O. and Jack, G. (2008) 'Poverty and the child's world: Assessing children's needs', *Poverty*, 129: 15–17.

Hacking, I. (1999) *The Social Construction of What?*, Cambridge, MA, Harvard University Press.

Harker, L. (2006) *Chance of a Lifetime: The Impact of Bad Housing on Children's Lives*, Shelter, London, http://england.shelter.org.uk/__data/assets/pdf_file/0016/39202/Chance_of_a_Lifetime.pdf [Accessed 12 May 2010].

Jack, G. (2000) 'Ecological influences on parenting and child development', *British Journal of Social Work*, 30: 703–20.

Jack, G. (2001) 'Ecological perspectives in assessing children and their families', in J. Horwath (ed.) *The Child's World*, London, Jessica Kingsley, pp. 53–75.

Lave, J. and Wenger, E. (1991) *Situated Learning: Legitimate Peripheral Participation*, Cambridge, Cambridge University Press.

Masten, A.S. and Powell, J.L. (2003) 'A resiliency framework for research, policy and practice', in S. Luthar (ed.) *Resiliency and Vulnerability: Adaptation in the Context of Childhood Adversity*, Cambridge University Press, Cambridge, pp. 1–29.

Meiers, S.J. and Tomlinson, P.S. (2003) 'Family-nurse co-construction of meaning: A central phenomenon of family caring', *Scandinavian Journal of Caring Sciences*, **17**(2): 193–201.

Mencap (2007) Disablist bullying is wrecking children's lives says Mencap, available online at http://www.mencap.org.uk/news.asp?id=2355 [Accessed 12 April 2010].

Parton, N. (2006) *Safeguarding Childhood: Early Intervention and Surveillance in a Late Modern Society*, Basingstoke, Palgrave Macmillan.

Rice, B. (2006) *Against the Odds: An Investigation Comparing the Lives of Children on either Side of Britain's Housing Divide*, London, Shelter.

Rogoff, B. (2003) *The Cultural Nature of Human Development*, Oxford, Oxford University Press.

Scottish Executive (2007) *Getting it Right for Every Child: Guidance on the Child's or Young Person's Plan*, Edinburgh, Scottish Executive.

Seden, J. (2006) 'Frameworks and theories', in J. Aldgate, D. Jones, W. Rose and C. Jeffrey (eds) *The Developing World of the Child*, London, Jessica Kingsley, pp. 35–55.

Sidebottom, P. (2001) 'An ecological approach to child abuse: A creative use of scientific models in research and practice', *Child Abuse Review*, 10: 97–112.

UN Committee on the Rights of the Child (2008) *Concluding Observations: United Kingdom of Great Britain and Northern Ireland*, 20 October 2008, CRC/C/GBR/CO/4.

Ungar, M. (2004) 'A constructionist discourse on resilience: Multiple contexts, multiple realities among at-risk children and youth', *Youth Society*, 35: 341.

Part I

Constructing and deconstructing practice

1

Wellbeing and the ecology of children's lives

Andy Rixon

It has become increasingly accepted that children's development and wellbeing are influenced by a wide range of factors in the environment in which they live. This social ecological perspective proposes that a child's genetic make-up and individual characteristics interact with their immediate network but also with influences deriving from factors as diverse as their family's economic resources, the nature of community in which they live, and even what they encounter on television and the internet, in fact, features of a whole array of broad economic, social and cultural factors. As outlined in the Introduction to this book, this perspective is most frequently described by a number of concentric circles representing layers of influence, drawing on Bronfenbrenner's (1979) model of child development. Although these 'layers' are helpful to grasp the concept, their reality is complex, with interactions between the layers and some factors in a layer being more influential than others. It might also suggest that factors in the outer layers have only a peripheral impact, whereas, although family factors are likely to be the most influential, broad social influences – 'forces emanating from more remote regions in the larger physical and social milieu' (Bronfenbrenner, 1979, p. 13) – can also reach deep into the centrality of children's lives and have a significant effect on their wellbeing. This chapter will use this perspective to explore some examples of these 'forces' to illustrate the debates around them and their effects.

However, before discussing the impact of any factor on the wellbeing of children, when we, as a society, consider 'wellbeing', are we all thinking about the same thing? We are concerned for children's wellbeing but how do we know if they are 'well'? How do we define it, what tools are being deployed to measure it and how does this shape services for children? Wellbeing might appear to be a commonsense concept but, on closer inspection, the picture is more complex, with a range of definitions and constructions that will be highlighted below.

Finally, what are the implications, if any, for practice? The development of children's services will be shaped partly by different political and policy interpretations of wellbeing and of how these social, cultural and economic influences impact on children – not all interpretations of what is best for children are fully compatible with each other. For practitioners who have to operate within these services, this 'big picture' shapes their everyday work yet can often seem to be something not just outside their control but outside their frame of reference. The final question the chapter will consider is whether practice with children, young people, and their families can take account of the wider influences upon it.

Wellbeing?

What as a society we believe is 'good' for children partly depends on what we believe about the nature of children and childhood and this is neither static nor uncontested. Views on children and their development vary between cultures and over time (Seden, 2006; Timimi, 2009). The ecological perspective has proposed a framework within which the development of children's lives can be viewed but it does not necessarily define what is good or bad for children. However, assumptions about this are important, given that they are central to decisions about policy, the shape of services for children and, in turn, the day-to-day decisions taken by practitioners tasked with assessing and ensuring children's wellbeing.

Axford (2008) has explored some of the definitional complexities of wellbeing and their implications for children's services. He has proposed that there are at least five different conceptual approaches to the way in which children's wellbeing is currently defined – those of need, rights, poverty, quality of life and social exclusion – all of which have their own further definitional problems. A closer look at one example, that of 'need', drawing on Axford's analysis, helps to illustrate the problem being drawn attention to.

'Need' has for many years been a key concept in work with children and their families – of central importance in assessment and as a way of distributing resources. This stems largely from the centrality of 'children in need' in the Children Act 1989, the Children (Northern Ireland) Order 1995, and the Children (Scotland) Act 1995, including the requirement for local authorities to establish the number of children in need in their area and to 'safeguard and promote' their welfare. In 2000, the Department of Health first estimated that out of 11 million children in England, there were 4 million 'vulnerable' children, and of these 300–400,000 children were 'in need' at any one time (DH, 2000). Further research in 2008 suggested children in need numbered 416,400 (Mahon, 2008). Once the scale and nature of need has been identified, this is intended to provide the basis for services being 'needs led'. In reality, measuring levels of need has been notoriously difficult for local authorities to achieve and the link to the planned prioritisation of resources is often unclear (Tisdall and Plows, 2007; Axford et al., 2008).

The main focus within legislation, in relation to defining the wellbeing of children, is on health and development and their likelihood of a 'reasonable standard' being achieved or 'significantly impaired' – all terms which themselves require further layers of interpretation. The key practice tools for children identified as being in need are the assessment frameworks, which are used to assess the 'welfare' (DH, 2000) or 'total wellbeing' (Scottish Executive, 2007) of children. These frameworks describe themselves as following an 'ecological' model and identify 20 or more 'dimensions', some focusing on the child's developmental needs, some on the ability of parents and carers to meet those needs, and some on the wider environment including school, community, and finances. The English *Common Assessment Framework for Children and Young People* was introduced as a standardised approach to conducting assessments of children's 'additional needs' (Children's Workforce Development Council, 2009).

Axford (2008) also pointed out that several different aspects of 'need' are frequently deployed in studies that attempt to measure it including individuals articulating their own needs (categorised as 'felt need'), measuring the level of demand for services (expressed need), using socio-demographic indicators of service recipients (comparative need), and a focus on outcome measures of key indicators like health, nutrition and education (normative need). In practice, studies often use a mixture of measures, such as surveys of children and their family's own views on their needs, alongside the presentation of more 'scientific' data using quantified dimensions of need, such as family relations and housing (Axford, 2008, p. 22).

A key point here is that the shape of children's services and modes of practice will vary depending on the approach taken to classifying and measuring wellbeing. Children who are 'poor' are not necessarily 'in need' and not all socially excluded children are poor and vice versa, so a service or strategy targeting one group will miss a proportion of the other (Axford, 2008). It is also possible to argue that a rights-based approach to wellbeing does not emphasise the relational aspects central to a good quality of life or reducing social exclusion. A right to protection may result in strategies that lead to services focused on checklists of standards and procedures rather than the actual quality of care provided (Axford, 2008).

Ultimately, behind these different approaches lie different ideas about children and young people – different constructions of childhood. The extent of the weight placed on children's views is likely to be less in an assessment based on need, since this approach has tended to view children more as the needy, passive 'objects' of professional expertise and recipients of services rather than active 'agents' with views and knowledge of their own. As a result, practice (and practitioners) may be more or less aware of power relations and therefore place more or less emphasis on empowerment. In fact, the differences could be more radical – Moss and Petrie (2002) have argued that portraying children as passive and needy and therefore requiring protection has been very much the dominant discourse of children's services. They questioned how these services might look if children were seen as 'strong, rich in resources and competent' (Moss and Petrie, 2002, p. 56) and argued that services could then be reconceptualised as 'spaces' co-constructed with children.

Attempts have also been made to use a variety of measures to gain a more multidimensional understanding of wellbeing. Bradshaw (2008), for example, described a model using 53 indicators clustered under eight headings – material situation, housing, health, education, children's relationships, civic participation, risk and safety, and, importantly, children's subjective wellbeing. This multidimensional approach was adopted by UNICEF when reporting on the wellbeing of children in rich countries (Bradshaw et al., 2007). Although the figures used for this report were challenged by the UK government as being out of date (Murphy, 2007), the UK was ranked as having the lowest child wellbeing indicators out of 21 industrialised countries overall (UNICEF, 2007).

This UNICEF report highlighted the subjective wellbeing of children and young people and clearly illustrates how the order of countries in the 'league table' of wellbeing according to this criterion does not match that of other more formal measures such as education and health and safety. Research in the UK suggests that life events and the quality of relationships are highly significant factors in subjective wellbeing, for example levels of family conflict and experiences of bullying (Rees et al., 2009). Children and young people's accounts of their wellbeing may frequently be at variance with the views of adults and the priorities of policy makers. But wellbeing also needs to be understood from within their experience, which perhaps suggests the need for a more sophisticated understanding to provide an insight into how children and young people define their wellbeing and how services could respond more appropriately.

Poor, excluded, unequal

Some children described how they tried to help reduce poverty-related stress for their parents by limiting what they asked for, including keeping school trips secret from parents because they did not want them to have the worry of paying for them or to face the stress of having to decide whether they could be afforded. At the same time, children were also upset by the deprivation, and by missing out on experiences and things their friends had. (Hooper et al., 2007, p. 61)

Within the ecological framework, socio-economic circumstances can exert a powerful influence on the lives of children. Although there are debates around the right way to define this socio-economic 'issue', its impact on children is clearly recognised as a political and policy concern. This section will explore this as one illustration of the impact of the broader context on children and their wellbeing.

Poverty is another of the lenses through which the wellbeing of children can be viewed and services shaped (Axford, 2008). Although definitions vary, it is widely understood as a negative influence on many of the key aspects of children's lives, including parenting (Ghate and Hazel, 2002), communities (Palmer et al., 2005; Hudson et al., 2007), health outcomes (Salway et al., 2007) and educational outcomes – aspects of which are already apparent when children are as young as three years old (Hirsch, 2007). By the end of the twentieth century, the UK had the highest rate of children living in poverty in Europe (Bradbury and Jänetti, 1999). Tackling child poverty was declared a priority by the Labour government in 1999, planning to halve it within 10 years and eradicate it by 2020.

Also, although average incomes are a common measure of poverty, its real impact needs to take into consideration its chronic or short-term nature as well as other factors such as 'place', that is, comparisons with families around them (Hooper et al., 2007). The overall figures for child poverty can also disguise how different sections of the population are disproportionately affected; while 15% of children in the UK are from Black and minority ethnic groups, they make up 25% (over 700,000) of children who are in poverty. Within these figures, further significant variations can be found between the experiences of communities of different ethnic origins (Platt, 2009).

Understanding poverty and its impact has also led to attempts to identify more specific indicators of a child's material situation, for example those proposed by Bradshaw (2008), which include not just income poverty and parental unemployment but also more specific measures of child deprivation, such as the lack of their own bedroom, a computer, holidays last year and less than 10 books in the home. This is reflected in the UNICEF report (see Figure 1.1).

Although in 1999 the Labour government highlighted child poverty and made explicit commitments about its reduction, its preferable terminology in this area reflected the view that the real issue was one of 'social exclusion':

Social exclusion is a complex and multi-dimensional process. It involves the lack or denial of resources, rights, goods and services, and the inability to participate in the normal relationships and activities, available to the majority of people in a society, whether in economic, social, cultural or political arenas. It affects both the quality of life of individuals and the equity and cohesion of society as a whole. (Levitas et al., 2007, p. 25)

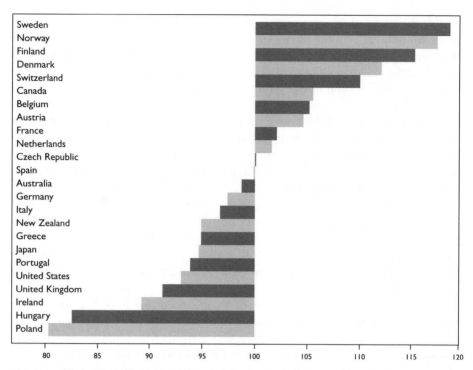

Note: Five components were selected to represent children's material wellbeing. Figure 1.1 averages each country's score over the five components and is scaled to show each country's distance above or below the average (set at 100) for the 24 countries featured.

Source: UNICEF, 'Child Poverty in Perspective: An Overview of Child Well-being in Rich Countries', Innocenti Report Card 7, UNICEF Innocenti Research Centre, Florence, 2007, Figure 1.0, p. 4. Reproduced with kind permission.

Figure 1.1 The material wellbeing of children

This language potentially adds extra dimensions of marginality to our understanding:

> Social exclusion opens up our understanding of the dynamics of poverty to embrace social relationships, citizenship and the ability to realise citizen's rights and entitlements. (Ridge, 2002, p. 143)

The focus on social exclusion led to a policy strategy of 'extending opportunities' rather than tackling the redistribution of resources. This emphasised the enabling of employment as the primary mechanism for reducing child poverty, although in fact, levels of 'in-work' poverty remained high (Palmer et al., 2005). Social exclusion also emphasises a geographical dimension, which leads to government interventions often focusing on particular communities.

While statistics demonstrate that there are links between poverty, exclusion and outcomes for children, the understanding of the relationship to wellbeing is heightened by listening to the experiences of children themselves – from within the 'state of childhood' (Ridge, 2002, p. 6). In a study by Ridge (2002), children whose family were in receipt of benefits were more likely to be worried about bullying and 'fitting in' with their peers than other children. Much of their difficulties stemmed from lack of access to financial resources limiting travel to see friends, the ability to go on school trips, and to afford the 'right' sort of clothes so as to avoid being made fun of:

> If you don't wear the right stuff you're like different and that of the crowd, just different. It's right to have the right clothes. (Carrie, 15) (Ridge, 2002, p. 67)

> I would have gone on this B adventure camp and it was like £10 for the deposit and mum didn't have the money and all the spaces went. (Nicole, 13) (Ridge, 2002, p. 75)

This also emphasises that there is a 'current' cost to children's lives and wellbeing beyond the outcomes frequently discussed in terms of the impact on their adult 'futures'.

A further perspective on this socio-economic issue suggests that it is not just poverty but the level of inequality in a country which is influential in terms of outcomes for its citizens. At the start of the twenty-first century, in addition to high levels of child poverty, the UK was also one of the most unequal societies among all the developed nations (Ridge, 2002). Inequality is not just a comparison of incomes but is also starkly portrayed in ownership of assets, for example shares and property – home ownership is particularly important in the UK context (Gill and Jack, 2007). While the degree of child poverty was reduced during the 2000s in line with its prioritisation by the government, income inequality continued to grow.

The case for inequality being an even more important influence on wellbeing than poverty is proposed by Wilkinson and Pickett (2009), who used international comparisons to show that health and social problems are more closely related to inequality than average income (see Figures 1.2 and 1.3). It is still the case that poverty is important:

> However, as well as knowing that health and social problems are more common among the less well off within each society ... we now know that the overall burden of these problems is much higher in unequal societies. (Wilkinson and Pickett, 2009, p. 20)

Therefore the negative impact of inequality is not just on the most disadvantaged children and adults but on all members of society. In this analysis, the 'health and social problems' for which this holds true include drug use, obesity, educational performance, violence and imprisonment. The proposed mechanism is that inequality has a corrosive effect on society, weakening community life, reducing trust and heightening sensitivity to social status and social anxiety; in essence, 'inequality gets under the skin' (Wilkinson and Pickett 2009, p. 31).

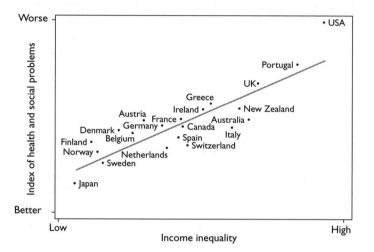

Figure 1.2 International comparison of health and social problems relative to income inequality

Source: Wilkinson and Pickett (2009) *The Spirit Level: Why More Equal Societies Almost Always Do Better.* Allen Lane.

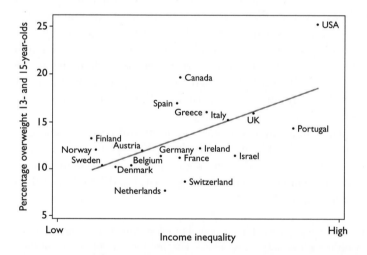

Figure 1.3 Childhood obesity in relation to income inequality

Source: Wilkinson and Pickett (2009) *The Spirit Level: Why More Equal Societies Almost Always Do Better.* Allen Lane.

Although the mechanism through which the impact of inequality works has been contested (Goldthorpe, 2009), the case for the powerful effect of inequality on children's wellbeing is compelling, reinforcing how broad economic policy can have a powerful impact on the lives of individual children.

The commercialisation of childhood?

> All families in OECD countries today are aware that childhood is being reshaped by forces whose mainspring is not necessarily the best interests of the child. At the same time, a wide public in the OECD countries is becoming ever more aware that many of the corrosive social problems affecting the quality of life have their genesis in the changing ecology of childhood. (UNICEF, 2007, p. 39)

Children's lives interact with many other more diffuse and interrelated socio-cultural and economic influences. The impact on children's wellbeing is even more difficult to assess, given the lack of research and lack of agreement on what is good or bad for children in terms of their engagement with, for example, new technologies or our prevailing culture of consumerism. Social commentators certain that the 'commercialisation of childhood' is all-pervasive, contributing to poorer mental heath, obesity and inappropriately early sexualisation, are not hard to find (for example Palmer, 2006; Compass, 2007), but substantial evidence can be difficult to establish. Some of these debates are long-standing, for example the impact of television, but often reoccur as new technologies are embraced by children bringing benefits but also risks. What we believe children need protecting from and why again depends at least in part upon, and challenges, our differing constructions of childhood.

What is increasingly not in doubt is that consumption is central to the identities of children and young people of all ages. Consumption of clothes and other commodities are key to self-image, gender identity, and negotiating social positions and friendships (Russell and Tyler, 2002; Croghan et al., 2006; Pole et al., 2006). The experiences of children quoted above (from Ridge's 2002 study) highlight the problems of being able to buy the 'right' clothes. Similar findings were reflected in research by Croghan et al. (2006), where the inability to buy the right labels and brands in a culture of conspicuous consumption not only heightened the experience of social exclusion, but this 'style failure' was also associated with being labelled with a negative identity:

> In these accounts money, style and social worth were inextricably linked, so that the ability to buy desirable consumer goods became a kind of *moral* ability, an indication of intrinsic worth. Thus, not having money made young people increasingly subject to the ascription of a negative identity, with all its attendant negative assumptions. (Croghan et al., 2006, p. 473)

> Sadie: If some people dress scraggy and stuff you think oh they ain't got a lot of money or whatever – tramps. (Bradford School, Birmingham, year 12) (Croghan et al., 2006, p. 473)

The culture of consumerism, with its associated branding, advertising and role modelling, exerts a powerful effect both on children but also on their families to provide the necessary products. That children and young people are positioned as consumers is now a feature of the dominant economic philosophy in the UK.

Children are also the recipients of unmediated commercial pressures from many thousands of television adverts per year. This is despite the fact that questions have been raised suggesting that two- to three-year-olds are not able to distinguish between advertisements and television programmes (Kunkel et al., 2004 in Piachaud, 2008) and that young children may not understand that adverts are not always truthful and they are therefore 'fundamentally unfair because of young children's limited comprehension of the nature and purpose of television advertising' (Kunkel et al., 2004, p. 23 in Piachaud, 2008).

Livingstone (2004, 2006), summarising research on the links between advertising and children's food preferences, argued that the impact of advertising is obvious to many people:

> It will doubtless be pertinent to policy considerations, if not to the academic debate, that the public will never find it credible that an industry that spends huge sums each year advertising food to children on television does so with no actual (or intended) effect on children's food consumption. (Livingstone, 2004, p. 29)

However, Livingstone agreed that rigorous evidence is hard to produce because the outcomes are multiply determined rather than by simple cause and effect. For example, what children eat is closely related to the practices within their immediate family; however, influence is also exerted through their exposure to eating in school, on the high street and through advertising. The older children are, the more likely they are to encounter these latter influences and, increasingly frequently, to make their own decisions about their eating habits. From an ecological perspective, concern about topics such as obesity must try to consider the implications at all these levels and the interactions between them, including recognition of an intersection with the earlier discussion of poverty and inequality.

Despite the complexities of the research, a review of this issue, specifically in relation to food promotion and consumption, concluded that

> there is a modest body of fairly consistent evidence demonstrating the direct effect of food promotion (in the main, television advertising) on children's food preferences, knowledge and behaviour. (Livingstone, 2004, p. 28)

It also concluded that if policy in relation to children should be guided by the 'precautionary principle', that is, erring on the side of caution if there is evidence of probable influence, then limited action was justified. In 2007, the British media regulator Ofcom began a phased introduction of restrictions on the advertising of food and drink products that are high in fat, salt and sugar (HFSS) in and around programmes with particular appeal to children. Ofcom believed that these measures would result in children under 16 being exposed to 41% fewer advertisements for HFSS products, while for children under 9, the reduction would be 51% (Ofcom, 2007a). Of course, advertisers have many other avenues open to them, through the internet, 'viral' marketing, text messaging, and even directly to schools through sponsorship. Computers and sports equipment have frequently been acquired by schools in exchange for supermarket vouchers sometimes to be collected from HFSS cereal and snack foods. Adopting the 'precautionary principle' has led to more extensive action being taken in other countries. For example, in 1991, Sweden legislated to ban television advertisements aimed at children under 12, and to prevent anyone appearing on children's television from appearing in any kind of advertisement, although here too advertising reaches children through other, less regulated sources. It also established a consumer ombudsman (Ofcom, 2007b).

In relation to children's exposure to various forms of media and technology, an important feature in the twenty-first century is that children's access, through the internet and use of their own television sets, is often unrestricted and unsupervised, arguably reducing the potential buffering effect of children's immediate families (Ofcom, 2009; Hasebrink et al., 2009). Periodically, anxiety in society (and the media) is high in relation to the nature of the material children and young people see, the type of activities they engage in and with whom, and the length of time they spend engaging in them, as opposed to being 'active' and 'outdoors'. The nature of the change – such as children's vastly increased exposure to sexualised and pornographic images – seems unarguable even if there is a lack of consensus on the extent of the risk this poses, the extent of the impact or how to respond.

Another element of these debates concerns the issue of children's agency: Can they be helped to make up their own minds? One response to concerns about media influence has been that rather than stricter regulation, children, as 'consumers', need to be – or need to be taught to be – more media literate (Buckingham, 2009). These arguments have been rehearsed in relation to the use of internet and video games – an area of concern sufficient for the UK government to commission research on the subject. This research report concluded that the emphasis should be on 'self-regulation' by providers and the 'empowerment' of children and families:

> Having considered the evidence I believe we need to move from a discussion about the media 'causing' harm to one which focuses on children and young people, what they bring to technology and how we can use our understanding of how they develop to empower them to manage risks and make the digital world safer. (Byron, 2008, p. 2)

Sometimes recommendations lean the other way. A Home Office-sponsored review of the sexualisation of young people argued that there is evidence of the profound negative effects of sexualised images and messages in terms of mental and physical health, attitudes and beliefs (Papadopoulos, 2010, p. 6), and recommended an extension of regulation and control:

Games consoles should be sold with parental controls already switched on. Purchasers can choose to 'unlock' the console if they wish to allow access to adult and online content ... This idea should be extended to 'child friendly' computers and mobile phones where adult content is filtered out by default. (Papadopoulos, 2010, p. 16)

The topics discussed in this section are likely to continue to be subjects of debate. Some of the issues are challenging because they are in new forms and are fast changing, and questions still remain about how we should respond to this uncertainty. Timimi (2009, p. 10) argued that 'aggressive forms of neo-liberal free market principles deserve further scrutiny' and furthermore suggested that:

What we do need, however, is a wider debate that engages the public with politicians, in which knowledge about children's development, mental health, protection, and their relationship to culture should be included. (Timimi, 2009, p. 22)

Ecological practice?

If practitioners listen carefully to the children and parents they work with talking about their lives, they will become aware that, on many occasions, children and their parents adopt what is essentially an ecological perspective. Their descriptions often move between different levels of explanation or interpretation of their difficulties and, crucially, they often identify some of the connections between factors in different areas of their lives. (Gill and Jack, 2007, p. 53)

While it is possible to identify factors in the broader economic, social and cultural ecology of children's lives and debate their impact on wellbeing, what account can be taken of the sorts of issues this chapter has been exploring by practitioners and their practice in children's services? Although the various assessment frameworks noted above have recognised the importance of broader community and environmental factors such as 'income' and 'families social integration' (DH, 2000), 'enough money' and 'belonging' (Scottish Executive, 2007), this does not necessarily mean that these dimensions of children's lives are given sufficient weight in assessments or subsequent plans (Jack and Gill, 2003). Practitioners are given little support with this – government documents listing the core skills and knowledge required in the children's workforce have made little reference to the need to understand or work with the wider social context of children and young people's lives (Gill and Jack, 2007).

It is possible that practitioners themselves do not always see the relevance of some of these factors or feel that they are the sorts of issues beyond their range of influence. Practitioners' own views on child poverty were investigated by Cameron et al. (2008, p. 8):

'Poverty' was not commonly recognised as a relevant or appropriate construct for practitioners working with disadvantaged children and families on the ground and indeed many practitioners in this research did not immediately see the relevance of discussions on child poverty to their own roles (even those who work with disadvantaged families).

This may seem surprising, although it was not that practitioners (including, in this instance, teachers, Jobcentre Plus workers, Connexions advisers, health visitors, social workers and welfare rights advisers) did not see the impact of poverty but defined and discussed the issue in terms of 'disadvantage' and 'children in need', seeing poverty as a somewhat extreme term. Practitioners' lack of specific reference to poverty may partly be influenced by broader public perceptions. A survey for the Department of Work and Pensions found that 41% of respondents thought there was 'very little' child poverty in Britain (Kelly, 2008). In fact, within British society as a whole, views on child poverty have not been overwhelmingly sympathetic to this policy or practice perspective – in the same survey, asked why there were families with children 'in need', responses were spread between 'injustice in our society' (25%), an 'inevitable part of modern life' (31%) and 'laziness or lack of willpower' (27%) (Kelly, 2008, p. 3). Certainly, this represents a barrier to be overcome in terms of broad public support for stated government aims of ending child poverty and making it 'everybody's business' (HM Treasury, 2008).

Practitioners saw the reasons for family poverty and disadvantage as multifaceted, not just relating to material circumstances but also to factors such as parenting attitudes and behaviours. However, Cameron et al. reported that through the process of discussing poverty as part of the research, practitioners did increasingly see its relevance to their work:

> Many found that they in fact had a lot to say on the subject and were surprised at their own knowledge and experience in the area. Indeed, for some there was in essence a real 'lightbulb moment' as they began to see the links between practitioners' roles and broader efforts to tackle child poverty. (Cameron et al., 2008, p. 9)

Recognising the links between poverty, social exclusion and their practice is an important first step for practitioners but how is it possible to take this into consideration? What would practice that was informed to a greater extent by this perspective look like? To begin with, as the quote at the start of this section proposes, an ecological approach is not something completely alien to many families as they can see the interconnectedness of different aspects of their lives and the influences on them. This suggests that there may be plenty of scope for practitioners to engage in discussions with families drawing on the relevance of issues such as community and forms of disadvantage as well as working with their individual situation. This requires practitioners to practise at a number of different levels or for a number of practitioners to coordinate and combine their interventions.

As an illustration, Gill and Jack (2007) cited work with a minority ethnic community in a largely white disadvantaged estate on the periphery of a city. Individual work here was supplemented by a support group bringing families of the same ethnic group together. At a community-wide level, research was undertaken on one particular issue of concern – police response times – which led to them being reviewed and improved. Schools from the estate were also linked to a school in the multiethnic inner city as a creative response to constructing social inclusion.

An important element of this approach is the co-construction of practice solutions through placing greater weight on the subjective interpretations by families of their own situations. This also promotes the idea that 'children, young people and their families are not passive victims of the pressure of their situation' (Gill and Jack, 2007, p. 10). They also suggested that practitioners need to focus on the meaning of the communities in which they work and different interpretations of it, for example children's views of their community may well differ from that of adults. Practitioners should also be prepared to engage with politicians, funders, agencies and the media about issues such as child poverty (Gill and Jack, 2007).

Other socio-economic or cultural influences such as those discussed above are perhaps even more difficult for practice to take account of. However, as with poverty and inequality, practitioners perhaps first need to see the potential impact. Critically reflective practitioners can develop a perspective that understands that an encounter with an individual child, young person or family has a broader context. For example, work with young people with eating disorders has a context that could mean exploring with them the constructs in society of what it means to be healthy, or challenging the powerful and gendered images of 'ideal' bodies (Robb, 2007). The same may be true of the way that other aspects of the lives of families are affected by prevailing economic and cultural beliefs, whether through consumerism, or even issues such as the way children and young people in general are portrayed in the media. Such an approach at least makes these factors explicit and legitimises their exploration. Sharing understandings can be a starting point for contesting problems and constructing responses.

Final thoughts

The main aim of this chapter is to encourage a broad view to be taken of influences on the wellbeing of children and young people. While agreeing how to define wellbeing in order to shape services for children is complex, the selective examples explored above illustrate some of the contemporary debates about the nature of the impact of factors in the social ecology of children's lives. There is the potential for practice to be enhanced by a willingness to consider the possibilities of ecological practice, while recognising that many of the arguments about the wellbeing of children and young people must also be had in the wider political arena.

References

Axford, N. (2008) *Exploring Concepts of Child Well-being: Implications for Children's Services*, Bristol, Policy Press.

Axford, N., Green, V., Kalsbeek, A. et al. (2008) 'Measuring children's needs: How are we doing?', *Child & Family Social Work*, 14: 243–54.

Bradbury, B. and Jänetti, M. (1999) *Child Poverty across Industrialized Nations*, Innocenti Occasional Papers, Economic and Social Policy Series no.71, Florence, UNICEF Innocenti Research Centre.

Bradshaw, J. (ed.) (2008) 'Child poverty and well-being', *Social & Public Policy Review*, 1(1), available online at <http://www.uppress.co.uk/socialpolicy_pdf/Bradshaw.pdf> [Accessed 16 April 2010].

Bradshaw, J., Hoelscher, P. and Richardson, D. (2007) *Comparing Child Well-being in OECD Countries: Concepts and Methods*, Innocenti Working Paper No. 2006-03, Florence, UNICEF Innocenti Research Centre.

Bronfenbrenner, U. (1979) *The Ecology of Human Development: Experiments by Nature and Design*, Cambridge, MA, Harvard University Press.

Buckingham, D. (2009) 'The appliance of science: The role of evidence in the making of regulatory policy on children and food advertising in the UK', *International Journal of Cultural Policy*, **15**(2): 201–15.

Byron, T. (2008) *Safer Children in the Digital World: The Report of the Byron Review, Children and New Technology, Executive Summary*, available online at <www.dcsf.gov.uk/byronreview/pdfs/Executive%20summary.pdf> [Accessed 16 April 2010].

Cameron, D., Freyer-Smith, E., Harvey, P. and Wallace, E. (2008) *Practitioners' Perspectives on Child Poverty*, Research Report DCSF-RR058, available online at <www.dcsf.gov.uk/research/data/uploadfiles/DCSF-RR058.pdf> [Accessed 16 April 2010].

Compass (2007) The commercialisation of childhood, available online at <http://clients.squareeye.com/uploads/compass/documents/thecommercialisationofchildhood.pdf> [Accessed 16 April 2010].

Croghan, R., Griffin, C., Hunter, J. and Pheonix, A. (2006) 'Style failure: Consumption, identity and social exclusion', *Journal of Youth Studies*, **9**(4): 463–78.

Children's Workforce Development Council (2009) *The Common Assessment Framework for Children and Young People: A Guide for Practitioners*, Leeds, CWDC.

DH (Department of Health) (2000) *Framework for the Assessment of Children in Need and their Families*, London, TSO.

Ghate, D. and Hazel, N. (2002) *Parenting in Poor Environments: Stress, Support, and Coping*, London, Jessica Kingsley.

Gill, O. and Jack, G. (2007) *The Child and Family in Context: Developing Ecological Practice in Disadvantaged Communities*, Lyme Regis, Russell House.

Goldthorpe, J. (2009) 'Analysing social inequality: A critique of two recent contributions', *European Sociological Review*, advance access published online on 22 October, doi:10.1093/esr/jcp046.

Hasebrink, U., Livingstone, S., Haddon, L. and Ólafsson, K. (2009) *Comparing Children's Online Opportunities and Risks across Europe: Cross-national Comparisons for EU Kids Online* (2nd edn), LSE, London, EU Kids Online.

Hirsch, D. (2007) *Chicken and Egg: Child Poverty and Educational Inequalities*, London, Child Poverty Action Group.

HM Treasury (2008) *Ending Child Poverty: Everybody's Business*, HM Treasury.

Hooper, C., Gorin, S., Cabral, C. and Dyson, C. (2007) *Living with Hardship 24/7: The Diverse Experiences of Families in Poverty in England*, York, Frank Buttle Trust.

Hudson, M., Phillips, J., Ray, K. and Barnes, H. (2007) *Social Cohesion in Diverse Communities*, York, Joseph Rowntree Foundation.

Jack, G. and Gill, O. (2003) *The Missing Side of the Triangle: Assessing the Importance of Family and Environmental Factors in the Lives of Children*, Barkingside, Barnados.

Kelly, M. (2008) *Public Attitudes to Child Poverty: Research Summary*, London, Department for Work and Pensions.

Kunkel, D., Wilcox, B.L., Cantor, J. et al. (2004) *Task Force on Advertising and Children*, Washington DC, American Psychological Association.

Levitas, R., Pantazis, C., Fahmy, E. et al. (2007) *The Multi-dimensional Analysis of Social Exclusion*, London, Social Exclusion Task Force.

Livingstone, S. (2004) *A Commentary on the Research Evidence Regarding the Effects of Food Promotion on Children*, prepared for the Research Department of Ofcom.

Livingstone, S. (2006) Does TV advertising make children fat? What the evidence tells us, *Public Policy Research*, **13**(1): 54–61.

Mahon, J. (2008) *Towards the New Children in Need Census*, Research Report DCSF-RW039, London, DCSF.

Moss, P. and Petrie, P. (2002) *From Children's Services to Children's Spaces*, London, Routledge Farmer.

Murphy, J. (2007) Unicef report: Reaction in quotes, available online at <http://news.bbc.co.uk/1/hi/uk/6359887.stm> [Accessed 16 April 2010].

Ofcom (2007a) Ofcom publishes final statement on the television advertising of food and drink products to children, available online at <http://www.ofcom.org.uk/media/news/2007/02/nr_20070222> [Accessed 16 April 2010].

Ofcom (2007b) The international perspective: The future of children's programming research report – Online annex, available online at <http://www.ofcom.org.uk/consult/condocs/kidstv/international.pdf> [Accessed 16 April 2010].

Ofcom (2009) Children's web access, available online at http://<www.ofcom.org.uk/consumer/2009/10/more-children-have-broadband-in-the-bedroom> [Accessed 16 April 2010].

Palmer, S. (2006) *Toxic Childhood: How the Modern World is Damaging our Children and What We Can Do About It*, London, Orion.

Palmer, G., Carr, J. and Kenway, P. (2005) *Monitoring Poverty and Social Exclusion*, York, Joseph Rowntree Foundation.

Papadopoulos, L. (2010) *Sexualisation of Young People Review*, London, Home Office.

Piachaud, D. (2008) 'Freedom to be a child: Commercial pressures', *Children, Social Policy & Society*, **7**(4): 445–56.

Platt, L. (2009) *Ethnicity and Child Poverty*, Research Report No 576, London, Department for Work and Pensions.

Pole, C., Pilcher, J., Edwards, T. and Boden, S. (2006) *New Consumers?: Children, Fashion and Consumption*, Cultures of Consumption Findings Series, London, ESRC/Birkbeck University of London/Arts & Humanities Research Council.

Rees, G., Bradshaw, J., Goswami, H. and Keung, A. (2009) *Understanding Children's Well-being: A National Survey of Young People's Well-being*, London, Children's Society.

Ridge, T. (2002) *Childhood Policy and Social Exclusion from a Child's Perspective*, Bristol, Policy Press.

Robb, M. (2007) *Understanding Youth: Perspectives, Identities and Practices*, London, Sage/OU Press.

Russell, R. and Tyler, M. (2002) 'Thank heaven for little girls: "Girl heaven" and the commercial context of feminine childhood', *Sociology*, **36**(3): 619–37.

Salway, S., Platt, L., Chowbey, P. et al. (2007) *Long-term Ill Health, Poverty and Ethnicity*, York, Joseph Rowntree Foundation.

Scottish Executive (2007) *Getting it Right for Every Child: Guidance on the Child's or Young Person's Plan*, Edinburgh, Scottish Executive.

Seden, J. (2006) 'Frameworks and theories', in J. Aldgate, D. Jones, W. Rose and C. Jeffery (eds) *The Developing World of the Child*, London, Jessica Kingsley, pp. 35–54.

Timimi, S. (2009) 'The commercialization of children's mental health in the era of globalization', *International Journal of Mental Health*, **38**(3): 5–27.

Tisdall, K. and Plows, V. (2007) *Children In Need: Examining its Use in Practice and Reflecting on its Currency for Proposed Policy Changes*, University of Edinburgh, Submission to the Sponsored Research Programme, Scottish Executive Education Department.

UNICEF (2007) *Child Poverty in Perspective: An Overview of Child Well-being in Rich Countries*, Innocenti Report Card 7, Florence, UNICEF Innocenti Research Centre, available online at <http://www.unicef-irc.org/publications/pdf/rc7_eng.pdf> [Accessed 13 May 2010].

Wilkinson, R. and Pickett, K. (2009) *The Spirit Level: Why More Equal Societies Almost Always Do Better*, London, Allen Lane.

2

Constructions of normative families

Lindsay O'Dell

In this chapter I use a social constructionist and a social ecological perspective to argue that understandings of 'normative' families, within which children and young people develop, shift through time and across different contexts. Ideas about what constitutes families are given to us in a variety of ways such as through legislation, policy, social science (including psychology) and through popular culture and cultural practices. How we construct families and children has an impact on the design of services and ways of working. I will argue that practice is constructed through understandings of families, how families are viewed and what roles and functions families perform. In this chapter I use the terminology of 'normative' and 'non-normative' purposefully to examine assumptions at play in understanding what are seen as 'normal' or 'abnormal' families. It is argued that by assuming an ideal or normative form, families that are in some way different from this norm will be judged as deviant and failing. In this chapter, three key areas are discussed: what constitutes a normative family and how other families are different; understandings of non-normative families; and the implications of these other issues for practice.

What is a normative family?

For many years, the typical, or 'normative' family structure in the UK, and in many western countries, has been seen as a 'nuclear' family consisting of a heterosexual couple caring for their (biologically related) children (Crabb and Augoustinos, 2008). This has been noted in policy, for example Dodd et al. (2009) argued that Australian government policy reflects the normative assumption of 'family' as a heterosexual couple with one main breadwinner, usually male, and one main carer, usually female. In the UK, it has been noted that in recent years there has been a resurgence in policy and media discussions of the view that a two-parent family is the best institution for children to grow up in (Walker et al., 2008). The contemporary situation is mixed, with some conservative commentators discussing the demise of the traditional family and family values, whereas others are addressing and celebrating the diversity of family life (Hargreaves, 2006). However, the assumption of a normative family structure as a nuclear family of two biological parents and their children is 'pervasive and influential' (Dodd et al., 2009, p. 175).

In this chapter, two examples of what can be viewed as 'non-normative' families will be drawn on: 'language brokers' – children and young people who translate for their families; and children and young people who live in lesbian, gay, bisexual or transgendered (LGBT) families. It is important to note that neither group are by definition problematic. However, both are good examples of how ideas about normative families have changed through time and in different contexts. Lesbian and gay parenting has, until recently, been an invisible aspect of some families' lives. It is key to note that in the UK homosexuality was illegal and defined as a psychiatric illness until the 1970s. Hence research into LGBT parenting is very recent. However, changes in attitudes, combined with changes in medical ethics and advances in reproductive technologies, have produced new configurations of normative families. LGBT families are often constituted as a result of a 'third parent', who could be a surrogate mother, donor father or as a result of a previous heterosexual relationship (Harris, 2008), and therefore the notion of an extended family is the norm for children and young people living in LGBT families.

The second example also illustrates how changes in society bring with them issues for children and young people. Recent immigration has led to many children and young people living in families where the adults do not speak English proficiently. Newly immigrant children and young people learn the language and cultural conventions of their new country much faster than their parents and older family members, usually because of attending school and interacting with their British peers, and so are used to translate for their family and are a resource for them (Orellana, 2009; Cline et al., in press). 'Language brokers' are defined as children who engage in activities where they mediate between two (or more) different languages, which is often part of a transitional situation for migrating families (Cline et al., in press). This is outside the normative expectation of childhood in the UK, where it is assumed that adults speak for their children rather than the other way round (O'Dell et al., 2006).

It is evident that understandings of a normative family have undergone profound changes over time. Increasing family change in the UK has been noted over the past 50 years (Walker et al., 2008, p. 430). Family structure in society has changed from 'convergence to divergence' (Boh et al., 1989, cited in Walker et al., 2008); from a society of largely nuclear families to one in which there are a number of diverse family types. Rapid changes in society, including increased economic migration, the dispersal of the extended family and changes to family law, have created situations in which more children and young people live in families that have been viewed as non-normative (Cline et al., in press). UNICEF estimated that 30% of British children live in either single-parent or reconstituted families (Walker et al., 2008). Many commentators have noted increased numbers of single-parent, step-parent, LGBT parents and other family forms:

> Gay and lesbian families, single-parent families, families without children, families caring for nonbiological children, and extended family configurations are increasingly part of the cultural landscape. (Sotirin and Ellingson, 2007 p. 455)

A common assumption when thinking about families is to draw on a biological explanation to define what are seen as normative families. Normative families are assumed to be biologically connected and so the ties between children and their parents are seen to be due to their biological relatedness (Hargreaves, 2006). Genetics, it has been argued, marks out 'real' families and marginalises other family forms (Crabb and Augoustinos, 2008). However, the relationship between biological and cultural aspects of family is increasingly complex, with advances in fertility research and genetics: 'learning about the facts of life will not, these days, necessarily tell us more about kinship' (Strathern, 1995, in Hargreaves, 2006, p. 262). Similar developments in the social construction of scientific knowledge also point to the complexities of genetics, which

> force us to recognise that any congruence between natural and cultural categories is not determined by the 'facts of nature' but that these 'natural' categories are themselves subject to cultural construction. (Atkinson et al., 2001, p. 6)

An alternative view is that kinship and a feeling of belonging within a family is not about biological connection but is about the social bonds formed over time in families. It has been argued that family relationships are 'established through everyday practices, such as naming and residence' (Atkinson et al., 2001, p. 21). Anthropologists have described this as an 'enacted practice' (Sotirin and Ellingson, 2007), where a sense of family is achieved through activities such as naming family members (mum, dad, aunt and so on) and the enactment of these social roles.

Children and young people are aware of normative family functioning and expectations. For example, in Gilby and Pederson's 1982 research (reported in Rigg and Pryor, 2007), children were asked to make a 'typical' family using cardboard figures given to them by a researcher. The majority of the children constructed a nuclear family with the cardboard figures. Research conducted by Morrow (1998) asked 8- to 14-year-olds: 'What is a family?' and 'What are families for?' She found that younger children considered factors such as the presence of children in the relationship, marriage and contact between family members as essential for a family, whereas older children looked at the quality of the relationships between people. What is evident from these studies is that families are seen by children and young people to have a variety of functions, which include care and the quality of relationships between people. While the normative family is recognised by children, they are also aware of variations from this norm that are also encompassed by their definitions of a family.

In a study by Walker et al. (2008), children and young people who were growing up in single-parent families were asked about their lives. The children identified some instances in which living with only one parent can be a positive experience for them. Obvious examples are where the family has separated because of instances of abuse but also where children have been witness to parental conflict, the removal of one parent can reduce conflict and stress in the home. Isabel, a 16-year-old young woman, articulates a sense of her family being outside the norm but also a strengthened family bond as a result:

> You look after your family more which makes you more of a closer family whereas some people who live in *normal* families, they're not as close. If you're a single-parent family, you must have had a rough patch somewhere so it kind of brings you together as a family. (Isabel, 16, rural interviewee) (Walker et al., 2008, pp. 432–3, emphasis added)

This is not to idealise a particular family form but rather to argue that it is the relationships within the family and not the family structure itself that determines children and young people's experiences of family life.

Theorising non-normative families

In this section, a social constructionist argument will be drawn on to discuss how ideas about normative families and children are constructed and measured.

A social constructionist perspective argues that the dominant, taken-for-granted view of society is reflected in family structures: 'the generally accepted societal views that are often unspoken and taken for granted (although at times forcefully argued) about what a "normal" or "functional" family is' (Dodd et al., 2009, p. 175). A social constructionist critique of the role of psychology, and other social and medical sciences, discusses how these disciplines produce activities and practices that theorise, identify and document normal, functional children and families. This is usually achieved by identifying what are seen as 'deviations' from the assumed normal ways of behaving, functioning and so on to document the 'abnormal' and thereby implicitly validating the 'norm' (Rose, 1985). Normative behaviour, functioning and roles are often implicitly assumed rather than articulated. Alternative family forms are often compared to a nuclear family and seen as deficient in some way. For example, LGBT families have been seen as not 'real' families and thus a problematic environment for children to grow up in. It has been argued that this 'deficit' view of LGBT families is 'inaccurate, misleading and discriminatory' (Crabb and Augoustinos, 2008, p. 304). There is a growing body of research that has documented the outcomes for children and young people growing up in LGBT families, many of which find no significant difference between children in LGBT families and those brought up in traditional nuclear families (Winter, 2008). There is evidence that children of LGBT families do well at school and participate in everyday activities of school (Winter, 2008).

Constructions of childhood are bound up with conceptions of what constitutes a 'normative' family and what can be expected of 'normal' parenting. The assumption within the dominant western construction of childhood is that children grow up through a gradual development of skills, autonomy and cognitive ability. Children are therefore assumed to be lacking in the skills needed to function in the world so are dependent on adults and in need of protection (Rose, 1990, cited in Crafter et al., 2008). It is evident that ideas about family roles and responsibilities differ across cultural contexts. Young people in all societies are expected to take on increasing levels of responsibility but the timings of these and the beliefs about them vary in different cultural communities (Dorner et al., 2008). This is evident in discussions of responsibility within families. In the UK, and other western societies, parents, other adults and society generally are seen to have a responsibility *towards* children. However, ideas about responsibility have been treated differently in different parts of the world. For example, where children are seen as more active in their environment and are seen to have responsibility towards the society they live in:

> This alerts us to the socially constructed nature of childhood in respect of children's activities – in sub-Saharan African countries, children's responsibilities are acknowledged in legal instruments, such as the African Charter on the Rights and Welfare of the Child. Article 31, entitled responsibilities of the child, stipulates that 'Every child shall have responsibilities towards his [sic] family and society, the State and other legally recognised communities and the international community' (OUA/African Union 1990). (Morrow, 2008, p. 20)

The dominant construction of family in the West is one in which parents take responsibility for their children. This has been noted in relation to many types of family. In Morrow's (2008) research on children's understandings of family, she found that many children and young people interviewed talked about looking after siblings. Morrow found that 'about half' of the 12- to 14-year-old young people in her study talked about mutual support and reciprocity in family relationships. She, and others, have argued that reciprocity in relationships between family members is rarely visible but often takes place within families.

A sense of reciprocity and mutual responsibility has also been noted in families that are seen to be in some way non-normative. When children engage in activities that are different from the expected norms of childhood, such as translate for their families, they are seen to be unusual and problematic (O'Dell et al., 2006; Early et al., 2007). However, if families are seen as a place of mutual dependence (as is common in many cultural settings), then it makes sense that children contribute to the family:

> Viewed as an interdependent script, everyday language brokering may be seen as a normal expectation of the child–adult relationship rather than a parent ceding control of family decisions. (Dorner et al., 2008, p. 521)

Similarly, in discussing work with young people who care for a parent with mental health difficulties, Grant et al. (2008) argued that it is important to understand the interdependency and mutual sense of obligation in families:

> The project recognised other demands on people's lives and took a family-centred view that acknowledged the importance of attachments and obligations felt by young people that were part of interdependent relations in families, supporting the views and evidence provided by an increasing body of research. (Grant et al., 2008, p. 279)

A social constructionist argument is that the measurements and instruments used to measure abnormal functioning, children and families are not neutral objects but are themselves part of a system of values, ideologies and cultural assumptions. This was evident within Phoenix's research investigating adults who experienced childhoods that could be seen as non-normative. The project aimed 'to advance knowledge of the factors that produce adult citizens who are "unremarkable" in not requiring social work intervention despite having childhood experiences often viewed as non-ideal' (Phoenix, 2009). She focused on children who had experienced a move from the Caribbean to join their parents in the UK and grew up in a family of mixed ethnicity or were sometimes translators for their parents. Phoenix discussed the ways in which her respondents' families were seen as problematic and 'deficient' because of their children's (assumed) problems, which were related to practitioners' assumptions about what they saw as the families' inadequate parenting and punitive punishment of children. The children were routinely given intelligence tests that measured a disproportionate number of newly immigrant West Indian children as 'educationally subnormal'. However, as illustrated by the extract below, there has been much criticism of intelligence testing because of its reliance upon knowledge gained within a particular cultural context; thus children with educational and cultural experiences similar to those of the test compilers were most likely to achieve high marks in the test:

Geoff Palmer arrived in London from Jamaica in 1955 ... a month before his 15th birthday ... His mother took him to the local school, where he was given a routine IQ test. 'I'd just travelled 5,000 miles from Jamaica. The test asked me "How does Big Ben indicate the time"' he chuckles. 'The question meant nothing to me. Absolutely nothing.' He was told he was 'educationally subnormal' (ESN) ... Palmer's saving grace was his cricketing prowess. He was spotted by the local grammar school head and awarded a place. Today he is Professor Geoff Palmer, OBE, of Heriot Watt University, one of only a handful of black chemistry professors in Britain. (Curtis, 2005, cited in Phoenix, 2009, p. 105)

Phoenix's work illustrates clearly that the measures used to judge children's development and parenting are a product of the cultural and historical context within which they are produced.

What does this mean for the co-construction of practice?

In this section, I discuss how a social constructionist and a social ecological perspective can be helpful in understanding and working with diverse families. Several implications for practice are discussed.

It is important to understand how families are viewed in society because this impacts on practitioners and their work with children, young people and families:

the professional construction of families reflects and inscribes the lay understanding of family members themselves, as well as general European-American cultural beliefs concerning kinship, reproduction and family. (Atkinson et al., 2001, p. 9)

In addition, it is important to note that in describing normative families, there is an implied view that the norm represents the ideal family for children to grow up in:

Considerations of how families play out their role within services that espouse a family-centred perspective need to be understood within these wider understandings, as well as the meanings attached to 'family' and to how a 'functional family' or 'good parent' is presupposed to be a caring subject. (Dodd et al., 2009, p. 177)

The construction of normative functioning held by practitioners may not be the same view as that held by the family they are working with. For example, Dodd et al. (2009) interviewed families who were caring for a disabled child and also 23 allied health professionals, including occupational therapists and social workers, who worked with the families. Dodd et al. (2009) argued that parents with specific qualities such as an authoritative parenting style (rather than an authoritarian, strict, hierarchical form of parenting or a permissive, laissez-faire style) were seen as the most able to provide support for the development of young children with disabilities. In their study, Dodd et al. (2009, p. 182) noted that allied health professionals work in ways which 'incorporate particular ideas about individual responsibility and how "ideal" families should function'. They argued that an ideal family was seen as one in which the family takes responsibility for the care of their disabled child, including organising and facilitating professional interventions. This view of a normative family does not acknowledge the differing levels of ability of individual families to manage these complex demands or to maintain a high level of energy and motivation. Therefore many families may simply not have the resources to match up to the assumed ideal family or to support a disabled child. In the extract below, the mother of a disabled child talks about the conflict between a view of her role as carer for her disabled child and her other, conflicting demands:

> It's a hard thing isn't it? In some families, or some situations, that [child's disability] might be all you have to worry about, but – that's probably not true. Everybody has other things – [such as] money issues in a family, there's everything. It's like, it's not just that [child's disability] and I feel like ... some days I just find it a struggle to get through the day. But that's just me – and I find with M [child] I feel like saying NO – this is just too hard. You know? (Dodd et al., 2009, p. 178)

The view of a normative family as one that interacts and actively engages with practitioners may be seen as an ideal family. However, care needs to be taken in understanding other families who do not engage in the same way. As the quote above shows, families have competing priorities and concerns. This is also evident in families where adults rely on their children to translate for them. In the NHS, there are interpreters and a national telephone interpreting service, but Cline et al. (in press) have noted that frequently families do not use established systems, preferring informal methods of translation, often relying on children and young people in the family to translate. There are many complex reasons why a family would involve a child as an interpreter. It may be because of a lack of trust in institutions, a concern about the confidentiality of the discussion, where translators are often part of the community group the individual is also a member of, and because of a preference for relying on a family member who will know the individual and their needs well. In addition, families may not be seen to fully participate in their children's schooling, for example not attending parents evenings. While this may be interpreted as a lack of interest on the parents' part, there may be many complex reasons to explain why they do not engage with their children's schooling and attend parents evenings. This may be due to embarrassment about the parents' ability to speak English and it may also be because the child is not bringing home information from school about invitations to school events (Edwards and Alldred, 2000).

It is important to recognise that a sense of identity is constructed partly through understanding our biological heritage. This may be an important issue for children and young people who live away from their biological families. As has been argued earlier in this chapter, biological ties and parenthood are linked, so the genetic parent is assumed to be a 'real' parent even if the individual is a donor (Hargreaves, 2006). This has impacted on policy and practice, for example in young people's right to know the identity of a biological parent who was a donor. Being open about a child's biological heritage is an important aspect of working with children born as a result of a donor (Hargreaves, 2006). This is demonstrated in the advice given by the Partnership Focus Group (2008):

> The lessons learned from the experiences of adopted adults about the importance of knowing about their genetic and biographical heritage and open communication within families is just one of the powerful messages for parents of donor-conceived children ... [It is vital that such children] have the opportunity and choice to access information they may need to make informed decisions that could profoundly affect their lives.

The assumption that 'blood is thicker than water', that biological bonds produce the best family context for children and young people is evident in practice, for example the preference for placing children in an extended family is partially based on this assumption. Equally, it is also key to recognise that many families and children do well without biological connections and that an increasingly large number of children and young people are living in such family structures. The current advice for adoption and fostering (from across the four nations), given by the British Association for Adoption & Fostering in its *First Questions: Adoption*, emphasises the wellbeing of the child and their developmental needs: 'ideally a new family should meet all a child's emotional, identity, health and developmental needs' (BAAF, n.d.).

Now I will return to the example of language brokers to illustrate that decisions about children and young people's lives are complex and require in-depth understanding of the roles and functions within families. There is research evidence to suggest that language brokering is a normative activity for many children and young people. There are many examples of positive experiences from brokering for the family reported in research projects. For example:

> We went all the way to 14th Street for an outdoor market. My dad wanted to buy some shoes for work so I had to ask a guy who sells them if he had [some] in my dad's size. I felt really good about it because he got a good deal on them. (Miguel, 7th grade, 2002) (Dorner et al., 2008, p. 532)

> It's fun, you get to do a lot of things, you get to help out. Sometimes, on Saturdays, they need help, because sometimes some families go there [to school] to check out the place, so they want somebody that knows a little bit more about, to go around the school sometimes. (Dorner et al., 2008, p. 528)

There have also been some reported benefits to the family as a whole. For example, it has been noted that some children of immigrants lose their heritage language for a variety of reasons, such as resistance, rejection and through lack of use, but being a language broker draws 'youth closer to their cultural and linguistic heritage' (Dorner et al., 2008, p. 529). However, language brokering itself may also cause difficulties and challenges for children and young people. There are instances when children and young people translate that may be judged as inappropriate, for example where a language broker translates very bad news to a parent such as a diagnosis of terminal illness or a refusal to grant asylum. In these instances, the child is positioned in ways that are inappropriate and will be stressful and upsetting to a child. Similarly, many children and young people who perform the role report that they enjoy language brokering, however, for others the tasks are too stressful and cause anxiety (Cline et al., in press). Therefore, an understanding of the whole family context is necessary when working with the individual child. It is not enough to know that the child translates for their family but under what circumstances and how they feel about the role.

Drawing on a social ecological perspective, the context within which children and young people live has an impact on how they see their family. For example, the reactions of others in the broader community can have a significant impact on the emotional and psychological health of children and young people. It is important to recognise that although there is a diverse range of family structures in the UK, many families still face prejudice and discrimination. For example, there is some evidence from the US to suggest that young people who live in LGBT-headed families report feeling less safe at school than other young people (Russell et al., 2008). Similarly, for children and young people who are language brokers, the reactions of others influence their experience. There is evidence of negative reactions to language brokers by teachers, health workers and the young people's peers (Cline et al., in press). However, the activity is seen as normative in contexts where other children and young people are also language brokers or have experience of this in the past. Patterns of immigration and settlement mean that, where there is the possibility of choice of area to live, families from similar regions often settle in the same area and send their children to the same school. Therefore, children may be in contact with others who share similar experiences to themselves:

> well my friends all speak Spanish, it's normal for us because everyone has to do the same thing and for others, no, they think it's alright. But sometimes they're like 'why do you have to miss school to translate for your mum, can't she get someone else?' so sometimes I'm like 'yeah whatever' innit? I don't really pay attention. (Cline et al., in press)

However, there are tensions between the reactions of others from outside their community as the children move from their community to a broader context:

I feel important! I feel useful because I speak the languages and so on … it is also very embarrassing for me because no one my age does that with their parents. That is … I mean, Carmo does. The Portuguese all do, but the English don't … It is to the contrary. Very often when they go to the doctor, their parents go with them, but I have to go with my parents. It is different. (Abreu et al., 2004, p. 122)

Final thoughts

In this chapter I have argued that ascriptions of normative functioning and normative families are premised upon culturally relative norms rather than universal standards. The task for practitioners is to understand the basis upon which judgements are being made, to disentangle *different* family structures from instances where the care (or lack of it) within a family of any kind can become problematic. This requires going beyond an ascription of the family as normative or not and working with the family to understand how children are being cared for within it. It is often assumed that the norm is unproblematic, that normative families provide optimum conditions for children. However, there are many instances where normative families do not provide adequately for their children, where children are abused and neglected.

Drawing on a social constructionist and social ecological perspective, I have argued that these are obviously more than individual decisions – meanings about 'normative' functioning are socially produced. Therefore, the experience of the child is not solely as a result of the family itself but often reactions to the family structure too. Meanings about 'different' families may impact upon the lives of the family itself, for example where a lesbian-headed family lives in an area where homophobia is common, or for a child who translates for their family in an area where there are not many who share the same cultural heritage.

References

Abreu, G. de, Silva, T. and Lambert, H. (2004) 'From crying to controlling: How Portuguese girls adapted to their secondary school in England', in G. de Abreu, T. Cline and H. Lambert (eds) *The Education of Portuguese Children in Britain: Insights from Research and Practice in England and Overseas*, London, Portuguese Education Department, pp. 103–29.

Atkinson, P., Parsons, E. and Featherstone, K. (2001) 'Professional construction of family and kinship in medical genetics', *New Genetics and Society*, **20**(1): 5–24.

BAAF (British Association for Adoption & Fostering) (n.d.) *First Questions: Adoption*, available online at <http://www.baaf.org.uk/info/firstq/adoption.shtml> [Accessed 18 May 2010].

Cline, T., de Abreu, G., O'Dell, L. and Crafter, S. (in press) 'Recent research on child language brokering in the United Kingdom', *mediAzioni* special edition on child language brokering.

Crabb, S. and Augoustinos, M. (2008) 'Genes and families in the media: Implications of genetic discourse for considerations of the "family"', *Health Sociology Review*, 17: 303–12.

Crafter, S., O'Dell, L., de Abreu, G. and Cline, T. (2008) 'Young people's representations of "atypical" work in UK society', *Children & Society*, **23**(3): 176–88.

Dodd, J., Saggers, S. and Wildy, H. (2009) 'Constructing the "ideal" family for family centred practice: Challenges for delivery', *Disability & Society*, **24**(2): 173–86.

Dorner, L.M, Orellana, M.F. and Jiménez, R. (2008) '"It's one of those things that you do to help the family": Language brokering and the development of immigrant adolescents', *Journal of Adolescent Research*, **23**(5): 515–43.

Earley, L., Cushway, D. and Cassidy, T. (2007) 'Children's perceptions and experiences of care giving: A focus group study', *Counselling Psychology Quarterly*, **20**(1): 69–80.

Edwards, R. and Alldred, P. (2000) 'A typology of parental involvement in education centring on children and young people: Negotiating familialisation, institutionalisation and individualisation', *British Journal of Sociology of Education*, **21**(3): 435–55.

Grant, G., Repper, J. and Nolan, M. (2008) 'Young people supporting mothers with mental health difficulties', *Health and Social Care in the Community*, **16**(3): 271–81.

Hargreaves, K. (2006) 'Constructing families and kinship through donor insemination', *Sociology of Health and Illness*, **28**(3): 261–83.

Harris, C. (2008) 'The Village People', *Advocate*, 1011: 38–43.

Morrow, V. (1998) *Understanding Families: Children's Perspectives*, York, Joseph Rowntree Foundation.

Morrow, V. (2008) 'Responsible children and children's responsibilities? Sibling caretaking and babysitting by school-age children', in J. Bridgeman, C. Lind and H. Keating (eds) *Responsibility, Law and the Family*, Farnham, Ashgate, pp. 105–24.

O'Dell, L., de Abreu, G., Cline, T. and Crafter, S. (2006) *Young People's Representations of Conflicting Roles in Child Development*, Children and Adolescents as Language Brokers, ESRC Seminar Series, London, Institute of Education.

O'Dell, L., Crafter, S., de Abreu, G. and Cline, T. (in press) 'Constructing "normal childhoods": Young people talk about young carers', *Disability & Society*.

Orellana, M.F. (2009) *Translating Childhoods: Immigrant Youth, Language and Culture*, New Brunswick, NJ, Rutgers University Press.

Partnership Focus Group (2008) *Briefing for the Human Fertilisation and Embryology Bill*, April, available online at <www.baaf.org.uk/about/campaigns/embryologybriefing.pdf> [Accessed 18 May 2010].

Phoenix, A. (2009) 'De-colonising practices: Negotiating narratives from racialised and gendered experiences of education', *Race, Ethnicity and Education*, **12**(1): 101–14.

Rigg, A. and Pryor, J. (2007) 'Children's perceptions of families: What do they really think?', *Children & Society*, 21: 17–30.

Rose, N. (1985) *The Psychological Complex*, London, Routledge.

Russell, S., McGuire, J.K., Lee, S.-A. et al. (2008) 'Adolescent perceptions of safety for students with LGBT parents', *Journal of LGBT Youth*, **5**(4): 11–27.

Sotirin, P. and Ellingson, L.L. (2007) 'Rearticulating the aunt: Feminist alternatives of family, care and kinship in popular performances of aunting', *Cultural Studies Critical Methodologies*, **7**(4): 442–59.

Walker, J., Crawford, K. and Taylor, F. (2008) 'Listening to children: Gaining a perspective of the experiences of poverty and social exclusion from children and young people of single-parent families', *Health and Social Care in the Community*, **16**(4): 429–36.

Winter, E. (2008) 'The new constituency: Welcoming LGBT-headed families into our schools', *Independent School*, **68**(1): 94–9.

3

The surveillance of children, young people and families

Lisa Arai

This chapter explores the ways in which some children and young people, their families and even entire communities are surveilled, considered socially problematic and made the subjects of intervention by welfare, health, crime prevention and other agencies. It considers how, and why, this happens, and explores what it might mean for practitioners (who are themselves subjected to scrutiny by others) working with children and their families. As a social scientist with a public health research background, my interest in surveillance grew out of my research on a highly scrutinised social group and the target of a number of social and healthcare interventions: pregnant and parenting teenagers and their children.

The chapter describes the context in which specific groups are the subjects of scrutiny, the emergence of the surveillant state and principal forms of surveillance. The surveillance of children and families is discussed to examine why and how this happens. The dilemmas and issues raised by surveying children, young people and families, as well as responses to these, which might arise in practice with children and families are considered. Some of the key themes and potential problems for service delivery are brought together as final thoughts at the end of the chapter.

The rise of the surveillant state

Contemporary, postindustrial societies have been described as anxious about a number of external and internal threats to their order including those posed by challenges to their economies in a globalised world, far-reaching and ethically complex medical and scientific developments, the possibly catastrophic consequences of climate change and the internal dangers posed by 'subversive' citizens who reject the values of the societies they live in (Beck, 1992). It is against this macro-level backdrop that the rise in surveillance of individuals and groups – including children and families – has occurred.

Surveillance of populations is not a novel phenomenon: governments have always been interested in monitoring citizens and their activities. Foucault (1977) has described the emergence of the 'disciplinary society', one focused on the surveillance of citizens and the regulation of all aspects of their behaviour. Foucault's work has been extensively used in analysis of contemporary forms of surveillance (Haggerty and Ericson, 2000), especially in relation to his reworking of the concept of the 'panopticon', the all-seeing prison where inmates are perpetually observed yet remain unaware of who is observing them or when they are doing so. As Haggerty and Ericson (2000, p. 606) stated, Foucault extended the idea of the panopticon and proposed that it 'served as a diagram for a new model of power which extended beyond the prison to take hold in ... other disciplinary institutions ... such as the factory, hospital, military, and school'.

Contemporary surveillance: an overview

Surveillance can be either centralized or diffuse, hence the debate over whether surveillance 'state' or 'society' is the more appropriate term for modern forms of surveillance (Garrett, 2004). Importantly, surveillance is more than the visual:

> A literal definition of surveillance as 'watching over' indicates monitoring the behaviour of persons, objects, or systems. However surveillance is not only a visual process ... Surveillance can be undertaken in a wide range of ways involving a variety of technologies. (House of Lords Select Committee on the Constitution, 2009)

It is in respect of technology, referred to above, in its 'electronic turn' (Garrett, 2004), that surveillance in contemporary, developed world societies is qualitatively different to that of previous eras. The twenty-first-century surveillance of people, groups and places is usually linked to electronic and other technologies and is especially linked to the development of databases (Lyon, 2003). It was noted earlier that governments have always been interested in the surveillance of their citizens, yet the use of such technologies has facilitated surveillance on a scale hitherto unseen:

> The processing of personal data has always been part of public administration ... But contemporary uses of surveillance and data processing can be distinguished from those of the past in extent and the intensity with which information is analysed, collated, and used. (House of Lords Select Committee on the Constitution, 2009)

Databases usually contain personal biographical information that can be easily retrieved, analysed, added to and edited. This data can often be linked to data held elsewhere so that a comprehensive informational snapshot of a citizen's life is created (Anderson et al., 2009). Clarke (1987) has usefully referred to this aspect of surveillance as 'dataveillance', which he described as the 'systematic use of personal data systems in the investigation or monitoring of the actions or communications of one or more persons'.

Modern surveillance is different to older forms of surveillance in another, crucial way. In part because the technology can facilitate it, it is possible for many more people to be the subjects of surveillance than was possible in the past. Mass (or 'passive') surveillance, such as that made possible by CCTV, by its very nature affects most sections of the population including people engaged in everyday activities such as shopping or driving. 'Targeted' surveillance, on the other hand, is aimed at specific individuals or groups of individuals, for example those suspected of engaging in, or plotting, acts of terrorism.

Contemporary forms of surveillance, while apparently offering benefits to citizens (protection from real or imagined threats, ease of access to public services), are believed to be damaging to civil liberties such as the right to privacy and freedom from excessive state intrusion into family life (Crossman et al., 2007). Commentators have also expressed concerns about the reliability, safety and security of databases. Databases can never be made entirely safe from those with criminal intentions, and the wrong information can be entered into databases, data can be inappropriately accessed or even mislaid altogether. In 2007, for example, the child benefit records of 25 million British citizens contained on two discs were lost.

Ultimately, surveillance of citizens that is considered disproportionate and unwarranted has the potential to fundamentally alter the relationship between the citizen and the state, and it is this aspect of surveillance that troubles many commentators (Crossman et al., 2007). In this respect, 'joined-up' government (National Audit Office, 2001) can be seen as a kind of Faustian bargain, where, in return for ease of access to services and social, health and other entitlements, citizens have to relinquish a good deal of their personal information and their privacy, as well as face the risk of this private information being lost, stolen or misused by criminals.

While surveillance may seem omnipresent (and omniscient), it is undermined by those who resist it by refusing to comply with its stipulations (for registration of personal information, for example), or who campaign for changes to legislation so that citizens are better protected against the effects of pervasive monitoring by the state (Martin et al., 2009). Contemporary forms of surveillance also encompass 'inverse' or 'sousveillance', where those being watched can become the watchers (Mann et al., 2003). The 2009 scandal over British MPs' expenses, which revealed widespread exploitation of the system of parliamentary allowances by politicians, was a powerful example of inverse surveillance, and one which led to changes in the allowance system. The scandal only emerged because freedom of information legislation permitted scrutiny, for the first time, of MPs' expenses by the electorate.

The surveillance of children, young people and families

Although mass surveillance has increased and, to some degree, everyone is affected by it, some groups are more 'problematic' than others and 'solutions' involve greater monitoring, scrutiny and regulation of their behaviour. The subjects of surveillance by the state and its agents have traditionally been the poor and dispossessed, especially those receiving welfare (Gilliom, 2001; Broadhurst et al., 2007). There is a long history of surveillance of those who are economically dependent on the state or other bodies; a central focus of the Poor Laws, which operated in England and Wales until the introduction of the National Assistance Act in 1948, was the monitoring of the poor and destitute (Solar, 1995).

Surveillance is not power neutral: it functions within the existing framework of power relations; those with money, status and other resources can bypass many forms of surveillance. Economically and structurally, powerless groups usually possess little political power (Schneider and Ingram, 1993) and are less able to resist surveillance than more powerful groups. The wealthy are never likely to be in a position, for example, where they are obliged to provide information to the state about the intricacies of their sexual relationships – such as how many nights a week a lover stays at their home – as others are sometimes obliged to do in the process of making applications for welfare benefits.

However, while the poor are still monitored more than others, social policy commentators have observed that, over the past two decades, there has been an increase in surveillance of *all* groups, even those who previously would not have been considered socially problematic (Parton, 2006). In the last decades of the twentieth century, the monitoring of children, young people and their families has increased and intensified as governments have sought to respond to perceived threats to (and from) children, as well as more general concerns about child welfare and family life.

In respect of threats to children, calls for greater surveillance of families (especially those that are 'problematic' or where there have been child protection concerns) have been made throughout the latter decades of the twentieth century, often in response to the deaths of children at the hands of abusive carers (Parton, 2006; Munro, 2007). However, during Labour's period in government from 1997–2010, there were 'significant policy and legislative changes aimed at shifting the incident driven focus of child protection in England' (Broadhurst et al., 2007, p. 454). Parton (2006) observed that in England the publication of the

Laming Report, written in the wake of Victoria Climbié's death in 2000, and the implementation of the *Every Child Matters* policy and the Children Act 2004 signalled the start of a more pro-interventionist change in the relationship between the caring professions and children and families. However, Parton located the origins of this change in an earlier period. From the mid-1990s onwards, the idea of intervening early in the life of children who might later become problematic was becoming more accepted, and proponents of early intervention were increasingly able to refer to a growing body of research on the childhood antecedents of anti-social or criminal behaviour. Poor outcomes for children were seen to be related to factors such as poverty, parental unemployment and maternal depression, and if these factors were dealt with through intervention at a crucial stage in a child's life, then children could be diverted from a life of anti-social behaviour or crime.

In addition to the growth in research on early life adversity and the growing popularity of the idea of early intervention – as well as the memory of past, high-profile tragedies like the murder of the British toddler James Bulger by two young boys known to be 'at risk' because of their chaotic family backgrounds – other developments were also significant in the move towards what Parton (2006) has described as the 'preventive-surveillance' state. Greater surveillance of children and their families can also be linked to developments in IT and the popularity of ideas about joined-up government allowing citizens seamless and efficient access to an array of public services.

Garrett (2004) links the increased surveillance of children not only to the belief that children need to be protected (and that the criminal proclivities of some children need to be contained so that others are protected from them), but also to the belief that young people need to be properly prepared for the world of work so that they can function in the 'flexible' labour market. So, while the curtailment of criminal and anti-social behaviour among the young has always been given as a reason for monitoring their behaviour (and there have been many initiatives introduced under the auspices of the Youth Justice Board that are significant in this respect), surveillance of the young is often justified by reference to a need to ensure their (more general) welfare and wellbeing, as well as specific aspects of it such as their educational attainment and employability.

Responding to practitioner 'failings'

Two young brothers were in the care of social services and may already have been reported to the police when they allegedly attacked and tortured two children … leaving one for dead. The boys, aged 11 and 10, had been placed with foster carers by Doncaster Council, whose child protection services were accused recently of a litany of failings. (Norfolk, 2009)

This extract, which describes aspects of crimes committed by two young boys in the north of England in 2009, draws attention to three salient issues: the very young age of the attackers; the nature of their offences; and the fact that they were known to the police and social care services – and were in fact in the care of the latter at the time the offences were committed. Savage acts of violence committed by 'feral' young children, incompetent practitioners and badly performing services are key motifs of the late twentieth and early twenty-first century and also help explain the acceleration of moves to monitor children and families. Parton (2006) attributed the emergence of the preventive-surveillance state in part to the growth of defensiveness among social care professionals as a result of high-profile practitioner 'failings'.

The deaths of Victoria Climbié in 2000, mentioned briefly above, and Peter Connelly ('Baby P') in 2007 are particularly instructive in this respect. Both children died in the London borough of Haringey, both had been seen by numerous health and social care professionals over a period of time, and yet, in both cases, the abuse the children were suffering, and which eventually led to their deaths, was not identified. In the case of Baby P, the practitioners who had worked with his family were attacked for their professional 'incompetence' in the media and elsewhere. *The Sun* newspaper ran a petition calling for the sacking of the social workers involved in Baby P's case and death threats were even made against some of them (Garrett, 2009).

In the midst of the (often hysterical) reaction to the death of Baby P, there were calls for (even greater) intrusion by the state into the private lives of families, especially those families that were already known to social services and might be considered 'dysfunctional' (Garrett, 2009). Lord Laming's Report (2009), which was written after Baby P's death and evaluated the progress that had been made to protect children since Victoria Climbié's death, referred to the need for more sharing of information, given the large numbers of children who were in need:

> Policies, legislation, structures and procedures are, of course, of immense importance, but they serve only as the means of securing better life opportunities for each young person. It is the robust and consistent implementation of these policies and procedures which keeps children and young people safe. For example, organisational boundaries and concerns about sharing information must never be allowed to put in jeopardy the safety of a child or young person. (The Lord Laming, 2009, p. 2)

Since the first Laming Report in 2003, greater information exchange had been seen as central to the protection of children (Burke, 2009), and is pivotal to the wider idea of joined-up and 'transformational' government. The Children Act 2004 stipulated the creation of 'information hubs' where data on English children could be collected, stored and accessed by a variety of practitioners involved in their care. These hubs became 'ContactPoint', a key element of the *Every Child Matters* programme, for storing information about every child up to age 18 in England. However, in response to civil liberties concerns, the coalition government elected in 2010 committed itself to scrap ContactPoint. At the time of writing, it is unclear what it will be replaced by. A similar system operates in Scotland, although there are some differences between the two systems in terms of their flexibility and accessibility (Freeman, 2009).

While the need for the enhanced surveillance of children and families to be facilitated by electronic means was considered necessary in light of high-profile child deaths such as Victoria Climbié's, Anderson et al. (2006) observed that Victoria's death might not have been averted simply by amassing more information about her situation: she was already well known to health and social care professionals. What the latter failed to do, however, was to make sense of the information known about her:

> If one of the core problems in accurately identifying children who are suffering, or are at risk of suffering significant harm, is the level of professional expertise in understanding data (rather than a lack of data per se), then providing more data does not seem to be the most obvious strategy for improving practice. In fact it may be counterproductive. (Anderson et al., 2006, p. 17)

Anderson et al. raise the (very real) possibility that practitioners may be swamped with information about children. And, while the information on Contactpoint was initially quite sparse (name, date of birth, schools attended and so on), there are vast amounts of information about every child in the country stored in other databases. All this is easily accessible to those who have the authority, and it is the practitioner's job to make sense of this information:

> a child's entire education or health record could be despatched to another practitioner in less time than it would take to type the covering email. Information that would once have occupied a large room full of filing cabinets can be fitted on to a USB stick, or an entire database of 11 million records downloaded on to two CD-Roms. (Dowty and Korff, 2009, p. 7)

Predicting the problematic

The origins of the preventive-surveillance state (Parton, 2006), then, and the greater surveillance of children and families lie in a number of places:

- greater recognition that the roots of anti-social or criminal behaviour are located in early childhood and that this should be where intervention is concentrated
- the desire to safeguard children, promote their wellbeing and stem anti-social tendencies so they develop into healthy and happy citizens, able to contribute to their communities and participate in the flexible economy

■ advances in IT making the storage and linkage of vast amounts of information in searchable databases possible
■ practitioner responses to much-publicised service 'failings' in the wake of child deaths.

These developments have occurred against a backdrop of wider, pervasive social anxieties about all kinds of natural, biological, technological and social risks (Beck, 1992), which has led to increased surveillance of all citizens.

Despite widespread calls for greater surveillance of the family, more intrusion into the lives of 'problem' families and more sharing of information, concerns have been expressed about the surveillance of children and their families. These are often focused on the civil liberties of individuals (including children), and their right to consent to the sharing of their private data, for example, or their DNA being held on the national DNA database, and the right of the family to remain private and free from excessive state intrusion. Some analysts have warned that contemporary forms of surveillance risk seeing all parents as potentially abusive (Parton, 2006). The possible dangers of storing personal information on databases have already been mentioned above.

There is another set of anxieties that is often referred to by commentators. Contemporary forms of surveillance often go beyond monitoring through the (relatively simple) collection of data into a realm that once belonged only to science fiction. The idea of early intervention was mentioned above, but it is the related concept of *prediction* that is significant here. At the beginning of the twenty-first century, social policy is oriented around the idea that, with the right kind of surveillance, the ongoing collection and analysis of diverse personal data gleaned from a variety of sources and the application of expert knowledge or expertise, governments can now predict who will become socially problematic and steps can be taken to intervene to prevent it. Early intervention policies have been popular with governments of all parties across the four nations of the UK, including the New Labour governments and the coalition government elected in 2010. In a much-quoted statement, Tony Blair, the former British prime minister, even suggested that early intervention might start before a child is born:

> Tomorrow's potential troublemakers can be identified even before they are born, Tony Blair has suggested. Mr Blair said it was possible to spot the families whose circumstances made it likely their children would grow up to be a 'menace to society'. He said teenage mums and problem families could be forced to take help to head off difficulties ... Mr Blair [said] ... there was a group of people with multiple problems. There had to be intervention 'pre-birth even', he said. (BBC News Online, 2006)

In *A Report on the Surveillance Society* (Surveillance Studies Network, 2006), it was suggested that the overall themes of a future surveillance society will be of 'pervasive surveillance', which will be largely directed at monitoring the mobility of people, things and data, and at 'predicting and pre-empting behaviour' (p. 64).

The consequences of the surveillant state: implications for practice

In Parton's view of preventive-surveillance state, the relationship between parents, children, practitioners and the state is fundamentally different to that which existed before (Parton, 2006), yet there is little research on how the intensive and technologically aided surveillance of children and their families will impact on public service use, on the role of the practitioner, or the relationship between practitioners and their clients. Given this, what are the implications of greater surveillance for those who work with children and families, both for the practitioner and for the users of services? Does this change in the way practitioners work pose dilemmas for them? How, for example, can they reconcile their welfare role with their surveillance role? Before some of these issues are considered, a point made briefly earlier should be reiterated.

Being able to work across agencies and sectors in a more joined-up way, being in a position to make best use of the most up-to-date technology so that time is saved and resources better targeted, and being able to access personal data quickly so that important decisions can be made about the welfare of children and families – all these can potentially have a positive impact on the way that practitioners work, and on their practice with children and families. Children and young people and their families are heavy users of all kinds of health, social care and education services, and come into contact with myriad practitioners. It makes sense to offer them the most relevant and appropriate services, and it makes sense for practitioners to be well informed about their clients' needs (Kelsey, 2009). Moreover, practitioners working with colleagues from other sectors, who all have access to reliable information about the children in their care, are in a better position to protect the most vulnerable children, those who are at risk of abuse or neglect.

These are some of the obvious benefits to joined-up working and their importance cannot be understated. However, recognition of these positives should not divert attention from the possible pitfalls of enhanced and technologically aided surveillance, described earlier in this chapter. With this in mind, what are the implications of greater surveillance of children and families?

The first set of possible implications are that, for most practitioners working with children and their families (and unless things change), there will probably be an even greater shift to a surveillance role, and this will continue to have an impact on the dynamics between practitioners and service users (Anderson et al., 2006;

Parton, 2006). Once the scale and scope of surveillance (as well as any negative impacts it might have) are fully understood by those accessing services, the dynamics between practitioners and those they are working with will inevitably be affected. Of particular concern to individuals accessing services is the possibility of their private information being transferred to other organisations or practitioners (Anderson et al., 2006). Consent would be required for this to occur, but service users may feel pressurised to give this, or be afraid of the consequences of withholding it. This undermines the principle of confidentiality between practitioner and client that is central to the integrity of many services (Munro, 2007).

Two related points should be made. First, practitioners have always had dual roles: help or support offered by the practitioner has always involved some degree of surveillance, even if it is at the level of data collection (Trotter, 2006). Second, both as practitioners and service users themselves, practitioners are also the objects of surveillance by others. The activities of social workers, in particular, are highly monitored by regulatory bodies (the General Social Care Council in England and the Scottish Social Services Council in Scotland), as well as by managers, colleagues, the general public and the media. Similarly, the Office for Standards in Education, Children's Services and Skills (Ofsted) inspects the performance of English schools and teachers.

The recognition that surveillance is not a one-way street but can take many forms, function on a number of levels and be subverted or resisted in a variety of ways is reflected in the coining of terms like 'sousveillance' or 'inverse' surveillance, mentioned above, and 'uberveillance' or 'omni-veillance' (Michael and Michael, 2007), the latter referring to an all-pervasive, ever-present state of surveillance.

In some respects, social care practitioners, in particular, are operating in an 'omni-veillant' professional environment: they have an obligation to monitor the activities of others, ostensibly for their welfare, yet are themselves highly scrutinised. They have to make the most profoundly important decisions about the lives of children – whether a particular 'at risk' child should remain with its parents or not, for example – but, because opportunities for them to work truly autonomously are limited and their decisions are so heavily scrutinised, they may feel constrained in their decision making (Burke, 2009). The consequences of making the 'wrong' decision can be so great that, out of fear, the practitioner might adopt a more procedural practice approach rather than a reflective and more creative one in their interaction with clients (Munro, 2007).

Another possible consequence of the move towards the preventive-surveillance state is that some practitioners may come to feel that information collecting rather than relationship forming is not why they entered the caring professions, and this might affect morale and impact negatively on staff retention and recruitment. This is a serious concern, given the high number of social worker vacancies and evidence of low morale among many social care professionals (McGregor, 2009).

A second set of implications is that, from a service user perspective, there is an increasing risk that service users will fail to engage with services. If service users are distrustful of practitioners, and believe that they are being scrutinised, there is a danger that they will not use services. This is likely to be particularly true of those who already have some involvement with social services and who fear the loss of their children (Canvin et al., 2007), or who are considered to be 'hard to reach' (Munro, 2007). There is some evidence that these fears are not unfounded: in Sure Start areas, there is an increased number of child protection 'Section 47' notices, that is, those where children are thought to have suffered, or might be likely to suffer, significant harm (Broadhurst et al., 2007), and Sure Start workers have reported informing social services about children they think may be at risk without their parents' knowledge (Canvin et al., 2007).

What will happen when individuals do not access services for fear of scrutiny by practitioners, or anxiety about what data might be collected, how it might be linked up with other data and used? If individuals withdraw from health and education services, there is a possibility that a service 'underclass' will emerge (Garrett, 2004; Munro, 2007). Another possible implication is that service users might engage in 'disguised compliance', where clients are seen to be cooperating with practitioners, but are in reality hiding information and manipulating practitioners.

There are at least two things that could be done to (begin to) address these concerns. First, the law on data protection, client confidentiality and the circumstances under which the transfer of information occurs could be strengthened and additional training could be made available to practitioners on their obligations in this respect. This might provide greater reassurance for service users. Children and young people need to be made fully aware of their rights in relation to their own data and regarded as competent to consent to data sharing where they can demonstrate sufficient maturity to do so. Dowty and Korff (2009, p. 27) recommend that:

> all local authorities [be] required to train practitioners in the assessment of children's capacity and competence to understand the reason for and the implications of sharing their data with specified organisations or individuals; and that they regularly review situations in which a child under 16 has given consent without parental involvement in order to ensure that correct procedures are being followed.

The European Court ruling that the retention of DNA data on the national DNA database contravened the European Convention on Human Rights signalled recognition of the importance of the rights of individuals to ownership of their personal data. The court noted that the dangers of unnecessary data retention were particularly 'damaging' for children and young people (Standing Committee for Youth Justice, 2008).

Second, another way to deal with the risk of people not accessing services is to make them accessible anonymously (Anderson et al., 2009). This might appeal to young people especially, for whom confidentiality is a major consideration, although it may lead to other dilemmas for practitioners.

Final thoughts

The rise of the surveillant state has been described in this chapter. This has been considered in relation to children and young people, and there has been some exploration of why children and families are subjected to greater scrutiny than they were in the recent past. As the subjects of surveillance, children and young people are monitored in relation to their general development, their behaviour and activities, their health status and their educational attainment. Information about diverse aspects of their lives is now routinely collected and stored on vast databases, the contents of which can be readily retrieved by a variety of practitioners. Information linkages can be made with other databases, so that a 'fuller picture' of a child's life emerges. Yet, contemporary forms of surveillance have moved away from the simple collection of data into a world of prediction. Using this data, statistical profiling might suggest that individual children or young people are at risk for some reason, and that early (possibly even antenatal) intervention is necessary long before a problem becomes apparent. Being described as a risk to society before birth and made the subject of early life intervention has profound implications for children and wider society.

Equally important is the growth of a state of omni-surveillance, which affects practitioners as well as their clients. Practitioners are a heavily surveilled group, their activities regulated by external organisations and their actions scrutinised by the public and the media. They find themselves in the difficult position of attempting to provide the best care for individuals in need while subjected to intense monitoring by others. This can affect their capacity to make informed decisions.

There have been many concerns expressed about the increasing surveillance of children and the family, and the vast amounts of data collected in health, education and social care settings every day. A balance has to be struck between the rights of the individual (children and young people included) to privacy and the rights of the family to be free of excessive state intrusion and, on the other hand, the need to safeguard children and young people. Practitioners are in a difficult position having to balance dual responsibilities of helping and monitoring. They themselves are subject to intense forms of surveillance, which can undermine their confidence and affect their abilities to deal with children and families. There is a danger that a hard-to-reach group will emerge: people who will not use services and will not engage with practitioners. There is also a danger that forms of surveillance, especially those that are technologically aided and which aim to pre-empt some forms of behaviour, will be seen as a panacea. Yet, even the most intensive and pervasive forms of surveillance cannot eliminate all forms of risk.

References

Anderson, R., Brown, I., Dowty, T. et al. (2009) *Database State*, York, Joseph Rowntree Reform Trust.

Anderson, R., Brown, I., Clayton, R. et al. (2006) *Children's Databases Safety and Privacy: A Report for the Information Commissioner*, Foundation for Information Policy Research, available online at <http://www.cl.cam.ac.uk/~rja14/Papers/kids. pdf> [Accessed 22 March 2010].

BBC News Online (2006) Blair to tackle 'menace' children, 31 August, available online at <http://news.bbc.co.uk/1/hi/5301824.stm> [Accessed 22 March 2010].

Beck. U. (1992) *Risk Society*, London, Sage.

Broadhurst, K., Mason, C. and Grover, C. (2007) 'Sure Start and the "re-authorization" of Section 47 child protection practices', *Critical Social Policy*, **27**(4): 443–61.

Burke, L. (2009) 'A broken profession or a broken society?', *Probation Journal*, **56**(1): 5–8.

Canvin, K., Jones, C., Marttila, A. et al. (2007) 'Can I risk using public services? Perceived consequences of seeking help and health care among households living in poverty: qualitative study', *Journal of Epidemiology and Community Health*, 61: 984–9.

Clarke, R. (1987) Information technology and dataveillance, available online at <http://www.rogerclarke.com/DV/CACM88.html> [Accessed 5 March 2010].

Crossman, G. with Kitchin, H., Kuna, R., Skrein, M. and Russell, J. (2007) *Overlooked: Surveillance and Personal Privacy in Modern Britain*, London, Liberty.

Dowty, T. and Korff, D. (2009) *Protecting the Virtual Child: The Law and Children's Consent to Sharing Personal Data*, London, Action on Rights of Children, available online at <http://www.archrights.org.uk/docs/NYA(4)arch_16.2.0%5B2%5D.pdf> [Accessed 22 March 2010].

Foucault, M. (1977) *Discipline and Punish: The Birth of the Prison*, New York, Vintage.

Freeman, I. (2009) 'Electronic sharing of information on children: The Scottish and English experiences', *Journal of Integrated Care*, **17**(2): 22–6.

Garrett, P.M. (2004) 'The electronic eye: Emerging surveillant practices in social work with children and families', *European Journal of Social Work*, **7**(1): 57–71.

Garrett, P.M. (2009) 'The case of "Baby P": Opening up spaces for debate on the "transformation" of children's services?', *Critical Social Policy*, **29**(3): 5333–47.

Gilliom, J. (2001) *Overseers of the Poor: Surveillance, Resistance, and the Limits of Privacy*, Chicago, University of Chicago Press.

Haggerty, K.D. and Ericson, R.V. (2000) 'The surveillant assemblage', *British Journal of Sociology*, **51**(4): 605–22.

House of Lords Select Committee on the Constitution (2009) *Select Committee Second Report of 2008-9, Surveillance: Citizens and the State*, London, TSO.

Kelsey, T. (2009) 'Long live the database state', *Prospect*, no. 161, available online at <http://www.prospectmagazine.co.uk/2009/07/longlivethedatabasestate/> [Accessed 22 March 2010].

Laming, The Lord (2009) *The Protection of Children in England: A Progress Report*, London, TSO, available online at <http://publications.everychildmatters.gov.uk/eOrderingDownload/HC-330.pdf> [Accessed March 2010].

Lyon, D. (2003) 'Surveillance as social sorting: Computer codes and mobile bodies', in D. Lyon (ed.) *Surveillance as Social Sorting: Privacy, Risk, and Digital Discrimination*, London, Routledge, pp. 13–31.

McGregor, K. (2009) 'Poll by social work employment agencies reveals fall in morale', *Community Care*, available online at <http://www.communitycare.co.uk/Articles/2009/10/13/112843/morale-among-social-workers-at-a-five-year-low.htm> [Accessed 5 March 2010].

Mann, S., Nolan, J. and Wellman, B. (2003) 'Sousveillance: Inventing and using wearable computing devices for data collection in surveillance environments', *Surveillance and Society*, **1**(3): 331–55.

Martin, A.K., van Brakel, R.E. and Bernhard, D.J. (2009) 'Understanding resistance to digital surveillance: Towards a multi-disciplinary, multi-actor framework', *Surveillance and Society*, **6**(3): 213–32.

Michael, K. and Michael, M.G. (2007) *The Second Workshop on the Social Implications of National Security: From Dataveillance to Überveillance and the Realpolitik of the Transparent Society*, University of Wollongong, Australia.

Munro, E. (2007) 'Confidentiality in a preventive child welfare system', *Ethics and Social Welfare*, **1**(1): 41–55.

National Audit Office (2001) *Joining Up to Improve Public Services*, London, TSO.

Norfolk, A. (2009) 'Edlington boys held for "torture" of children were in care', *The Times*, 7 April, available online at <http://www.timesonline.co.uk/tol/news/uk/crime/article6048032.ece> [Accessed March 2010].

Parton, N. (2006) *Safeguarding Childhood: Early Intervention and Surveillance in a Late Modern Society*, Basingstoke, Palgrave Macmillan.

Schneider, A. and Ingram, H. (1993) 'Social construction of target populations: Implications for politics and policy', *The American Political Science Review*, **87**(2): 334–47.

Solar, P.M. (1995) 'Poor relief and English economic development before the industrial revolution', *Economic History Review*, **48**(1): 1–22.

Standing Committee for Youth Justice (2008) *Keeping the Right People on the DNA Database: Response on Behalf of Standing Committee for Youth Justice*, available online at <http://www.crae.org.uk/assets/files/SCYJ_HOconsultation_NDNAD%20090807%20FINAL.pdf> [Accessed 5 February 2010].

Surveillance Studies Network (2006) *A Report on the Surveillance Society*, available online at <http://www.ico.gov.uk/upload/documents/library/data_protection/practical_application/surveillance_society_summary_06.pdf> [Accessed 30 March 2010].

Trotter, C. (2006) *Working with Involuntary Clients: A Guide to Practice*, Crows Nest, NSW, Allen & Unwin.

4

Public policy, children and young people

Pam Foley

The focus of this chapter is children and social policy as it is played out at the meeting point of policies, children, young people and their families. It also looks at the roles of some key catalysts, notably the media. Choices, enacted through social policy, remain under the control of individual national governments, despite being subject to global influences and some EU treaties (http//europa.eu/index_en.htm). Tradition, culture and values coalesce to create different responses to similar developments across Europe (Cohen et al., 2004). There is also an increasing divergence in different parts of the UK. Internal UK governments are increasingly able to create their own particular set of social policies and to make decisions. While it is unlikely to be formally announced, incremental changes now underway could result in an increasingly hybrid welfare system evolving in different parts of the UK. Policies affect the lives of children and young people; recently these have involved such developments as the significant expansion of early years education, a greater measurement of outcomes and attainment in schools, moves towards the integration of children's services and the increasing cost of higher education. Decisions about welfare and education lead to differences in services, in the workforce, and in those underlying concepts and understandings of children, young people and families with which services and workers work.

The initial parts of this chapter look at where policy that affects children and young people comes from and what can influence its development. As a social scientist, I focus here on the ways a belief in families as resilient, resourceful and self-reliant is balanced with the intervention/provision/protection roles of the state. These roles of the state are complex not least because of the ways they necessarily merge and overlap. In the second half of this chapter, I look at how policy for children and young people develops in the real world, how different policies gain momentum, how certain policies are forefronted, sidelined and sometimes dropped, and how policies tackle some large and deep-rooted issues that affect children and young people's lives now and in the future. The chapter aims to deconstruct and explore some of the ways in which public policy emerges from the dialogue between policy makers, state organisations and agencies that work with children, young people and families, and children, young people and families themselves.

Children, young people, politics and policies

Children, young people and families are always high on any political agenda. They feature strongly, for example, in political discourse concerning economic growth, employment and unemployment, welfare, health, crime, the education system and demographic change. Governments must try to reconcile social stability with change, economic competition and growth, while protecting and nurturing the next generation. There is uncertainty about what to base decisions on and what to prioritise and compromise on. In addition, policies have intentional and unintentional consequences, introducing a further element of uncertainty.

Inevitably, there are complex compromises to be made in a society that is diverse, mobile and individualistic. While state institutions have the means to intervene in the lives of children and families, even when its desired outcomes are made unusually clear, such as in the *Every Child Matters* group of policy documents (DfES, 2004), there are usually doubts about what will work, whether the right outcomes have been targeted, and whether the right balance has been struck between the responsibilities of parents and the responsibilities of the state towards children. And as social policy for children and families usually involves a commitment to the spending of large amounts of public money, mistakes are costly.

Nonetheless, a steady stream of policies emerge, which raise important questions about the welfare, care and education of children and young people, about parenting and working lives, and about the values and practices of those who work with children and families. Particular phrases may be reiterated, such as 'hardworking families', which may capture the relationship the state hopes for between itself and children and families. The usefulness of such phrases is mixed; 'hardworking families' creates an antithesis for who, in turn, another set of policies then emerges. The widely used phrase 'best interests of the child' is problematic as a tool, as it is both impossible to know with any certainty what is in a child's 'best interests' and 'best interests' necessarily exist within a specific social and cultural framework (Thomas, 2002). This means that working with best interests presents further practical and ethical questions for practitioners, along with the set of values and ethics they have already chosen to use themselves.

At its most basic, the purpose of public policy for children and young people is to deliver a good standard of care, health, welfare and education through initiating, directing, funding, providing and regulating a range of services and practitioners. However, there is fundamental disagreement about whether the state's main duty is to children and young people more directly, or whether its main duty is to families as social units that include children. A child cannot be isolated from their family and society. Whatever the problem for the child, it almost always relates to what is happening to the adults around them. So the best children's services can only work well for individuals if other adult issues are simultaneously tackled, such as the child whose parent is in prison, whose parents disregard education, whose parent has drug or alcohol problems, or the child whose mother experiences domestic violence. Paradoxically, a state can also continue to instigate damaging processes from which it then needs to protect children. So, for example, a government can both create a space in which free-market economic systems are largely unhindered and create services for those left behind or discarded by that system. Social policies for children and young people therefore often include both economic and social goals: the *Every Child Matters* policy framework, for example, identified certain outcomes as key to wellbeing in childhood and later life – being healthy, staying safe, enjoying and achieving, making a positive contribution and achieving economic wellbeing (DfES, 2008).

Public policy can be at the forefront of social change, more often trails social change, and can even attempt to reverse certain social changes. Consequently, policies for children, young people and families get caught up in strong currents of shifting social attitudes and are scrutinised by a sceptical, sometimes hostile media. While the makers of public policy for children and young people can look for 'evidence-based policy', this rarely seems able to provide reassuring or definitive answers. Not all evidence is trusted or trustworthy, evidence may be thin and ideas that work on a small scale as pilots may fail when scaled up and rolled out nationally. In addition, the importation of policies and models of practice from other nations may not work. As policies involve both enabling choices made by some families (for example whose childcare is paid for) and the sanctioning of other families' choices (for example faith schools), they become involved with the private and public lives of individuals and individual families. They need to reconcile both private and public objectives; for example educational policy involves reconciling the demand by society and the economy for a certain level and kind of education, with the abilities, desires and aspirations of individuals, so the national curriculum, which could take the form of a minimum curriculum, is instead detailed and prescribed, with subjects explicitly divided and narrowly assessed.

This may all be difficult enough but these policies are also judged using subjective terms such as 'good parenting' and a 'good childhood'. Governments can be judged for their particular policies that have most affected the lives of children, for example the legacy of the Conservative governments of the 1980s and 90s of high levels of child poverty and the failure of the Labour governments that followed to reverse widening income inequality. The publication of cross-national data, seeming to take a name and shame approach, can be another powerful influence. The UNICEF report *Child Poverty in Perspective: An Overview of Child Well-being in Rich Countries*, for example, described its purpose as 'to encourage monitoring, to permit comparison, and to stimulate the discussion and development of policies to improve children's lives' (UNICEF, 2007, p. 2). As the UK was ranked last of the 21 OECD (Organisation for Economic Co-operation and Development) countries, the opening statement of the report had a particular sting for those reading it here:

> The true measure of a nation's standing is how well it attends to its children – their health and safety, their material security, their education and socialization, and their sense of being loved, valued, and included in the families and societies into which they are born. (UNICEF, 2007, p. 1)

International comparisons such as this can reveal each country's strengths and weaknesses but, crucially, also underline that children's wellbeing is 'policy susceptible'. Comparative data representing choices made by similarly economically advanced nations may be used 'as a broad and realistic guide to the potential for improvement in all OECD countries' (UNICEF, 2007, p. 2). In the end, policies for children and young people must convince those who pay the taxes that support the enactment of policies and those on the receiving end of policies that they are fair, effective and good for the individuals concerned. Just how much they are seen as fair and effective becomes clearer as policy goes out into the real world.

Policies: only as good as the politics that support them?

Out in the real world, policies becomes diluted, enfeebled or strengthened. There can be a clear connection, for example, between public/media anxieties and the strengthening of the determination of policy makers to get tough, but little connection between the reality and the public perception of the extent of juvenile crime and children's offending behaviour (Goldson, 2003). The incidence and seriousness of youth crime becomes amplified within the public perception and, in response, Goldson (2003) argued, an increasingly punitive set of policies and legislation has been forefronted, underpinned with notions of risk factors themselves linked to the legitimisation of early intervention that continues to ignore the wider social structural context. The momentum of growth within the early years sector was strengthened by early years policy becoming educationalised, that is, taken into the school system, raising further questions about who should pay for it and what type of practitioners were needed to provide it. Aspects of education policy offer further examples of how policy evolves. Aspects of school policies have been questioned by those who point to the experience of specific groups of children for whom the educational system still does not work. Others have pointed out that educational policies and educational systems need to recognise the difference between the world of the family and the world of the classroom (Evans, 2006). Some working-class children and young people are disconnected at both personal and public levels from the education system and are yet to find a way for it to work well for them (Evans, 2006). Ways of thinking within educational institutions seem alien to them. Schools need to work with the possibility that educational achievement is not always part of how a child or young person is valued at home and these children and young people subsequently cannot then know until it is too late how it is valued in the wider society. As a result, they are excluded by others and exclude themselves (Evans, 2006). Policies can be undone by an inability to recognise that individuals bring with them different assumptions, expectations and anticipations. Other trends in educational policy have been criticised for forefronting academic achievement as the main means to address social exclusion in adulthood. A greater focus on measurable achievement has, to some, meant the weakening of education as a means to develop deeper social, emotional and ethical understanding (Ridge, 2006). Policy and practice have been developed in partial response to such criticism, resulting in the introduction of the Social and Emotional Aspects of Learning (SEAL) programme to schools (DCSF, 2005).

The influence of the media on policy makers, political thinking and therefore social policy will be immediately apparent to most people. Its influence on public policy for children and families on such subjects as child protection, education, additional educational needs, parenting and youth justice are subject to considerable comment and debate (Parton, 2006). Without space to cover this in any detail here, it will perhaps suffice just to make two points. The first point is how crucial it is to be aware of the extent to which the media shapes how we think and feel about support and services for children, young people and families. The second point concerns how the media shapes our thinking about what the state can, and should, do.

The powerful contribution of the media to the social construction of childhood, youth, parenting and families has been pointed out by many commentators and researchers. The media gives us the language with which to think about these issues and how to respond to them. Right across the media, childhood, youth and family life are powerfully evocative, disturbingly uncertain and profoundly ambiguous. Different parts of the media (such as print, films, advertising, TV and so on) make significant contributions to ideas about children, childhood, young people, parents and families. Inevitably, its language seeps through to the heart of thinking about, and the development of, social policy. If policy is part dialogue, part commentary, the media largely provides the language which can shape the questions and the answers. The language of politics could be said to be co-constructed with the media. This can mean that the constant and fast-changing dialogue and commentary about childhood and family life is not fully thought out. The shorthand used by journalists, for example, can be startlingly punitive (underclass, feral children, sink estates and so on) and can short-circuit thinking (zero tolerance, hardworking families, 'broken Britain' and so on). But because social policy involves people's private and public lives, a free flow of ideas through debate and dialogue is essential. Issues associated with children, young people and families need to be contested but in ways that make the contest a fair one. Otherwise, questions about inequalities can be submerged by questions of individualism or personal freedom, rights are displaced by talk of duties and responsibilities, and 'inclusion and exclusion' obscures the reality of who is dominant and who is dominated.

My second point concerning the media, children and families is perhaps less visited. The politics of children and young people is, I have argued, largely constructed through the media and an idea about the proper role of the state in our lives is one such construction. The ways in which we think about 'the state' affect the ways we think about how a society should respond to children and young people. With the prefix 'welfare', the state has been understood by previous generations as a positive force in people's lives, particularly for the young and old. Now the word 'state' and descriptions of its purpose are almost entirely used without that prefix or another reasonably positive one, and 'welfare' has been replaced with a series of pejorative prefixes or adjectives – 'the nanny state', 'the bureaucratic state', 'the surveillance state', 'arbitrary state interference', 'an ineffective state', 'big government', 'faceless bureaucracy', or 'social engineering'. Pushing back the state is seen by some as liberating and some describe any government as 'the problem not the solution'. Strengthening society, rather than being equated to making progress towards a fairer society, is linked to the weakening of the state. Advocates of a weaker state deplore how vertical links between the state and citizen seem to have replaced the horizontal links between people and now people look to the state for solutions rather than to each other. They call for an end to what they describe as the relentless incursion of the state into the lives of individuals. These opinions seem to be rarely if ever balanced in the media by a view of 'the state' as a political community, expressing a level of collective responsibility, organised under a democratic government, and as a protective, supportive presence in people's lives.

So what would make a fairer, less fearful contest of ideas about policies for children and young people? The media cannot be held entirely to blame for a low level of political debate concerning children and young people. It seems to be able to provide ways of thinking about issues that strike a chord with many people. Perhaps the place to start could be not accepting the language that is provided, which restricts the debate before it has started, such as the language that seeks primarily to position the state as a necessary evil, or that positions people in relation to services merely as consumers, with choice:

> The notion of users of social care services exercising rational choice in a way which is consistent with the notion of economic agents maximising personal benefits ignores the reality of the way in which people come to be in the position of 'needing' such services and the way in which such services are used. (Barnes and Prior, 2000, p. 85)

This has to mean more bottom-up policy making and greater consideration of the power relations that inevitably feature in determining the responses of policy makers (Lister, 2007). As we still collectively maintain the NHS, a state pension and a state education service, for most people, the expectation follows that the state, shouldering a level of responsibility for meeting a range of needs, will play an important part in almost everyone's lives.

We also have real examples of policy for any debate about children and young people's services to analyse and build upon. The Sure Start programme has successfully identified communities as capable of delivering policy and acting as generators of solutions, rooted in the places where problems need to be understood and addressed (DCSF, 2010). It is also important that more ways are found for the collective voice of children and young people to be part of the debate by being active citizens voicing their own values, perspectives and experiences and using these to take action in their own right or contesting those who have power over their lives (Kay et al., 2006; Percy-Smith and Thomas, 2010). There are international examples that can make changes to existing political structures; for example the introduction of children's commissioners in the UK, as part spokespeople, part lobbyists and part ombudsman, who are being given an increasingly wider remit including activity within the youth justice sector. It would also be possible and probably advisable for all proposed policies affecting children and young people to be systematically scrutinised for their direct or indirect impact on children as individuals, on specific groups of children and/or on children and young people generally, using 'child impact statements'. Policies including immigration, crime, transport, housing and childcare manifestly affect children and young people who are not able to vote for one set of policies as opposed to another. Child impact statements could lift up children and young people's preferences, rights and needs so they become distinguishable from those of adults. All proposed legislation and policies affecting children and young people could be considered by the UK government for their impact on children's rights before they are adopted (CRAE, 2009), just as the Scottish Executive (2001) has committed itself to 'childproof' legislation to make sure it has the most positive possible impact on children and young people.

However it is done, child impact statements, reworking policies using new models of working, or learning from past experience, children and young people will continue to be profoundly affected by choices made through social policy. The quality of policies has to be directly related to the quality of debate and deliberation from which they develop. It is to some of these effects of social policy decisions that the final part of this chapter now turns.

Social exclusion, social mobility and social inequalities

Successive governments find themselves asking similar questions about children, young people and families. If the family is the cornerstone of society, what strengthens families? What are the continuities needed by our society and what does one generation owe to the next? What needs to change? If higher levels of education and employability are agreed aspirations, what are the best means of achieving these? What about child poverty, children's happiness and safety?

The answers to such questions can, of course, vary fundamentally. Politicians with solutions are drawn to data and theorists who support their general approach. At times, governments feel strong enough and committed enough to radically reshape public services for children and young people. Educational policy in the 1960s and 70s, for example, opened up education intellectually to new ideas and socially to a wider group of people. Comprehensive schools and the expansion of higher education created real social mobility and temporarily a more equal society (Blanden et al., 2005). Through the social and economic policies of the governments of the 1980s and 90s, funding for public services contracted, leading not only to a deterioration of public services overall but also to greater social divisions as private provision was positioned alongside state schools, public transport, recreational centres, public libraries and museums. Rolling back the state in the 1980s led to an exceptional rise in inequalities. Since then, governments have spent significant amounts of money on public services particularly for children and young people, most notably through early intervention programmes, major school rebuilding programmes and the expansion of higher education. They also attempted to reverse some of the wider social divisions that had arisen with actions such as abolishing museum charges and renovating city centres. Some long-term goals were also acted upon, most conspicuously the attempt to abolish child poverty.

Social policy affecting children and families that came out of New Labour thinking focused on three main approaches:

1 Public services needed a serious injection of public money, and children, young people and families depend upon the quality of public services.
2 Childcare was central to the economic regeneration of Britain, as the market

participation of mothers was seen as an essential component of the 'hard-working family'. Although the purpose of early years services remains contested by parents, practitioners and policy makers, now the question of whether the state should pay for early years services for three- and four-year-olds is not.

3 The organisation and modernisation of public services would not only address the deterioration in public services but these should be connected up in order to address the linked social problems that make up 'social exclusion'.

Social exclusion as a concept drove a number of policies and sought to emphasise education and work as key to individual advancement and social cohesion. Recognising that deep-rooted social and economic problems were connected, such as material disadvantage, marginalisation, poor access to goods and services, poor health and wellbeing, lack of social and cultural capital, a lack of self-determination, and disengagement from public decision making, tackling social exclusion has been and is likely to remain a focus for UK governments. Across Western European governments, similar policies emerged, as fears of fragmented societies and cultures influenced policy makers, with a fear of social division being stronger than a fear of uniformity.

However, the focus on social exclusion was always a highly contested approach. There have been fierce debates about whether it was a progressive idea or simply language that diverted attention from the pervasive blight of material inequalities. Among opponents to the idea was Lister (2003), who offered another analysis, characterising the changing construction of the citizen by the state in the 1990s as the 'social investment state'. What we were seeing was children being prioritised as citizen workers of the future, with 'opportunity' identified as promoting social inclusion and equality rather than addressing disparity of income (Lister, 2003, 2007) or the distribution of wealth or health on class lines. To some, however, there were strengths of using the concept of social exclusion. It made sense to some social groups, such as people with mental health difficulties who experienced social exclusion and whose experiences were not adequately explained by material inequalities (Morris et al., 2009). Social exclusion has also been thought to be useful, in that it focused on the processes by which people become excluded and led to a greater focus on how people within certain social groups then ended up leading unnecessarily unfulfilled lives (Morris et al., 2009).

Some important questions remain for those working with public policy for children and young people. How much can be asked of particular state agencies and public sector workers? How can schools address poverty and inequalities, when these are rooted in economic systems and with origins beyond national borders? To what extent should children's services be always informed by an understanding of the wide range of contextual and interpersonal factors that affect the lives of individual children and young people? How crucial is it for children and young people that social mobility has stagnated? Comparisons of children born in the 1950s and the 1970s have found declining social mobility in the UK. Norway has the greatest social mobility, followed by Denmark, Sweden and Finland (Blanden et al., 2005). These researchers found declining social mobility to be in part due to the strong incremental relationship between family income and educational attainment in the UK. While the graduate proportion of people from the poorest fifth of the population of the UK had increased from 6% to 9%, the percentage of graduates in the richest fifth had increased from 20% to 47% (Blanden et al., 2005). Interestingly, this research was taken up by the media and formed the basis for a renewed attack on comprehensive schools, with the argument that the (partial) end of educational selection at age 11 had reduced opportunities for children as the brightest lost their only escape route from mainstream state schools.

Perhaps the biggest question remains whether, as social inequalities in Britain had worsened, this was the most significant of the Labour governments' legacies? In Wilkinson and Pickett's (2009) *The Spirit Level: Why More Equal Societies Almost Always Do Better*, a book widely read across the political spectrum, research data from over 30 years was put forward to support their argument that social inequality, above all others, is the one measurement that should have been the focus of economic investment and social policies of the past decade and more. Wilkinson and Pickett (2009) argue that almost all social ills, including ill health, the lack of community life, violence, drug abuse, obesity, mental illness and large prison populations, are more prevalent in less equal societies such as the UK. Recent decades of social policies have failed to address this fundamental issue because they have attempted to treat problems and client groups one at a time rather than to act to diminish the prevalence of social problems overall. Wilkinson and Pickett's evidence is clear:

> It is remarkable that these measures of health and social problems ... and of child wellbeing among rich countries, all tell us so much the same story. The problems in rich countries are not caused by the society not being rich enough (or even by being too rich) but by the scale of material differences between people within each society being too big. What matters is where we stand in relation to others in our own society. (Wilkinson and Pickett, 2009, p. 25)

Across the richest countries of the world, Wilkinson and Pickett (2009) argued that there is no connection between national wealth and things that really matter to most people such as good health, low levels of crime or close communities. These are, say Wilkinson and Pickett (2009), warped by economic stratification and each person in a society benefits or suffers from the extent of its inequalities. Perhaps the governments of the 1990s and 2000s, as they battled with the number and purpose of their social policies, and struggled to avoid missing a plethora of self-imposed targets, failed to realise just how important inequality was.

Final thoughts

Public policy is required to address the deep-seated problems faced by individuals, families, or whole communities. Social policies need to be applied to aspects of life, including childhood and family life, about which most people have opinions and beliefs about what is the right thing to do in certain circumstances. These views can be firmly held. Since the state has many responsibilities towards children and young people, its policies need to be constantly debated using a wide range of viewpoints, ideas and modes of thought beyond those proffered by the more vociferous parts of the media. Practitioners, researchers, academics, social commentators and politically engaged groups, including voluntary agencies, and children and young people themselves are all part of this debate. Changes in a society should open up new questions and new solutions, not just raise anxiety levels. Public policy needs to remain subject to constant debate and dialogue and needs to be co-constructed with the organisations and agencies that engage with the policy and with children and families themselves. Only in this way can there be any hope of getting the balance right between the roles and responsibilities of children, young people and families and the roles and responsibilities of the state.

The art of politics, it could be said, is to do what you want to as a government, while persuading enough people that it is what they wish too. The media plays a significant part in providing debate and deliberation but this cannot be the sole or even the main source of evidence by which certain issues and their solutions are brought to the attention of politicians and policy makers. The quality of the debate is important, as who pays for, and who benefits from, political decisions means that the state has to act as an arbiter of the different interests of different groups within a society. Despite the complexities, the layers of public policies for children and young people must also present a coherent, coordinated and evaluated plan of action. They need to assist parents, develop universal and specialised services, allocate financial and other resources and build communities. At the same time, the very meaning of 'good outcomes' for children and young people needs, as I have argued above, to be constantly debated. Who should define and plan for desirable outcomes for children – policy makers, service providers, service users or the wider society? The answer, clearly, is all of these, since, in essence, public policy for children and young people is an important expression of, and embodiment of, each child's and each young person's relationship to their society.

References

Barnes, M. and Prior, D. (2000) *Private Lives as Public Policy*, Birmingham, Venture Press.
Blanden, J., Gregg, P. and Machin, S. (2005) *Intergenerational Mobility in Europe and North America*, Centre for Economic Performance, available online at <http://cep.lse.ac.uk/about/news/IntergenerationalMobility.pdf> [Accessed 4 June 2009].

Cohen, B., Moss, P. Petrie, P. and Wallace, J. (2004) *A New Deal for Children? Re-forming Education and Care in England, Scotland and Sweden*, Bristol, Policy Press.

CRAE (Children's Rights Alliance for England (2009) CRAE sends children's rights impact statement to Ed Balls, available online at <http://www.crae.org.uk/news-and-events/news/crae-impact-statement.html> [Accessed 11 June 2010].

DCSF (Department for Children, Schools and Families) (2005) *Social and Emotional Aspects of Learning (SEAL): Improving Behaviour, Improving Learning*, available online at <http://nationalstrategies.standards.dcsf.gov.uk/node/87009> [Accessed 8 March 2010].

DCSF (Department for Children, Schools and Families) (2010) *Sure Start*, <http://www.dcsf.gov.uk/everychildmatters/earlyyears/surestart/thesurestartprinciples/> [Accessed 11 June 2010].

DfES (Department for Education and Skills) (2004) *Every Child Matters: Change for Children*, London, TSO.

DfES (Department for Education and Skills) (2008) *Every Child Matters: Outcomes Framework*, available online at <http://publications.everychildmatters.gov.uk/eOrderingDownload/DCSF-00331-2008.pdf> [Accessed 30 March 2010].

Evans, G. (2006) *Educational Failure and Working Class White Children in Britain*, Basingstoke, Palgrave Macmillan.

Goldson, B. (2003) 'Taking liberties: Policy and the punitive turn', in H. Hendrick (ed.) *Child Welfare and Social Policy. An Essential Reader*, Bristol, Policy Press, pp. 255–68.

Kay, E., Tisdall, M. and Bell, R. (2006) 'Included in governance? Children's participation in public decision making', in E. Kay, M. Tisdall, J.M. Davis et al. (eds) *Children, Young People and Social Exclusion. Participation for What?*, Bristol, Policy Press, pp. 105–20.

Lister, R. (2003) 'Investing in the citizen-workers of the future', in H. Hendrick (ed.) *Child Welfare and Social Policy: An Essential Reader*, Bristol, Policy Press, pp. 449–62.

Lister, R. (2007) 'From object to subject: Including marginalised citizens in policy making', *Policy and Politics*, **35**(3): 437–55.

Morris, K., Barnes, M. and Mason, P. (2009) *Children, Families and Social Exclusion: New Approaches to Prevention*, Bristol, Policy Press.

Parton, N. (2006) *Safeguarding Childhood: Early Intervention and Surveillance in a Late Modern Society*, Basingstoke, Palgrave Macmillan.

Percy-Smith, B. and Thomas, N. (2010) *A Handbook of Children and Young People's Participation*, London, Routledge.

Ridge, T. (2006) 'Childhood poverty: A barrier to social participation and inclusion', in E. Kay, M. Tisdall, J.M. Davis et al. (eds) *Children, Young People and Social Exclusion: Participation for What?* Bristol, Policy Press, pp. 23–38.

Scottish Executive (2001) *For Scotland's Children*, available online at <http://www.scotland.gov.uk/library3/education/fcsr%20pt1.pdf> [Accessed 8 March 2010].

Thomas, N. (2002) 'Children, parents and the state', in H. Hendrick (ed.) *Child Welfare and Social Policy: An Essential Reader*, Bristol, Policy Press, pp.157–76.

Wilkinson, R. and Pickett, K. (2009) *The Spirit Level: Why More Equal Societies Almost Always Do Better*, London, Allen Lane.

UNICEF (2007) *Child Poverty in Perspective: An Overview of Child Well-being in Rich Countries*, Innocenti Report Card 7, UNICEF Innocenti Research Centre, Florence, available online at <www.unicef.org/media/files/ChildPovertyReport.pdf> [Accessed 25 July 2009].

Part **II**

Co-constructing practice with children, young people and families

5

Disabled children, their parents and their experiences with practitioners

Dan Goodley and Katherine Runswick-Cole

This chapter focuses on the experiences of disabled children and their parents/ carers. Our aim is to explore different understandings of disability, disablism (discrimination against disabled people) and ableism (societal preference for the ambitions of non-disabled people rather than disabled people) and to consider how these are constructed and experienced by children, parents/carers and practitioners in early childhood. We start by outlining a number of theoretical approaches that have influenced our exploration of parenting and childhood as part of our ongoing research project (Goodley and Runswick-Cole, 2010). We then briefly explain our study before introducing pen portraits of two mothers. Using the mothers' narratives as a guide, we explore the co-construction of disablism and ableism and consider how parents, in particular, confront these two forces in the context of 'virtual' and 'real' parents' support groups.

Theoretical approaches

Over the past 20 years there have been significant changes in the way that disability has been constructed. Traditionally, disability has been understood through what has been described as an 'individual pathology model of disability': disability is seen as the property of the individual, often characterized as a 'tragic problem' located within the person. The 'problem' of disability is often determined by medical practitioners and so the 'natural' response to disability has been a process of diagnosis, rehabilitation and, if at all possible, cure. Individual and/or medical models of disability have been challenged by the disabled people's movement and by the academic community. The focus has moved away from problem bodies and minds to a focus on exclusionary environments that are created by social factors, including economic, systemic, physical and attitudinal barriers (Campbell and Oliver, 1996). The social model of disability highlights the oppression of and prejudice against disabled people.

Central to a social model approach to disability is the distinction between disability and impairment: impairment, of itself, is not seen as being part of the problem, rather the problem is disability which is socially created (Oliver, 1990). In this approach, a person may have an impairment, but is disabled by society. Recently, social model accounts of disability have been challenged to include what Thomas (1999) and Reeve (2002) term 'disablism within', that is, disablism at a psychological and emotional level. However, the private psycho-emotional aspects cannot be disconnected from the public aspects of disablism which include socio-structural forms of oppression (Goodley, forthcoming).

Crucially, for us, Davis (2006, p. 3) drew our attention to the hegemony of the 'world of norms'. This is a world in which intelligence, height, weight and many other aspects of the body are measured in comparison to the 'norm'. 'Normal' human beings simply happen, whereas 'abnormal' human beings occur and sit outside the natural paradigm (Michalko, 2002). As Davis (1995) noted, disability is often absent from analysis and ability is presumed. This ensures that ableism often unconsciously underpins societal members' engagement with those considered not to fit dominant norms. Campbell (2009, p. 5) has cautioned against examining experiences of disability as the perspective of the 'Other' and encouraged researchers to acknowledge a 'common ableist homosocial worldview' that ableism is a widely accepted and often implicitly valued worldview. The consequence of analyses that presume ability is that children are expected to fit the idealised individual of ableist society. The 'problem' of failing to match up to the idealised norm is a problem for all dis/abled people. However, disabled people are often the ones expected to bear the complications of this failure.

Psychologists, psychiatrists, family doctors and other practitioners are typically consulted by parents/carers in the process of constructing the child's (ab) normality (Lasser and Corley, 2008). And practitioners work in situations which, we could argue, identify – perhaps construct – impairments. For example, in 1970 in the USA, the President's Committee on Mental Retardation (the preferred term in the UK is 'learning difficulty') produced a report entitled *The Six-hour Retarded Child*, which concluded that between 9 and 4, five days a week, a whole host of children were defined and reacted to as 'retarded children' purely on the basis of IQ scores (Langness and Levine, 1986, p. ix). In the US and the UK in the 2000s, we could argue that the hours have been extended beyond the seven hours as ideas around IQ become ever-more ingrained in families' home lives as well as the school context. Hardt and Negri (2000) argue that institutional boundaries – say between 'home' and 'school' – have been eroded as psychological ideas become ever-more part of our mundane, everyday lives. The influence of psychology in the lives of disabled babies and children leads us to our final resource: critical developmental psychology.

Like Davis, critical developmental psychologists have challenged the construction of the standardised, naturalised and normalised nature of childhood in western societies (Walkerdine, 1993). Walkerdine (1993) and Burman (2008) set out to expose the myth of the 'norm', and are sceptical about the truth claims of developmental psychology. Walkerdine (1993) describes developmental psychology as one of the 'grand meta-narratives of science' that constructs both 'the child' and the 'development'. For Burman (2008), developmental psychology, like other grand narratives, is deeply culturally embedded, representing the cultural white, western, middle class, masculine subjectivity of the mid-twentieth century. In this sense, 'the "developing child" is not a description of a "real" entity, but a discursive construction, albeit a very powerful one' (Walkerdine, 1993, p. 454). The 'developing child' is an ableist phenomenon: expected to normally develop, through a series of stages, towards an anticipated end goal of autonomy and independence. Burman (2008) urges us to move away from seeing the child as the developmental subject and to ask how, for example, global north ableist conceptions of childhood are spreading throughout the globe informing how practitioners and parents understand the child. Indeed, Davis (1995) and Campbell (2009) would insist that 'ableism' is an example of a colonial and globalising mode of production.

Social oppression theories of disability (Oliver, 1990), notions of ab/normality (Davis, 1995) and dis/ability (Campbell, 2009) and critical developmental psychology (Walkerdine, 1993; Burman, 2008) have all influenced our analysis and it is to the aims and methods of the study that we now turn.

Description of the study and methodology

The data for this chapter is taken from ongoing fieldwork being conducted between 2008 and 2011 in the north of England by researchers from Manchester Metropolitan University as part of a research project *Does Every Child Matter, Post Blair? The Interconnections of Disabled Childhoods*, which is being funded by the Economic and Social Research Council (Goodley and Runswick-Cole, 2010). The research has a number of aims:

1 To examine the extent to which *Every Child Matters* and related policies are reflected in the provision of enabling environments for children and families in the contexts of health, social care, education and leisure.

2 To consider how disabled children, in particular, are supported to achieve the *Every Child Matters* outcomes to be 'healthy', 'stay safe', 'enjoy and achieve', 'make a positive contribution' and 'achieve economic wellbeing'.

3 To understand how the 'parent', 'practitioner' and 'disabled child' are constructed across contexts, over time, nested in a host of policies and practices and how these relate to notions of 'good' parenting, 'good' practitioner practice and 'well-adjusted' children.

In practice, we are interested in how disabled children and their families 'grow up' and how practitioners influence this growing up in communities, schools, the family, health and social care settings.

The data for this chapter is drawn, in the main, from two mothers' retrospective narrative accounts of parenting their disabled children. The interviews were open-ended and covered a range of issues related to the families' experiences of health, social care, education and leisure. The mothers spoke very openly and in depth about their families. Both stories presented here were told by mothers of disabled children to Katherine, the researcher, who is also a mother of a disabled child. We recognise that we can be accused of carrying out 'illegitimate interviews' (Oakley, 1981, p. 31): the interviewer shared with the mothers that she was also a mother of a disabled child; and the participants were able to ask questions back to the interviewer to the extent that there were times in the interviews where roles were 'reversed' as the mothers asked the researcher a series of questions. We broke the 'rules' of interviewing. However, we agree with Oakley that 'hygienic' research is neither possible nor desirable and that the rules we broke originate from a 'masculine' research paradigm that has traditionally celebrated more sterile research environments (Oakley, 1981, p. 31). While we are unapologetic about the interviewer sharing her own experiences of motherhood and disablism, we recognised that it was also important that there were many times of self-monitoring, when the interviewer 'held back', allowing the interviewee time to talk. Of course, we also accept that the elements of commonality between the participants and interviewer were complicated by differences constructed by class, ethnicity, age, and the status of the 'academic' researcher (McLaughlin et al., 2008).

In the course of the analysis of these narratives, we read and reread the mothers' stories, searching for themes or 'nodes' (Snow et al., 2004). This involved us subjecting narratives to points of analysis or themes that were drawn together as the data was collected (Snow et al., 2004). The range of analysis and discussion allowed ongoing consideration of whether we were developing the most appropriate forms of interview; it allowed us to capture the complexity of the cultures we were investigating; it highlighted new spaces to explore; it enabled us to reflect on our research questions and through it we began to make the connections between what we were finding and the broader theoretical ideas introduced at the start of this chapter. It also sparked debate and argument about how we each were understanding the narratives.

Exploring processes of disablism and ableism

Gayle is in her early forties and has one child, an 11-year-old son, Simon, who has been diagnosed with Asperger syndrome. Gayle works for the Home Office during term-time only. Her partner also works for the Home Office. Both Gayle and her partner are able to work flexibly so that someone is always there to take Simon to school or to pick him up. Simon's father lives 200 miles away from the family and visits in the school holidays. Simon is coming to the end of year six at primary school. He moved from one mainstream primary school to another because he was 'having difficulties at school', but Gayle says he has been 'treated as a naughty boy' at both schools.

Shelley is in her early fifties and has a 16-year-old daughter, Chloe, who has been diagnosed with a rare genetic syndrome. Shelley has worked for a voluntary housing organisation in recent years, but since becoming unemployed she has returned to higher education and is taking a social work qualification. Shelley is married and also has a 13-year-old son. Shelley fought for Chloe to attend mainstream school throughout her education and ended up going through the courts to achieve this. However, when Chloe was 16, there was no mainstream provision in school available in the city where they live and so Chloe had to attend special school. This was also the time when Chloe was given an additional diagnosis of autism, which was seen, by Shelley, as helpful for getting Chloe into the only special provision available, an autism special school.

In this section, we explore the process of the construction of impairment and disability in the lives of disabled children and their families and the impact this has on parents/carers and children. Ableist normativity (Campbell, 2009), the assumption that a child will be 'able' and 'normal', permeates every aspect of society so that even before a child is born, the impact of ableism can be felt by parents/carers. At antenatal classes, impairment is rarely discussed and when the topic is raised, impairment is soon constructed as an undesirable, and unlikely, outcome of pregnancy. Fetuses with impairments are situated outside the 'natural variation' (Michalko, 2002). For Shelley, the impact of disablism was evident in the first year of her daughter's life. Her daughter was given a diagnosis of global developmental delay by a paediatrician at the age of six months. Shelley described it as a 'useless' diagnosis that told her nothing, but, more significant, was the response to her daughter's impairment outside the walls of a medical institution. She told us:

> We had friends from the NCT [National Childbirth Trust] group who'd had babies at around the same time … but that support became fairly useless fairly quickly as it was obvious that their babies at a year were busy beginning to talk, walking and Chloe couldn't actually hold anything in her hands still and still hadn't got the upper body strength to sit unaided and was still being miserable and I was still being miserable!

The NCT group became for Shelley a site where impairment was magnified by the 'typically developing' children. Shelley gradually withdrew from the NCT group, which she described as being full of 'pretentious mothers' who were obsessed by development. The totalising narrative of developmental psychology (Walkerdine, 1993) was much in evidence at the NCT meetings:

> I did [go] but not very much because it was all these people endlessly going on about how wonderful it was that their baby was doing X, Y and Z.

If we follow the ideas of Davis (2006) and Campbell (2009), then we can understand the NCT group as embracing normal childhoods and promoting ableist thinking. Consequently, for parents of disabled children, the constant comparison of one child against a normative developmental trajectory can feel like an act of rejection and cultural violence. Interestingly, Shelley did resist one of the central assumptions of child development by challenging the significance of mother–child interactions, arguing instead that development:

> has nothing to do with what the mother does cos it is so heavily programmed into babies, you have to really, I mean you know all this, you have to really deprive a child to stop them sitting, crawling, standing, walking, climbing, being able to use their hands, basically sticking them in a playpen with no toys but even then they'll still be doing quite a lot of things but it was really uncomfortable being in that environment.

While the construction of impairment was evident in Shelley and Chloe's lives from her first year, for Gayle and Simon, the processes unfolded more slowly. Simon was a 'normal' baby, as a toddler he had one particular friend but didn't much like playing with other children and he liked a regular routine – bath, story, bed. It was his interaction with another institution, school, which radically changed the way his behaviour was constructed. In the context of a busy classroom, Simon was described as a 'naughty' boy. Concern about his behaviour at school led to the involvement of an early years assessment centre. Gayle told us that it was only at this point that she began to see Simon as different:

> you know, when you go for an assessment and they ask you all these questions, it was only at that point that I thought, 'Oh, okay, that's considered bizarre behaviour'. I didn't realise that.

At this point, Simon was given the label of Attention Deficit Hyperactivity Disorder (ADHD). Gayle felt that this label didn't properly reflect Simon's difficulties but she felt 'intimidated' by health practitioners and unable to challenge the diagnosis. However, the label of ADHD did allow her to access support from the ADHD nurse and support group. Interestingly, if Simon had been given a diagnosis of Autism Spectrum Disorder (ASD) at the same point, there was no ASD nurse available.

This highlights the experiences of parents who engage with medicalised constructions of their children in order to access support. Gayle remained unhappy with Simon's label of ADHD and when Simon was seven he was reassessed and given the label of Asperger syndrome, which Gayle felt better reflected his difficulties.

So, by the age of seven, Simon had been constructed in turn as 'normal', 'naughty', 'having ADHD' and finally as having 'Asperger syndrome and dyspraxia'. The sites of the construction of his labels included the home, the school and the clinic. Gayle highlighted the positive effects of this labelling that gave her access to Disability Living Allowance, to a statement of special educational needs, and to the ADHD nurse. Her story demonstrates how some diagnostic labels can function as powerful markers that provide a passport to services and support (Mallett and Runswick-Cole, 2009). However, the consequences for the family of the labelling process were far-reaching. Gayle now describes what she had previously seen as ordinary events through the lens of the label: her son's behaviour is an autistic 'meltdown'; a good bedtime routine is part of a 'structured' approach; and having fun on a bike is, now, an example of physiotherapy to strengthen Simon's 'core stability'. The child becomes known through the ever-folding of impairment discourses over their bodies. In short, the child becomes known more and more through disablist discourses, which understand them in terms of a host of potentially pathologising and reductive labels.

By contrast, Shelley's description of 'global developmental delay' as a 'useless label' is an example a medical label that fails to function, as it did not bring with it access to services or support. Eventually, Chloe was given a diagnosis of a rare genetic syndrome. The rarity of the label meant that, like 'global developmental delay', it failed to function; the passport to services and support available to Simon was not available to Chloe. There was no specific support group or nurse for children with global developmental delay and no access to specialist schooling or other provision. Significantly, it was an additional diagnosis of autism (a functioning label) at age 16 that allowed Chloe access to special school.

During the process of the construction of their children's impairments, both Shelley and Gayle turned to 'real' and 'virtual' support groups and it is to the impact of support groups in the lives of parents of disabled children that we now turn.

Confronting disablism and ableism: 'real' and 'virtual' parents groups, biological citizens and radical parenting

'Real' and 'virtual' parents groups have been seen as key mechanisms through which parents of disabled children are able to confront and resist the disablism they experience in their social worlds. McLaughlin et al. (2008) identified parents groups as a space where parents of disabled children could form alliances with each other. These alliances are typically characterised as being productive of mutually supportive relationships between parents. The spread of access to the internet has led to the rapid development of 'virtual' parent groups, where parents of disabled children are able to 'meet' with one another online. These online groups are complemented by the presence of parents groups on social networking sites and the presence of a parents organisation, which has a virtual office where you can call in for help and information in the virtual world 'Second Life'.

The existing literature about parents groups is generally positive (McLaughlin et al., 2008). Parents organisations provide necessary information and support and are considered to be particularly important for parents who are surrounded by non-disabled children of friends and families (Seligman and Darling, 2007). These findings were echoed by the mothers in our study. Gayle valued meeting other mothers of disabled children. This was where she learned about the process of getting a statement of special educational needs in school and also where she found out about her son's entitlement to Disability Living Allowance. Shelley described her discomfort at the NCT group and access to a virtual community was particularly important for her because this was the only way of her being in touch with parents of children with the same diagnosis as her daughter. She was wary of the impersonal nature of communication on the web, however, and was cautious about her postings:

> [Mock shouting] Life is hell! Yes, it will continue to be hell! [Laughs] Go shoot yourself now! No, no don't want to be negative 'cause this person's already depressed – do not make it worse!

For us, the distinction between 'virtual' and 'real' parents groups was less marked than the distinction between groups that organised around impairment labels and groups that had members whose children had a range of impairments. Several mothers in the study, like Gayle, joined impairment-specific groups. As the literature suggests, these groups were important to mothers in terms of finding information and support (Runswick-Cole, 2007). Sally told us that, without her autism parents group, she would not be able to go out with her young children. This was, in part, due to the high cost of leisure activities, which were subsidised by the funds raised by the group if she went with them, but more significant was the feeling that she could not take her children out without the support of being in a large group of disabled children. The staring, tutting and comments made by strangers on her parenting had made her lose confidence in venturing out into the wider community alone, examples of what Reeve (2002) and Thomas (1999) term 'psycho-emotional disablism'. This story is another example of a site of the construction of impairment beyond the school, home and the clinic, as families self-segregate and self-exclude as a reaction to their experiences of an intolerant and disabling world.

Appropriating Hughes (2009), we could argue that those parents groups that organise around specific impairments combine opportunities for information and support with 'biological citizenship'. This concept, adapted from the work of Rose (2001), refers to the practices of activism and community engagement through which individuals and others focus on the aspirations and ambitions related to a particular form of impairment. Parents groups offer an opportunity for parents to confer such citizenship on their children. Many parents clearly value the opportunity to engage with biological citizenship, but there are less positive aspects of the production of mutual support through impairment-specific groups. The first is that only the parents of children with the appropriate diagnosis can access support. Gayle attended a support group for parents of children 'newly diagnosed with ADHD'. For parents of children who have a 'useless' diagnosis or, indeed, no diagnosis at all, impairment-specific groups appear exclusionary. One mother, Natalie, in our study, whose daughter, Nadia, has a diagnosis of Down's syndrome, told us that she felt excluded by the Down's syndrome parents group because her daughter was seen as a 'slow developer'. It seems that the 'tyranny of developmentalism' (where the claims are developmental psychology are treated as universal truths, not social constructions) (Burman, 2008), the power of the norm (Davis, 1995) and the process of ableism (Campbell, 2009) were at work even at the Down's syndrome support group.

This led some parents to turn to groups of parents of disabled children who had a range of impairments. Natalie told us that Nadia could just be Nadia at this group, whereas she had been a 'slow developer' in the Down's syndrome group. In our study, these groups also tended to be parent led, whereas impairment-specific groups were often facilitated by practitioners, like the ADHD nurse in Gayle's example. Shelley felt this was significant:

I think in some ways ... because we didn't have a fixed outcome and we were financially self-supporting cos we all paid up whatever needed to be paid. And we got the capacity to arrange things. And it was something that could be people could come along to and knew that their child was accepted, they were accepted and they could say ... most things they felt like saying.

Shelley explained that tensions could arise within the parents group, particularly when it came to making choices about mainstream or special provision:

> I went to that one [special school] and that was lovely and that's where I want my child to go – there and nowhere else. And if I want that it is absolutely right, so everybody else must be wrong. I think that there's some of that.

Shelley also felt that parents' engagement with the processes of education, which meant that you had to fight for 'special' or fight for 'mainstream' schooling, entrenched parents' positions and exaggerated the gap between different approaches. This brings in a further layer of analysis. Parental engagement with special and inclusive education magnifies the complex overlap of these distinct positions. It is clear that even attempts to be inclusive in mainstream schools still rely on the specialist interventions of special educational needs coordinators, educational psychologists, and parent groups who may well bring in specialist knowledge around disability. This is increasingly the case with the rise of 'new disabilities' – such as ADHD, Asperger syndrome, autism, oppositional defiance disorder – where children in mainstream schools are becoming more and more susceptible to labelling and impairment-specific educational interventions.

Final thoughts

In this chapter, we have explored some of the processes of disablism and ableism in the lives of disabled children and their mothers. The sites of the construction of impairment include the home, the school, the clinic and the wider community. Disablism and ableism influence the co-construction of impairment created between parents/carers, children, practitioners and other members of the communities that disabled children inhabit. The concepts of dis/ability, ab/normality and development are all central to these constructions. These tensions are played out in a range of contexts, not least, in 'real' and 'virtual' parents groups, where biological citizenship is played out in ways that both include and exclude children and parents.

Thomas (1999, p. 48) suggested that 'agents' or 'carriers' of disablism are sometimes close to the disabled person and may include those closest to them, including family members and practitioners. However, those closest to disabled people are also in the best position to tackle the assumptions and practices of disablism and ableism. Practitioners have a unique opportunity to challenge the concepts of dis/ability, ab/normality and development and to create enabling forms of care in the lives of disabled children and their families. This project should start by unsettling deeply held views about what it means to be a 'normal child' (ableism), while refuting social, cultural, political, economic and psychological processes that exclude 'non-normal' children (disablism).

References

Burman, E. (2008) *Deconstructing Developmental Psychology*, London, Routledge.

Campbell, F.K. (2009) *Contours of Ableism: The Production of Disability and Abledness*, Basingstoke, Palgrave Macmillan.

Campbell, J. and Oliver, M. (1996) *Understanding our Past, Changing our Future*, London, Routledge.

Davis, L.J. (1995) *Enforcing Normalcy: Disability, Deafness and the Body*, London, Verso.

Davis, L.J. (2006) 'The end of identity politics and the beginning of dismoderism: On disability as an unstable category', in L.J. Davis (ed.) *The Disability Studies Reader* (2nd edn), New York, Routledge, pp. 231–42.

Goodley, D. (forthcoming) *Disability Studies: An Interdisciplinary Introduction*, London, Sage.

Goodley, D. and Runswick-Cole, K. (2010) *Does Every Child Matter, Post Blair? The Interconnections of Disabled Childhoods*, Manchester Metropolitan University, available online at <http//www.rihsc.mmu.ac.uk/postblairproject/> [Accessed 30 March 2010].

Hardt, M. and Negri, A. (2000) *Empire*, Cambridge, MA, Harvard University Press.

Hughes, B. (2009) 'Disability activisms: Social model stalwarts and biological citizens', *Disability & Society*, **24**(6): 677–88.

Langness, L.L. and Levine, H.G. (eds) (1986) *Culture and Retardation: Life Histories of Mildly Mentally Retarded Persons in American Society*, Dordrecht, Reidel.

Lasser, J. and Corley, K. (2008) 'Constructing normalcy: A qualitative study of parenting children with Asperger's Disorder', *Educational Psychology in Practice*, **24**(4): 335–46.

McLaughlin, J., Goodley, D., Clavering, E. and Fisher, P. (2008) *Families with Disabled Children: Values of Enabling Care and Social Justice*, Basingstoke, Palgrave Macmillan.

Mallett, R. and Runswick-Cole, K. (2009) 'The iconic case of autism: Celebrity in impairment specific research', paper presented at the Centre for Educational and Inclusive Research at Sheffield Hallam University, 17 April.

Michalko, R. (2002) *The Difference that Disability Makes*, Philadelphia, Temple University Press.

Oakley, A. (1981) 'Interviewing women: A contradiction in terms', in H. Roberts (ed.) *Doing Feminist Research*, London, Routledge & Kegan Paul.

Oliver, M. (1990) *The Politics of Disablement*, Basingstoke, Macmillan – now Palgrave Macmillan.

Reeve, D. (2002) 'Negotiating psycho-emotional dimensions and disability and their influence on identity constructions', *Disability & Society*, **17**(5): 493–508.

Rose, N. (2001) 'The politics of life itself', *Theory, Culture & Society*, **18**(6): 1–30.

Runswick-Cole, K. (2007) 'The tribunal was the most stressful thing: The experiences of families who go to the Special Educational Needs and Disability Tribunal (SENDisT)', *Disability and Society*, **22**(3): 315–28.

Seligman, M. and Darling, R.B. (2007) *Ordinary Families, Special Children: A Systems Approach to Childhood Disability*, New York, Guilford.

Snow, D.A., Morrill, C. and Anderson, L. (2004) 'Elaborating analytic ethnography: Linking fieldwork and theory', *Ethnography*, **4**(2): 153–5.

Thomas, C. (1999) *Female Forms: Experiencing and Understanding Disability*, Basingstoke, Macmillan – now Palgrave Macmillan.

Walkerdine, V. (1993) 'Beyond developmentalism', *Theory Psychology*, **3**(4): 451–69.

6

Counselling children: values and practice

Alison Davies

I am a child therapist who has worked within primary schools for a charity organisation offering school-based counselling. In this situation, children were usually referred by their teachers, who were concerned by the child's behaviour within the school, or about events at home and the potential impact of these on the child. I currently work privately in a therapeutic centre where the majority of referrals are made by parents and, occasionally, social services. I work with individuals rather than groups or families, and so the focus of my work is the internal world of the individual child. This is in the tradition of therapeutic intervention that uses individually focused models of counselling and psychotherapy. However, it is important to consider that every child is located in a specific cultural and historic context and is part of a unique social and family environment, all of which contribute to a child's behaviour and experience (Swenson and Chaffin, 2006). Increasingly, perspectives such as social constructionism or social ecology are informing practice with children.

This chapter will, first, outline some of the values of counselling, in particular embedding them within a social constructionist and a social ecological framework. It will then raise some common dilemmas faced by counsellors in practice.

Counsellors and children as co-constructors

Both social ecological and social constructionist perspectives are interested in the contexts within which individuals are located. Specifically, with regard to individuals who come for therapy, a social constructionist perspective would suggest that problems 'are produced or manufactured in social, cultural and political contexts' (Besley, 2002, p. 131). Children are often, within a school environment, labelled as 'problems'; the language used to describe these children contributes to the construction of the 'truth' about this child. These 'truths' become normalising – for the school community and for the child. A therapist working within a social constructionist framework aims to collaboratively construct a new 'truth' with the child.

Central to working within this perspective is that the therapist tries not to position themselves as 'the expert'. As Besley (2002) indicated, the therapist is not interested in diagnosing problems or prescribing solutions and treatments; instead, children are encouraged to find their own solutions to their problems. With the therapist's help, the child is encouraged to explore alternative stories about their lives and the choices they can make. The child and therapist are co-constructors in a new story that the child comes to tell about themselves.

This is demonstrated by my work with Zoe (all the names of individuals and places have been changed to protect confidentiality, and some personal details have been altered, where necessary, to further maintain anonymity), whose behaviour was of concern to her mother and teachers. Zoe's father had just left the family home and Zoe had become very withdrawn. In 10 weeks of counselling, Zoe hardly mentioned her father. Instead, the focus of the sessions was on a picture storyboard she was creating, based on the characters of Dr Who and his assistant Martha. The unfolding story centred on Martha's abandonment by Dr Who. Through the story, we explored how Martha felt as a result of Dr Who leaving. Initially, Zoe identified Martha as feeling angry and resentful and Dr Who as unfeeling and cruel. Towards the end of our time together, Zoe acknowledged that Martha was feeling hurt by Dr Who's leaving. Significantly, she could also acknowledge that Dr Who had not intended to hurt Martha and that, despite his leaving, Martha would always be important to him and that he would return to see her whenever he could. This 'story' took 10 weeks to unfold and although the interpretation of Dr Who's and Martha's experience as a metaphor for the child's own experience seems obvious, this was never discussed directly. At the end of the sessions, in which the child came to an accommodation of Dr Who's behaviour, she turned to me and said: 'I don't think I need counselling anymore, I feel more confident.' In this particular case, Zoe was able to explore her own, at times, negative feelings towards Dr Who/her father within the relatively safe framework of a story. Zoe quite literally authored her own story and, crucially, her own ending. I did not quiz her on her feelings about her father and did not offer advice on how to 'deal' with him or the current situation. However, working within her 'Dr Who and Martha' framework, she was able to explore how these characters felt and negotiate an acceptable ending. This accommodation of her situation within the counselling sessions seemed to impact on her life outside the sessions; her confidence at school increased and her teachers and mother reported her to be less withdrawn and anxious. Significantly, her relationship with her father also improved.

In encouraging the child to be active in co-constructing the counselling sessions, it is important that the counsellor is as non-directive as possible and adopts a child-centred approach. For this reason, I make minimal use of questions. Questioning can result in the therapeutic work being counsellor led rather than child led. Rather than following the counsellor's agenda for what they believe is important for the child, it is important that children are encouraged to think and make decisions for themselves and talk about what is important for them.

A child-centred approach to counselling empowers the child to tell their story, whether directly or metaphorically, through their play or story-telling. For therapy to be genuinely child centred, the therapist should join the child at their 'developmental level'. This can be achieved by the child and counsellor participating in play together. Typically, in child-centred therapy, a child will organise the activity, the storyline and the outcome (see Patrick, 2006). Role play with dolls and puppets, painting, picture storyboards and sand play can provide insight into the child's inner world and social relationships, as demonstrated by my work with Zoe.

In permitting the child to have a voice within the sessions, it is crucial that the counsellor and child 'stay with the child's perceptions' (Geldard and Geldard, 2008, p. 10). The counsellor can never assume what the child knows or feels and each child's experience should be seen as unique. As Walker (2005) stated, counsellors should ensure they do not generalise or make assumptions about the life, customs or beliefs of young people. For example, in the following case, it would have been easy for me to have assumed that Fatmah's painting of a white girl was just a drawing of an unspecified character. By staying within Fatmah's perceptions, this white girl came to have quite a different meaning from the one that I might have assumed. Whiteness seemed to mean 'non-difference' to Fatmah and the girl represented Fatmah as she felt before she came to the UK:

Fatmah had recently come to the UK from Southwest Asia. Although her mother was now in the UK, Fatmah had originally come on her own to stay with her aunt, leaving her mother and sister in her home country. Her mother had since had another daughter and was occupied by looking after the two younger sisters, who Fatmah seemed to resent. Fatmah was often blamed for causing trouble at home and her perception was that her mother saw her as different from her sisters. 'Why can't you be "good" like the others?' and 'Why do you have to be so different?' were questions that her mother reportedly asked. At school, Fatmah also felt 'different'. Initially, there was a language difference. When she first arrived, she had minimal English. She often talked of 'being left out', of other children not wanting to play with her. Repeatedly, in sessions, she painted a solitary girl in a desert landscape. Fatmah was always very particular about choosing the skin colour of the girl. She always chose a 'white' skin tone coloured paint. Initially she could not 'say' much about the girl and there was no 'story'. Not wishing to direct her story-telling, I refrained from asking questions about the girl. A few weeks into the counselling, Fatmah painted the same image and, pointing at the girl, said: 'That's me before I came to England. I wasn't different then.' The symbolism of the picture and statement was very powerful. Through the process of self-directed exploration, in a space which encouraged self-reflection, Fatmah was beginning to understand what was troubling her. Had I kept interrupting this process with questions which were potentially meaningless for her, then this shift in her understanding of her situation might not have occurred. It was also quite significant that after this identification with the girl in the picture, Fatmah was able to 'tell a story'. She was able to add her mother to the picture and explore how it felt to be with her mother and without her siblings. Slowly, Fatmah was able to add her siblings to the picture and, I believe, reach some accommodation of their existence. Indeed, her relationship with her younger sisters improved, and whereas at the beginning our time together, Fatmah was reluctant to talk about them, by the end of our work, she would readily talk about shared experiences with them. She also reported feeling much happier at home and this corresponded with increased levels of confidence at school and an ever-widening group of friends.

The role of counselling within a social ecological framework

Social ecology 'refers to the nested arrangement of family, school, neighbourhood and community contexts in which children grow up' (Earls and Carlson, 2001, p. 143). A possible source of tension when considering intervention with children is whether the focus for change should be on changing the child's internal processes or on changing social environments. Certainly, within the counselling sessions, it is likely that the counsellor will encounter 'problems' that relate to the various 'layers' within the child's social ecology. Fatmah, for example, had been separated from her mother and siblings and had come to a new country where, at first, she did not speak the language. Similarly, I have had counselling relationships with other children who have experienced a parent being sectioned under the Mental Health Act 2007 or imprisoned. Others live with the unpredictability of an addicted parent. Many of the children I worked with in the school setting were also living in relative poverty and had experienced being evicted from their homes. Counselling cannot directly resolve problems within the wider ecology of the child's life; however, it can work with children at the micro-level to encourage them to make appropriate choices for themselves and to work through ambivalent feelings they may have about their home environments. Shifts in a child's understanding and behaviour within the counselling situation can hopefully be transferred to wider social ecology and help with resilience building.

My work with Sean is an example of how counselling can indirectly help with wider issues in the child's life. Sean lived with an alcoholic father in what was quite a chaotic household. It was evident he had learned few appropriate boundaries. Faced with the necessary boundaries of a school system, he pushed against them violently. He would erupt angrily in class, insult teachers and frequently attempt to flee from school. His behaviour could be potentially harmful to others and himself, and led to sanctions by the school, such as the loss of playtime and detentions. His experience of boundaries was negligible in one situation, and punitive in another. Establishing firm but benevolent boundaries was a key theme in our work together. The progress we made regarding Sean's maintenance of boundaries was carried beyond the counselling sessions into the school environment; he became less angry in class, started to develop more positive relationships with his teachers and rarely left the classroom without authorisation.

Counsellors are also situated within different contexts, typically within schools, agencies or therapeutic centres, their practice being informed by the different protocols and other socio-cultural practices existing in these contexts. The counsellor's services are usually engaged by the school and/or the parents and this can provide potential sources of tension for the integrity of the counselling relationship, as the counsellor is not only accountable to the child. The therapeutic work is situated within family and school expectations of behaviour and outcomes. Parents and teachers may have a vested interest in the outcome of the counselling and want to see 'results'. Consequently, the counsellor must be prepared for enquiries regarding the progress of the counselling. It is important to establish clear professional boundaries with staff and parents from the beginning. I always make clear what information I am prepared to share before the counselling begins and make sure that the child is also aware of what information I will share.

In addition to local contexts, the counsellor's work is also situated within ethical and legal frameworks. As a member of the British Association for Counselling and Psychotherapy (BACP), the largest professional organisation for counselling and psychotherapy in the UK, I am bound by their ethical framework for good practice (BACP, 2009). A requirement of this framework is that I have regular supervision to discuss my client work. The supervisor is also bound by a professional ethical framework. Legally, counsellors are obliged to report any concerns regarding a child's welfare, specifically with regard to suspected incidents of abuse. Within the school system, I reported my concerns to my supervisor; we then completed a written record detailing our worries and passed this on to the nominated child protection lead within the school. Working privately, I raise concerns with the child protection lead at the centre who liaises with other child protection professionals and agencies.

The issue of power

There is inevitably a power imbalance within the therapeutic relationship. The therapist is often understood to be the 'expert' and is often experienced as the holder of the 'truth' about the client's personality or difficulties. This power imbalance is more acute when the client is a child. In addition, the counsellor, as an adult, represents authority. As the counsellor's services are usually engaged by teachers or parents, it is very possible that the child will perceive the counsellor to be in collusion with them. Indeed, working in schools, many children initially think of me as a teacher. It took one boy a couple of months to call me Alison and not 'Miss'. In other situations, when children say or do something which might be considered inappropriate, they look at me in anticipation of a reaction or punishment. For example, in one session in which we were painting, Sean wanted to use paints from the top shelf and insisted he got them himself. Unable to reach the top shelf, he started throwing other objects at the paints to bring them down. One by one the paint tubes fell to the ground. Engrossed in knocking down objects, he seemed to be enjoying himself. There was a real risk that he or I would be hurt. I did not wish to reprimand him or 'make' him stop, I wanted him to make that decision for himself. I reflected back to him that he seemed to be really enjoying himself and reminded him of our contract (a fundamental feature of counselling and one I shall discuss later). Sean thought about it and said 'maybe we might get hurt, or something might get broken' and he stopped. He picked up the paints, put them on the table and we started painting.

Children who present challenging behaviour have often had abusive or disempowering experiences, and it is vital to empower them in the counselling relationship. Many of these children have experienced broken attachments, trauma and deprivation. It is unsurprising that they have difficulty managing their behaviour or emotions. Typical reasons for referral include abuse, bereavement and loss, bullying, changes to family structure, neglect, parental illness, substance abuse or criminality, transfer to a new country and transfer to a new school (Place2Be, 2009). In all these situations, the children 'are done to'. They are rarely given choices and in this sense are passive recipients of their own circumstances. The counsellor must be aware of the potential for counselling to reinforce the child's powerlessness 'by pathologising children's problems and treating them as passive recipients of services' (Shooter, 2008, p. 15). Children often feel that they have been sent for counselling because they are inherently 'bad' or there is something 'wrong' with them. As Shooter

(2008) reflected, these feelings can be exacerbated if the counselling breaks down; in this situation, children will often feel they are to blame. For this reason, counselling should 'seek to uncover the child's strengths and build upon them' (Shooter, 2008, p. 15).

Part of the process of empowering children within counselling relationships is by creating a safe and contained 'space' (see Bion, 1962) within which they can explore their emotional worlds. For this reason, I establish a contract in the first session. This lays out clearly the expectations of both parties, and the boundaries within which the work will take place. The contract is established to keep the child and counsellor physically and emotionally safe. The contract is unique to each counsellor–client relationship and is negotiated by both participants, although this process is guided by the counsellor to ensure that certain ethical principles are adhered to and understood. However, it is crucial that the child is able to contribute to its creation and I aim to elicit as much of the framework as possible from the child, by asking questions such as: 'What would make you feel safe in here?' 'What would you like me to promise to do/not to do'? In this way, the child is active in the construction of boundaries that make them feel safe, which provides an opportunity to explore with the child any unhelpful expectations they may have of counselling.

The child is invited to make a representation of the contract in any form they wish (usually written or pictorial) but the following points are always included: the time and duration of the sessions; physical and emotional safety; and confidentiality. A regular time for the sessions is set and the child usually knows in the first session the intended finishing date. Some children have very little consistency in their life and have experienced abrupt endings. It is essential that these children can experience a safe and consistent framework and work towards a positive ending. I ask the child what would make them feel physically safe. Usually, they say 'you won't hurt me'. I also say that I would feel safe if they agree not to hurt me. I help the child to understand that they can play with anything within the room in whatever way they wish. However, I also explain that for us both to remain physically safe, we need to try not to damage the items in the room on purpose, stressing that accidents are fine.

My response to Sean's behaviour described at the beginning of this section was to refer him back to the contract we had made together. Of course, this is not always going to be the outcome of referring back to the contract. Sometimes children want to break the contract and push boundaries. I use this example more as an indication of how children, if trusted and empowered to 'do the right thing', might do just that. Here, Sean was able to construct and observe his own boundaries.

Another potentially disempowering aspect of counselling children is in the referral system. When adults undertake counselling, it is usually through self-referral. With children, however, the referral is usually made by a teacher or parent. A child may be unwilling to participate in the therapeutic work, or may be unclear about what it involves. They may also feel it is a punishment for being 'bad', and so one challenge for the counsellor is to reconstruct the child's understanding of what counselling and/or a counsellor is. Even if the child is open to the idea of counselling, within a school setting, the child has little say in selecting a counsellor or in negotiating the time or duration of the sessions. The setting of a suitable and convenient time and place within the school environment is dependent on the cooperation of the head teacher to allocate a room that is suitable for counselling, and to allow children to attend the sessions within class time, despite this possibly conflicting with the statutory entitlement that all children have access to the national curriculum. With pressure placed on teachers to produce good results, it might be that counselling sessions are encouraged to take place within lessons considered to be less academic, such as art or PE, even though these are lessons the child might really enjoy.

For example, I saw Lucy during assembly time. After some weeks, she became increasingly reluctant to come to counselling. Exploring this with her, it became clear her reluctance was due to her missing out on assembly – a time when 'gold stars' were given for 'good' behaviour or performance. Although allocated gold stars, she was not present to receive the public acknowledgement of her achievements and felt, understandably, disappointed by this. Lucy felt herself to be 'bad' in many ways and it was important to her sense of worth to feel validated by others. The teaching staff were able to understand the importance of this and a new time for the counselling sessions was arranged. This had an enormously positive impact on the therapeutic work with Lucy, as she felt that she had been really heard and understood, by both myself and the school staff. However, such flexibility is not always possible and, more often than not, children have little input as to when the sessions take place.

One way of empowering children is in the referral process. Within a school environment, it may be possible for the children to self-refer. Where I worked, we had a referral box where the children put their names if they wanted to speak to a counsellor. Subsequently a one-off meeting with a counsellor was arranged to assess the needs of the child.

The issue of consent and the situated counsellor

One criteria stipulated by the British Association for Counselling and Psychotherapy (2009) to ensure good standards of practice and care is keeping trust. This includes obtaining informed and explicit consent from the client and, with children, from the parent also. However, it can be difficult to gauge how much a young child truly understands the notion of consent. I adopt a principle of assent. If the child's behaviour or body language suggests they are becoming distressed, then I consider this as a possible indication they are withdrawing their assent/consent for the counselling to continue and will suggest stopping the session (and possibly sessions). Arguably, the child's 'assent' is given by empowering them to 'direct' their own sessions by making decisions and choices about where to sit, what to play and what to talk about.

Within a school setting, the permission of relevant staff is also required before counselling can begin. The need for parental and teacher consent can potentially raise issues of whose goals are being addressed in the counselling relationship. Certainly, practitioners are often engaged to work with children because they are displaying behaviour that is challenging for the adults and other children in some way. It is quite possible that a, perhaps, unstated condition of the engagement of the practitioner is to resolve this problematic behaviour in order to 'make life easier' for the adult. Integral to work that respects the autonomy of the client is respect for the client's goals for counselling. This can be particularly challenging when working with children, as the child may not have any particular goals for counselling and, if they do, these may not match the goals that the counsellor, working within a specific practice framework, will have. For example, a practitioner working with a child from a home where there is domestic violence might have the goal of providing the child with strategies to keep them safe. The child, however, might have the goal of wanting to keep their mother safe (Geldard and Geldard, 2008). Child-centred therapy places the child's needs at the core of the therapy and it is essential that the child's concerns are attended to, as well as ensuring the safety of the child at all times.

Issues of privacy and confidentiality

Another area posing dilemmas for the counsellor concerns privacy and confidentiality. Regarding the former, if the counselling takes place within the school during the school day, it is probable that other children (and teachers) will become aware a child is 'having' counselling. This raises potential issues of stigmatising the child, possibly inhibiting the child's willingness to attend. However, if the counselling service becomes embedded within the school culture, then the potential embarrassment about seeing a counsellor can be reduced. Alternatively, it may be feasible for children to leave the school premises to attend counselling sessions or for them to attend counselling outside school times.

One of the crucial ethical principles for a counsellor is to respect client confidentiality. It is essential that the child feels they can bring any concerns to the sessions and that these will not be passed on to others. However, the counsellor, working within professional, legal and ethical constraints, is unable to 'promise' they will never pass on any of the information the child gives them. I make clear that whatever the child says or does within the session remains private and will not be repeated to anyone except for my supervisor (someone who checks that I'm doing my work properly). I explain that the details of our sessions will not be shared with teachers and/or parents; however, some of the broader themes might be discussed with them, but only after consultation with the child. Crucially, I make explicit in the first session that there may be a time when I need to pass on details of our sessions. This will happen if I hear the child is being hurt and I will tell someone who will try to stop this happening. Similarly, if I hear that another child is being hurt, I will also have to tell someone else about this. However, I explain that I will not do either without discussing it with the child first. 'Keeping things private' can potentially raise anxieties for some children, especially those who have been abused, so I stress that if the child wants to talk to someone about what goes on in our sessions, they can.

Confidentiality is a difficult aspect of working with children. It takes a significant amount of trust for a child to tell you they are being hurt in some way, and breaking that trust by telling someone else can have a negative impact on the child. That is why it is so important to keep reminding the child of the confidentiality 'rules' in the contract. During one session, Adam looked anxious and kept tugging at his sleeves; he told me that he had a 'bad arm'. I asked him if he wanted to show me his 'bad arm' and initially he refused and continued to play. After some time, he came over to me and pushed up his sleeve. There was a huge bruise on his arm and I commented that it looked very painful and asked him if he wanted to tell me about it. Reluctantly, he said that his much older brother had done this to him. It emerged through gentle probing that this was not the first time his brother had hurt him. It also became clear that Adam was very scared of his brother. Adam seemed relieved to have finally told someone, but there was now a new anxiety about possible repercussions. I reminded Adam of what we had agreed in the contract; that I would have to report the bruise to someone who would try and make sure that this would not happen again. Adam was not happy with this and tried to persuade me not to tell anyone else. He especially did not want his brother to find out he had told anyone. I was unable to guarantee this to him and, at the end of the session, I completed the required documentation to register my concern for his welfare.

A more positive instance of sharing information came with my work with Luke. He was referred by his mother, who was worried about his 'aggressive tendencies'. She, other family members and his teachers perceived him as an aggressive child with the potential to hurt others. My own experience of him within the counselling sessions was of an angry boy but also a hurt and vulnerable boy. Luke's father had left the family home three years before and, as the eldest boy in the family, it became clear that Luke felt responsible for looking after his siblings and his mother. Indeed, it was often while 'standing up' for his brother at school that he became involved in fights. He felt very protective of his mum. Luke did not allow himself to feel vulnerable (and possibly was not allowed to). During one session, he admitted to having recurring nightmares in which his mother was being attacked and he could not protect her. We talked about his fears for his mum and he asked me if I would tell his mother about his night-mares. I suggested it might be something he would like to try first. Luke seemed unsure he could do this. However, the following week, he was keen to tell me he had told his mum all about the nightmares and she had been really understand-ing and caring. It felt to me he had finally become the child again and was able to express his vulnerability. Empowering Luke to share the feelings explored within the therapy with his mother was a pivotal moment for his emotional devel-opment; as a result of counselling, he was much more able to express his vulner-ability to those around him, rather than 'lashing out' in anger, and consequently, as his mother reported, family relationships greatly improved.

Final thoughts

As a counsellor, the focus of my work is the internal world of the child and central to that is the unique counsellor–client relationship. However, as I have outlined above, both the counsellor and child are situated within a wider system of social networks. My work is influenced by the contexts within which I work and the rules by which I am bound, whereas the child is nested within multiple contexts such as home, school and community. Problems that exist within these wider contexts include poverty, family breakdown, parental psychiatric illness, parental addiction and crime, all of which are potential risk factors in the devel-opment of emotional and behavioural difficulties. Generally, the remit of the counsellor does not, or cannot, extend to intervening in these wider 'layers' of the child's ecology. However, the therapist can, hopefully, facilitate change in the way the child 'acts on' the systems in their social ecology. Hopefully, by enabling the child to construct new understandings of their 'problems' and make useful choices within the secure environment of the counselling sessions, they will be able to transfer some of these skills beyond the therapeutic situation. Perhaps the optimum approach to intervention is a multidimensional one; one that focuses on the different systems within which the child is embedded as well as individually focused therapy.

References

Besley, A.C. (2002) 'Foucault and the turn to narrative therapy', *British Journal of Guidance and Counselling*, **30**(2): 126–42.
Bion, W. (1962) *Learning from Experience*, London, Heinemann.
BCAP (British Association for Counselling and Psychotherapy) (2009) *Ethical Framework for Good Practice in Counselling and Psychotherapy*, Lutterworth, BACP.

Earls, F. and Carlson, M. (2001) 'The social ecology of child health and well-being', *Annual Revue Public Health*, 22: 143–66.

Geldard, K. and Geldard, D. (2008) *Counselling Children: A Practical Introduction* (3rd edn), London, Sage.

Patrick, E. (2006) 'Koala, cat and me', *Therapy*, **17**(7): 9–12.

Place2Be (2009) Info for schools: Our range of services, available online at <http://www.theplace2be.org.uk/> [Accessed 25 November 2009].

Shooter, M. (2008) 'The elephant in the room: Counselling in the context of poverty', *Therapy Today*, **19**(3): 19–22.

Swenson, C.C. and Chaffin, M. (2006) 'Beyond psychotherapy: Treating abused children by changing their social ecology', *Aggression and Violent Behaviour*, 11: 121–37.

Walker, S. (2005) *Culturally Competent Therapy: Working with Children and Young People*, Basingstoke, Palgrave Macmillan.

7

Young people and mental health: resilience and models of practice

Wook Hamilton

Young people's mental health is a subject that has attracted a great deal of attention in recent years in the media, in policy and in the public imagination.

I am a trainer of practitioners who works with young people and their parents, and have a background working in mental health in the voluntary sector. In this chapter I will look at how young people are constructed in ways that render them 'dangerous', 'at risk' and in crisis. These persistent representations of young people also permeate the way young people think about themselves and how we think about and work with young people.

The chapter will also consider young people's mental health, its epidemiology and how it is constructed. I will argue that mental health is seen as not existing purely in individuals but is also part of the context in which they live and we will go on to consider how this can be addressed in practice. I will explore how the shifting semantics in mental health practice have helped to shape new policy trajectories that see mental health in its wider context as well as challenge the prevailing negativity. I will then look at some evolving practice models that draw in particular on resilience research and consider how these alternative models offer both challenges and opportunities for practitioners working with young people. In this exploration I will unpack some of the models and constructs that not only shape how we see young people, but how we then support them.

Young people and mental health: social constructions of young people

The experience of being a young person in the West in the early twenty-first century is very different from 100 or even 50 years ago. The rapid social and economic change of the twentieth century, its changing employment patterns, its affluence, and its policy focuses have changed what it means to be young. From the arrival of the 'teenager' as both a social identity and a marketing niche in the 1940s and 50s to the youth unemployment of the 1980s, these changes had an impact (France, 2007). Young people generally spend longer in education, they enter the workforce later, they get married and have children later, and in many ways see themselves as a distinct social group in a way unprecedented in recent generations. The life stage often termed as 'adolescence' has been marked and characterised by these changes, prompting debates about its changing and extending nature (Arnett, 2004; Graham, 2006; Devitt et al., 2009). For the purposes of this chapter, however, I am considering young people up to 18 years old.

Our contemporary fascination with young people expresses itself in the popular media as well as academic and policy discourses. These discourses, which so often have a tendency to problematise young people, have had a huge impact on how young people are constructed today and how in turn they feel about and see themselves. We will all be familiar with the extent of negative reporting about young people in the media. Research has suggested that over 70% of stories about young people are negative, most frequently featuring incidents of violence and knife crime, while positive stories tend to be about high achievers in either sport or education (Begum et al., 2004; Anderson et al., 2005). Many adults believe youth crime to be rising rather than falling. This growing concern over youth crime has been termed by some as a 'moral panic' (France, 2007), with media images ranging from the 'Black mugger' in the 1970s (Hall et al., 1978) to 'hoodies' at the beginning of the twenty-first century. Birkland (1997) argued that within this media preoccupation, the murder of James Bulger in the 1980s represented a 'focusing event', which constructed a 'collective agony' over the state of our youth (Birkland, 1997). Recent headlines, such as 'A decade of delinquency: Teen robberies, violence and drug crime soar to record levels' (Slack, 2009), show how current this trend still is.

Policy has played a key part in framing how young people are seen in contemporary society. Policy around young people took its cues in the 1970s and 80s from the political questions being asked about young people and unemployment, as well as concerns about youth crime. While some of these questions addressed themselves to the underlying causes, a tendency also emerged to look to individual 'failings' for answers, with its corollary of blame. Alongside these representations of young people in the media is an associated discourse surrounding the blaming of parents for the ills of youth. Policy developments that promote support for parents have often been conflated with these notions of parental blame by the media.

Despite the fact that youth crime in the UK has been falling (Coleman and Brookes, 2009), young people remain demonised in the public imagination, and youth crime is a hot political issue that constructs youth as a major problem: 'The youth question in late modernity therefore remains fixated with "youth as a problem" that still needs fixing' (France, 2007 p. 152). Policy developments at the beginning of the twenty-first century reframed the issue under the banner of 'social exclusion' and offered education as the solution. If crime and delinquency are linked with unemployment, the argument is posited, then young people need to be skilled and educated in order to join the workforce. Education then is the solution to social exclusion. This reconfiguration of the youth problem retains the tendency to blame the individual for their lack of 'inclusion'. As France (2007 p. 84) put it: 'It locates the causes [of social exclusion] as being lack of personal traits or the willingness to be included.'

If we look to who the 'underachievers' are or those excluded from education, however, we find an overrepresentation of working-class young people, of boys and in particular Black Caribbean and mixed race groups (Coleman and Brookes, 2009; Devitt et al., 2009). However, not all policy trajectories have rendered young people so passive, and recent initiatives, as I shall discuss later, offer a more empowering perspective on young people that runs alongside these trends.

The social construction of mental health

Before discussing the impact of the social construction of mental health on young people's mental health, it is useful to consider the meaning of mental health and ill health itself. Mental health and illness are highly contested terms (Szasz, 1967; Mental Health Foundation, 1999) – contested because of debates about how appropriate it is to understand mental health within the medical model of illness and because of the painful stigma that surrounds mental health issues.

In particular, psychiatry's overreliance on the medical model as an explanatory system has been challenged by many, from academics to service users. Any definition of mental health and ill health necessarily enters into these debates, with language itself reflecting these controversies. The term 'mental illness', for instance, implies a medical definition of mental health and has been rejected by some in the service user movement who prefer alternative terms such as 'mental distress', which emphasizes the experience of distress rather than the diagnosis of 'illness'.

Further questions arise if we consider patterns of mental health diagnosis in young people. Mental ill health is not evenly distributed throughout the population and patterns of diagnosis point to many differences in relation to gender, social class and culture. Girls, for instance, are much more likely to be diagnosed with depression and anxiety, and boys more likely to be diagnosed with conduct disorders (Coleman, 2007). Black young people (particularly girls) are more likely to be diagnosed with mental health difficulties, and Asian young people (particularly boys) are less likely to be diagnosed than their white counterparts (Coleman, 2007). Suicide rates are considerably higher among boys and lesbian and gay young people (Warwick et al., 2000). Mental health difficulties are also linked with poverty and disadvantage, with rates of mental health disorders twice as high among children brought up in lone-parent families and much higher among families where neither parent is working (Coleman, 2007; Coleman and Brooks, 2009). Similarly, young people brought up 'in care' are much more likely to experience mental health difficulties (ibid.). These variations demonstrate that mental health issues cannot be understood solely in terms of individual predisposition but that the social context in which a young person lives has a significant impact on their vulnerability to develop mental health difficulties.

Much academic and media attention has been given to the question of the apparent increase in mental health difficulties among young people (Collishaw et al., 2004; Philips, 2004). The evidence is mixed as to whether this is the case, but there seems to be an increase in stress and emotional distress among young people whether or not this is reflected in mental health diagnoses. These fears about the prevalence of mental health difficulties among young people have, however, undoubtedly fed into the sense of panic about the crisis in youth.

An important question to consider here is what the influences are on mental health in young people. Despite the controversies outlined above, most researchers would agree that the causes of mental health difficulties are multifactorial in origin, with biological, psychological and environmental factors all playing a part (Dogra et al., 2002). We do know that self-esteem and self-image, as well as the environment that a young person lives in, all can have a part to play in mental health difficulties (Dogra et al., 2002). Young people will necessarily internalise the representations of themselves described above to some extent. To put it crudely, as Mathew Owen (2009, p. 12) argued in an article in *Young-Minds*, 'if they're told enough times that they are hoody wearing immoral drunks who carry knives, then they'll start to believe it'. The literature from resilience research is helpful here; it both contributes to our understanding of the causes of mental health difficulties as well offering us different perspectives on young people, with some important practice implications.

Messages from resilience research

Resilience theory and research offers us a model that turns the question about the cause of mental health problems in young people on its head. Instead of asking what causes the problems, it asks: What protects young people from developing mental health difficulties, and what keeps them healthy despite adversity? This reframing of the question is significant and affects how we construct young people and how we then go on to think about how to support them.

Resilience can be defined as 'the capacity to transcend adversity' (Daniel et al., 1997, p. 14), or the ability to 'bounce back from significant difficulties'. One understanding of resilience is to see it as a quality or a trait that individual young people may or may not have. However, research has favoured an understanding of resilience as something that is not statically located in the individual alone, but a more dynamic process supported by a set of conditions. These conditions include an individual's traits, but also importantly include the family, community and environment (Garmezy and Rutter, 1988):

> Resilience involves a range of processes that bring together quite diverse mechanisms operating before, during and after the encounter with stress experience or adversity. (Rutter, 1999, p. 135)

It is this definition of resilience that is most useful for practitioners and offers up opportunities to 'promote' resilience in young people by working with all these dimensions of a young person's life.

Resilience research (such as Garmenzy and Rutter, 1988) asks what is it that affects the enormous variation in children and young people's responses to risk experiences and in particular what is it that has protected young people from developing difficulties. Within the literature on resilience, protective factors have been identified within these domains (Coleman, 2007, p. 11):

- *Individual attributes:* good intellectual skills, positive temperament, positive views of the self
- *Family attributes:* high warmth, cohesion, high expectations, parental involvement
- *Community attributes:* good schools, neighborhood resources, strong social networks.

A young person's capacity to be resilient is seen then as a chain reaction between these factors; something that is built on a combination of conditions and attributes that promote resilience.

The resilience model offers a different perspective on young people and mental health in a number of ways. The model recognises the interaction between the individual's health, the family and the community. It sees young people as having agency and allows the possibility of change. As such, the model is solution, not problem centred and opens up a range of interventions for practitioners. The resilience model has gained currency in recent years and has informed research and policy developments as well as practice interventions.

Policy and practice developments

Praise youth and it will prosper. (Irish proverb)

Resilience and wellbeing discourses have entered policy and practice in a variety of ways in the past two decades, offering new perspectives on approaches to working with young people. In this section, I will look at some recent policy and practice initiatives that have been inspired by a resilience perspective; preventive interventions will be considered as well as developments in the treatment of young people with mental health problems. Finally, I will consider what challenges and opportunities this poses to practitioners.

There have been significant policy developments across the UK in relation to children and young people (DfES, 2004, 2006; Scottish Government, 2006; Office of First Minister and Deputy Minister, 2006), all of which are rooted in a social ecological perspective:

> [*Youth Matters*] proposes that young people should have: More things to do and places to go in their local area – and more choice and influence over what is available; More opportunities to volunteer and to make a contribution to their local community. (Cockburn and Cleaver, 2008, p. 1)

It is fair to say that in many ways these policy developments signal a shift towards more holistic and resilience-based approaches to the delivery of children and young people's services. For example, a current mental health policy initiative, *New Horizons*, which aims to shape the next 10-year agenda in mental health, has a stated policy aim of 'building mental resilience in individuals, families and communities' (DH, 2009, p. 11).

The shifting use of language reflects these changes and terms such as 'emotional health', 'emotional literacy' and 'wellbeing' are becoming part of the discourse of children and young people's services (Coleman, 2007). This new terminology brings with it different constructions of young people's mental health and how to work with it. Wellbeing, for instance, can be defined as:

> a state of being with others, where human needs are met, where one can act meaningfully to pursue one's goals and where one enjoys a satisfactory quality of life. (Wellbeing in Developing Countries, 2008)

The term 'wellbeing' therefore assumes emotional health to be more than just the absence of mental ill health and includes aspirations of positive mental health. The term also recognises the role of social, material and psychological forces in the promotion of wellbeing, and in doing so shifts the focus away from individual pathology. It 'links the provision of basic needs with social relatedness, the exercise of meaningful agency and attainment of enhanced quality of life'. (Cockburn and Cleaver, 2008, p. 3)

The field of mental health promotion has provided an important vehicle for the implementation of the ideas about resilience and wellbeing. Many programmes in and outside government have been developed, which have furthered interest in the subject and initiated new service models (Coleman, 2007). Recent reviews of mental health promotion services for young people (cited in Coleman, 2007) found a wide range of programmes on offer, many within a school setting either with a whole school approach or classroom based. The focus and aims of these programmes varied, some having specific aims such as the reduction in self-harm or depression and some with broader aims of improving general mental health or self-esteem.

Initiatives such as SEAL (Social and Emotional Aspects of Learning) in England and Wales promote a model whereby the wellbeing of children and young people is seen as inextricably linked to their capacity to learn; it promotes a whole school approach with a focus on the school environment and the involvement of parents and the community (Weare and Gray, 2003). The National Healthy Schools Programme in England (NHS/DCSF, 2007) and initiatives flowing from the Schools Act in Scotland (Scottish Government, 2007) similarly focus on the promotion of emotional health and have furthered work in this area.

Another example of a more direct preventive intervention is the Penn Resiliency Program, which has a successful evidence base in the US and has recently been trialled with the support of the Department for Children, Schools and Families (DCSF), in parts of the UK. The UK Resilience Programme, as it is known here, is a curriculum-based intervention for year seven children involving a series of lessons over a number of months. This intervention is based on resiliency research and its intention is to help young people respond better to problems and to prevent future mental health issues through the building of resilience skills (The Young Foundation, n.d.). Initial findings from the evaluation show that it has had a significant impact on reducing symptoms of depression and anxiety among pupils that have taken part in the programme (Challen et al., 2009). Similar programmes are being piloted in Scotland with equally positive results, such as the FRIENDS for Life programme (Stirling Council, 2008).

The recent trend of transferring or importing programmes into a different cultural context has itself not always been easy and often further evaluation is necessary in these new contexts. Additionally, the efficacy of preventive interventions can often be hard to measure (Coleman, 2007). The more patchy evidence base of other interventions developed in the UK shows that programmes with more clearly defined aims tend to be more easily evaluated. A further issue in the evaluation of interventions is that in practice the success or failure of 'whole school' programmes, such as SEAL, often rest on the extent of 'buy in' among frontline practitioners, for example whether teachers in schools embrace the links between emotional health and education in their practice.

These emerging preventive interventions take their inspiration from the resilience model and its question of what protects young people from mental health problems and promotes their mental and emotional health. In this reframing of the question, the perspective shifts from seeing young people as the 'problem to be fixed' to a perspective that recognises and tries to address some of the environmental stressors which may contribute to young people's lack of 'wellbeing', and sees individuals as having agency in their capacity to build resilience. In this deconstruction and reconstruction of the question and the interventions that flow from it, challenges are made to the prevailing images of young people referred to at the start of this chapter. However, it could be argued that services are still more focused on 'interventions for mental ill health rather than the promotion of mental wellbeing' (Carter et al., 2006, p. 584). We will turn now to consider how interventions for mental ill health can also draw on ideas about resilience.

Resilience research also carries important messages for practitioners working directly with young people with mental health problems. Many service models and therapeutic disciplines have engaged with, or been influenced by, these ideas. I will consider some issues in family therapy, the multisystemic fostering model and also the practice of parenting support to consider some of these influences. Finally I will draw on ideas from resilience therapy to point to issues that are raised for all practitioners who work with young people.

The systemic perspective of family therapy sees a young person as part of a wider system and ideas from resilience research complement this model. Over the past few decades, family therapy has moved away from deficit models of the family towards being an increasingly strength-based approach 'recognising that successful interventions depend more on tapping into family resources than on therapist techniques' (Walsh, 2002, p. 130) and several treatment models have been developed from this perspective. Multisystemic therapy is a model developed in the US for working with 'anti-social youth' and has been adapted in the UK in a number of contexts. The model has an effective evidence base in the US and the DCSF is currently trialling a number of projects based on this approach in the UK context (Jones, 2009).

In South Wales, the Multi-disciplinary Intervention Service (MIST) Torfaen is an example of a project that has been developed using these ideas. The project recognises that children in foster care have a much higher risk of mental health problems and applies the model to a wraparound foster care service. The project works with 'Looked After' young people who present some of most challenging and risk-taking behaviour and who have typically been excluded from school and had several placement breakdowns. A key feature of the service is that it is multidimensional and multisystemic. In practice, for a team of practitioners, this means that:

> multiple interventions drawing on different psychological approaches are carried out concurrently with different configurations of the young person and their network ... [spanning] foster home, family home, school and community. (Street et al., 2009, p. 27)

Working with an attachment focus, the programme attempts 'to promote trust, self-esteem, self-value, autonomy and emotional literacy' (Street et al., 2009, p. 27); it prefers not to see young people in diagnostic terms and focuses more on what a young person needs. It also aims 'not to engage in stereotypical views and prejudices' (Street et al., 2009, p. 29), thereby not simplifying an individual's situation. In these ways this programme is engaged in promoting a young person's resilience by engaging with individual, family and community dimensions of their life. In its challenge to mental health diagnoses and stereotypical views, it recognises the potential role of these constructions of young people in perpetuating mental ill health. Importantly, this approach has been successful in its initial aim to move young people successfully from out of authority residential care to local foster care.

Another significant service development that links into resiliency work is the growth in parenting support. Prompted by research in the youth justice sector that linked young people's offending to parenting styles (Loeber and Stouthamer-Loeber, 1986; Utting et al., 1993), parenting support has now become an adjunct to many children and young people's services, including education and the voluntary sector, as well as the subject matter of policy (DfES, 2007). This development concurs with resiliency research, which identifies parenting as one of the most important resilience-promoting factors for young people. The evidence base for this work has largely been conducted in the US and Australia, although many of the programmes have been imported and trialled in the UK context as part of the Parenting Early Intervention Pathfinders government initiative (Lindsay et al., 2008).

While the evidence base is good for the practice of parenting support and parents of young people report that they want support, in practice it can be hard to engage parents in the process (Asmussen et al., 2007). This may well be largely because of the way in which the issues of parenting young people have been negatively constructed around a discourse of blame: 'though parents were now encouraged to seek support, this was against the backdrop of criticism and blame ... A sense of failure was then added to a fear of judgement' (Asmussen et al., 2007, p. 115). The additional issue of guilt is also often present when a young person has mental health problems (Hamilton and Shepherd, 2008).

The discourse of blame and failure is something that practitioners are encouraged to challenge as part of their work with parents. An important precursor to offering parenting support is to engage with these negative constructions and to reframe the support offered in a more positive way. Triple P, an evidence-based parenting programme from Australia being trialled in the UK, includes a comprehensive media strategy as part of its delivery programme that 'serves to normalise and destigmatise parenting difficulties' (www.triplep.net), thereby recognising and integrating this in the work.

Finally, I would like to draw on some of the messages from resilient therapy to consider issues for any practitioner working with young people with mental health issues. Resilient therapy is an approach that has been developed within a child and adolescent mental health services (CAMHS) setting and offers some important applications of resilience research for any practitioner (Hart and Blincow, 2008). The approach suggests that the 'strategic management of therapy ... [is as important as] ... micro-interventions in the moment' (Hart et al., 2007, p. 132). Hart et al. (2007) present some basic premises of practice or 'noble truths', which draw eclectically on a number of traditions and form the backbone of the approach: accepting, containment, commitment and enlisting:

- *Accepting* refers to the need for resilient therapists to engage precisely where the clients are by exploring the important details in a client's life
- *Containment* is drawn from the psychoanalytic idea of containment, recognising the therapeutic role of providing safety and boundaries for a client
- *Commitment* involves remaining alongside a client throughout their difficulties and challenges the tendencies in services for clients to be 'passed around'
- *Enlisting* is about creating a team surrounding the young person, whereby parents and others are educated to become 'co-practitioners' in the process.

In the case of Belinda, cited by Hart et al. (2007), a young woman in foster care whose history included rejection from her birth family and a history of mental health problems, Hart demonstrates how a resilient therapy approach ensured that all relationships that could be seen as 'hopeful attachments' were worked with. In Belinda's case, these included a social worker and her birth mother, resulting in therapeutic work being initiated with her birth mother and other extended family members, alongside work on her interpersonal strategies with others and attention to the wider details of her life.

Resilient therapy has implications not just for direct work with young people but also for strategic issues in services in a number of ways. This therapy challenges the professional defences that often operate in organisations working with the most disadvantaged children and young people, where there may be a tendency for a young person to be pathologised and moved on, or an overreliance on diagnosis for explanations rather than a 'dramatic response to adversity' (Hart et al., 2007). In this way, as Hart and Blincow commented (2008, p. 140): 'the developmental vocabulary of resilience can help practitioners avoid the exclusive search for pathology in accordance with a deficit model of child mental health' and offer a more positively framed starting point. To approach working with young people from a resiliency perspective, practitioners are also required not to undermine existing functional strategies and to enlist others in the work, thereby challenging some of the professional boundaries that may pull against this approach.

Final thoughts

In considering the way in which young people have been constructed in contemporary society, we find competing discourses of blame versus responsibility that in some ways plays out an age-old historical tension surrounding youth. However, our present-day concerns have a sense of urgency to them – the escalation of negative media reports about young people and the increase in emotional and mental health issues and the damaging stigma of mental health are issues that demand our attention.

Recent policy direction in relation to young people does in many ways take account of these issues and attempts to reframe both mental health and the demonisation of young people. However, policy can shift in line with changes of government priorities, and it relies on funding, services and individuals to deliver its objectives. As France (2007, p. 163) said:

> National policy may be an important arena, where social change is targeted as an outcome, but it is in the everyday practices and activities of individuals at the local level that real change takes place.

Resilience research can offer an alternative model, which can help to reframe and reconstruct young people who have mental health difficulties and with it a range of related intervention strategies.

However, as I have shown, there are competing definitions in the construction of the concept of resilience itself that have important ramifications. On the one hand, resilience, when defined as something someone either does or doesn't have, can lead to a potentially blaming, individualistic understanding of mental health, and the absence of problems is attributed to individual traits alone. On the other hand, if resilience is understood as process oriented, it opens up a way of seeing young people as co-constructed via an interaction between themselves, their family and environment. These differing definitions clearly have implications for practice.

The resilience model, and its invitation to challenge some of the prevailing negative constructions of young people, presents practitioners with some important issues to consider in their work with young people. Not only do we need to consider reframing how we see young people (and their parents) but we need to include them in the process of reconstruction. This includes asking young people what they need, including others as 'co-practitioners' in the process, and considering the messages inherent in any language we use.

The concepts behind 'multidisciplinary' work are stretched by some of these invitations: Can we consider the full range of ways in which a young person can be supported to build resilience, even if they fall outside the boundaries of our preferred, or role-defined mode of intervention? Do we consider how an interest in sport or a link with a distant but supportive relative has a role to play along-side talking therapy? Do we take an 'adult-centric view of what coping consists of in young people' and 'assume that talking is [always] the best way to promote better mental health' (Coleman, 2007, p. 56)? Are we able to listen to the detail of what is important to a young person even if it doesn't fit within our own constructs? And can we enlist others in the process without getting caught up in professional rivalry?

This way of seeing can present challenges for practitioners as well as being liberating. It can open up a wider vision and suggest creative new ways of working. It invites practitioners to turn the vicious circle of mental ill health into a virtuous circle towards health, by initiating small changes in a young person's internal and external world and to see young people in their wider context that we play a part in creating.

References

Anderson, S., Bromley, C. and Given, L. (2005) *Public Attitudes to Young People and Youth Crime in Scotland: Findings from the 2004 Social Attitudes Survey*, Scottish Executive.

Arnett, J. (2004) *Emerging Adulthood: The Winding Road from Late Teens Through the Twenties*, New York, Oxford University Press.

Asmussen, K., Corlyon, J., Hauari, H. and La Placa, V. (2007) *Supporting the Parents of Teenagers*, Research Report RR830, London, Policy Research Bureau.

Begum, A., Rushbrook, A., Rushbrook, C. and Arthur, D. (2004) *Media Portrayal of Young People: Impact and Influences*, London, National Youth Agency Young Researcher Network/National Children's Bureau.

Bentall, R. (2009) 'Diagnoses are psychiatry's star signs: Let's listen more and drug people less', *The Guardian*, 1 September.

Birkland, T.A. (1997) *After Disaster: Agenda Setting, Public Policy and Focusing Events*, Washington DC, Georgetown University Press.

Carter, B., Bradley, S., Richardson, R. et al. (2006) 'Appreciating what works: Discovering and dreaming alongside people developing resilient services for young people requiring mental health services', *Issues in Mental Health Nursing*, 27: 575–94.

Challen, A., Machin, S., Noden, P. and West, A. (2009) *UK Resilience Programme Evaluation: Interim Report*, London, DCSF.

Cockburn, T. and Cleaver, F. (2008) Wellbeing and Children's Association: Processes of Poverty and Social Exclusion in British Civil Society, paper presented to International Workshop 'Impact of Poverty and Social Exclusion on Children's Lives and their Wellbeing', 8–9 September, Bratislava, Slovakia.

Coleman, J. (2007) 'Emotional health and well-being', in J. Coleman, L. Hendry and M. Kloep (eds) *Adolescence and Health*, Chichester, John Wiley & Sons, pp. 41–61.

Coleman, J. and Brooks, F. (2009) *Key Data on Adolescence*, Brighton, AHPH/TSA.

Collishaw, S., Maughan, B., Goodman, R. and Pickles, A. (2004) 'Time trends in adolescent mental health', *Journal of Child Psychology and Psychiatry and Allied Disciplines*, **45**(8): 1350–62.

Daniel, B., Wassel, S. and Gilligan, R. (1997) *Child Development for Child Care and Protection Workers*, London, Jessica Kingsley.

Devitt, K., Knighton, L. and Lowe, K. (2009) *Young Adults Today: Key Data on 16–25 year olds, Transitions, Disadvantage, Crime*, Brighton, Young People in Focus.

DfES (Department for Education and Skills) (2004) *Every Child Matters: Change for Children*, London, TSO.

DfES (Department for Education and Skills) (2006) *Youth Matters: Next Steps*, London, TSO.

DfES (Department for Education and Skills) (2007) *Every Parent Matters*, London, TSO.

DH (Department of Health) (2009) *New Horizons: Towards a Shared Vision for Mental Health*, London, COI for the DH.

Dogra, N., Parkin, A., Gale, F. and Frake, C. (2002) *Child and Adolescent Mental Health for Front-line Professionals*, London, Jessica Kingsley.

France, A. (2007) *Understanding Youth in Late Modernity*, London, Open University Press.

Garmezy, N. and Rutter, M. (1988) *Stress, Coping and Development in Children*, Baltimore, MD, Johns Hopkins University Press.

Graham, P. (2006) *The End of Adolescence*, Oxford, Oxford University Press.

Hall, S., Criticher, C., Jefferson, T. et al. (1978) *Policing and Crisis*, London, Macmillan – now Palgrave Macmillan.

Hamilton, W. and Shepherd, J. (2008) *The Needs and Experiences of Parents of Young People who Have Mental Health Difficulties*, Brighton, Trust for the Study of Adolescence.

Hart, A. and Blincow, D. (2008) 'Resilient therapy: Strategic therapeutic engagement with children in crisis', *Child Care in Practice*, **14**(2): 131–45.

Hart, A. and Blincow, D. with Thomas, H. (2007) *Resilient Therapy: Working with Children and Families*, Hove, Routledge.

Jones, H. (2009) Evidence-based Interventions: At Least Do No Harm, presentation to Investing in Children Conference, London, February.

Lindsay, G. Davies, H., Band, S. et al. (2008) *Parenting Early Intervention Pathfinder Evaluation*, University of Warwick and Kings College, London, DCSF, available online at <http://www.dcsf.gov.uk/research/data/uploadfiles/dcsf-rw054.pdf> [Accessed 14 May 2010].

Loeber, R. and Stouthamer-Loeber, M. (1986) 'Family factors as correlates and predictors of juvenile conduct problems and delinquency', *Crime and Justice*, **7**(29): 29–149.

Mental Health Foundation (1999) *Brighton Futures: Promoting Children and Young People's Mental Health*, London, Mental Health Foundation.

NHS/DCSF (Department of Children Schools and Families) (2007) *The National Healthy Schools Programme*, London, DCSF.

Office of the First Minister and Deputy First Minister (2006) *Our Children and Young People – Our Pledge: Ten Year Strategy for Children and Young People in Northern Ireland 2006–2012*, available online at <www.allchildrenni.gov.uk/ten-year-strategy.pdf> [Accessed 12 March 2010].

Owen, M. (2009) 'Self-fulfilling prophesy', *YoungMinds*, 100, June/July.

Philips, M. (2004) 'Childhood's lost idyll', *Daily Mail*, 14 September.

Rutter, M. (1999) 'Resilience concepts and findings: Implications for family therapy', *Journal of Family Therapy*, pp. 119–14.

Scottish Government (2006) *Getting it Right for Every Child*, Edinburgh, Scottish Executive.

Scottish Government (2007) *The Schools Act*, available online at <http://www.scotland.gov.uk/Topics/Education/Schools/HLivi/foodnutrition> [Accessed 12 March 2010].

Slack, J. (2009) 'A decade of delinquency: Teen robberies, violence and drug crime soar to record levels', *Daily Mail*, 6 March.

Stirling Council (2008) *The Impact of the FRIENDS Programme on Children's Anxiety, Low Mood and Self Esteem: A Replication Study in a Scottish Setting*, available online at <http://www.scotland.gov.uk/Resource/Doc/1049/0086487.pdf> [Accessed 8 April 2010].

Street, S., Hill, J. and Welham, J. (2009) 'Delivering a therapeutic wrap-round service for troubled adolescents in care', *Adoption and Fostering*, **33**(2): 26–33.

Szasz, T. (1967) *The Myth of Mental Illness: Foundations of a Theory of Personal Conduct*, New York, Hoeber-Harper.

Utting, D., Bright, J., and Henricson, C. (1993) *Crime and the Family: Improving Child-rearing and Preventing Delinquency*, London, Family Policy Studies Centre.

Walsh, F. (2002) 'A family resilience framework: Innovative practice applications', *Family Relations*, 51: 130–7.

Warwick, I., Oliver, C. and Aggleton, P. (2000) 'Sexuality and mental health promotion: Lesbian and gay young people', in P. Aggleton, J. Hurry and I. Warwick (eds) *Young People and Mental Health*, Chichester, John Wiley & Sons, pp. 131–46.

Weare, K. and Gray, G. (2003) *What Works in Developing Children's Emotional and Social Competence and Wellbeing?* London, DfES.

Wellbeing in Developing Countries (2008) *Wellbeing, Poverty and Conflict*, Briefing Paper 1/08, available online at <http://www.welldev.org.uk/research/bp/bp1-08.pdf> [Accessed 14 May 2009].

Young Foundation, The (n.d.) *The Big Initiatives: Promoting Emotional Resilience among 11 to 13 year olds in Secondary Schools*, available online at http://www.youngfoundation.org/our-work/networks-and-collaboratives/the-local-wellbeing-project/more-info/the-big-initiatives-promo [Accessed 18 May 2010].

8

Domestic abuse and safeguarding children

Lisa Arai

Children's wellbeing needs to be positively fostered if they are to have happy and enjoyable childhoods. If children are to develop into well-balanced and healthy adults, they also need to be kept safe from a variety of possible threats to their welfare, such as those caused by structural factors like poverty and poor housing, as well as family-level factors such as neglect, exposure to a carer's substance misuse or physical, emotional or sexual abuse. One way in which children can be harmed is through exposure to domestic abuse. Children's exposure to domestic abuse has come to be regarded as a serious threat to their welfare and is now treated as a safeguarding issue in the UK and many other countries (Edleson et al., 2006; Humphreys and Stanley, 2006). Exploring this change in policy and practice is the focus of this chapter. I come to this issue as a social scientist with a public health research background whose work has been focused primarily on the health and wellbeing of children and young people.

In this chapter, background information about domestic abuse, including use of terminology, and an exploration of the context within which domestic abuse occurs are briefly presented. The concept of safeguarding and the treatment of domestic abuse as a safeguarding issue, as well as the possible limitations of this approach, are described next. The chapter goes on to suggest and discuss some practice solutions.

While it is recognised that domestic abuse can affect women *and* men, and occur in same-sex partnerships, the focus of this chapter is on abuse (emotional, physical and so on) of women by a male partner in a domestic setting where children are resident, since this is the most typical context in which domestic abuse occurs (Humphreys et al., 2008).

Domestic abuse: a brief overview

Domestic abuse has profound health, psychological and social consequences for those who experience it (Humphreys et al., 2008). In the UK, it has been reported that two women a week are killed by a partner or ex-partner (DH, 2005). Feminist groups, health and social care professionals and others have been at the forefront of campaigns to raise awareness of domestic abuse. These campaigns have led, over time, to changes in the ways that the police, medical personnel and the courts deal with domestic abuse, and to the creation of special police units, refuges and shelters (Burman and Chantler, 2005). In England in 2009, the Specialist Domestic Violence Court programme was extended. Justice Minister Bridget Prentice said:

> I am delighted to announce a further 18 Specialist Domestic Violence Courts ... This latest batch of accredited courts puts us well on the way to meeting the target of 128 Specialist Domestic Violence Courts by 2011. (Ministry of Justice, 2009)

In Scotland, there have been similar campaigns against domestic abuse and the creation of the National Strategy to Address Domestic Abuse in Scotland (Scottish Executive, 2003).

'Domestic abuse' can also be called 'domestic violence', 'intimate partner violence', 'spousal abuse', 'family violence', and can include elder abuse. The victims of domestic abuse used to be called 'battered wives' (and, less frequently, husbands), although, as Johnson (1995) pointed out, this definition tended to draw attention to the person affected by the abuse rather than the perpetrator and is now rarely used. The Home Office's much-cited definition is 'any violence between current and former partners in an intimate relationship, wherever the violence occurs. The violence may include physical, sexual, emotional and financial abuse' (DH, 2005). The term 'domestic abuse' is used in preference to 'domestic violence', since use of the latter can imply that domestic abuse is primarily about physical violence (DH, 2005). It is likely that there will never be unanimity about what constitutes domestic abuse, or what terminology to use; this varies across time and place and is highly dependent on social context.

The Home Office estimates that, in England and Wales, one in four women will be a victim of domestic abuse in their lifetime (Walby, 2004). Importantly, domestic abuse is usually seen as something that only affects women but a significant number of men report being victims of domestic abuse (Mankind Initiative, 2009).

Attempts to estimate the prevalence of domestic abuse are complicated by a number of factors, such as reticence to report it on the part of those affected and a reliance on data collected in women's shelters – both are likely to lead to an underestimate of the scale of the problem (DH, 2005). To address this, there have been attempts to measure the prevalence of domestic abuse in diverse settings. Screening for domestic abuse among women accessing antenatal care, for example, can produce different prevalence rates to those created using survey or other domestic data (see, for example, Bacchus et al., 2005). Assessing women's experience of domestic abuse in healthcare settings can also facilitate medical intervention so that better health outcomes for those at risk of domestic abuse might be achieved. However, a randomised controlled trial of screening for domestic abuse in Canada followed by provision of information to medical personnel (so that further intervention might occur where needed) found no difference between a screened and unscreened pregnant population in terms of their health or wellbeing post-screening (MacMillen et al., 2009).

Social ecological and social constructionist perspectives

Domestic abuse still tends to be seen as matter of individual pathology, as a problem caused by dysfunctional individuals (Hearn and Whitehead, 2006) and is often represented as something done by 'bad' males, who are distinct from, and inherently different to, the 'ordinary' male population. Yet the research evidence demonstrates that domestic abuse is strongly related to wider social factors and is not just about individual pathology (although this can be important). Hearn and Whitehead (2006, p. 40) observed that:

> there is continuing concern with the identification of abusive personalities and 'anti-social personality disorder/trait' among violent men ... But the fact that the forms and rates of men's violence vary considerably in different societies suggest that to reduce ... men's violence means changing society. For example, the homicide rate in the Russian Federation is over 20 times that in Norway. Societal variations and the social and legal policies, including reporting procedures ... are likely to be much more important factors affecting the level of violence than the outcomes of intervention with individual men.

Hearn and Whitehead's observation highlights the importance of understanding the ways in which gender is a socially constructed category, and how constructions of masculinity (and femininity) vary from one society to the next as well as across time. Their statement also draws attention to macro- and micro-level influences (and their interplay) on domestic abuse. Social ecological perspectives emphasise the interrelatedness of individual, community and wider cultural factors and do not seek to explain human behaviour as the *sole* consequence of individual psychology. Whitaker et al. (2009) observe that the literature on interpersonal violence is still focused primarily on factors associated with violence found at individual and family level, and that wider societal factors are largely ignored. Yet the latter can be highly significant. Macro-level, societal factors – those operating within peer or neighbourhood contexts or within the wider culture – that correlate with domestic abuse include:

- patriarchal societal norms
- economic inequality
- community norms accepting of the use of violence to resolve problems
- communities that do not have shelters or services for those suffering the effects of domestic abuse
- low social cohesion
- a high level of social disorganisation
- the existence of peer groups and peer norms that are accepting of aggression (see, for example, Raghavan et al., 2009).

While social ecological theories of domestic abuse are useful in describing the diverse influences on behaviour, it should be briefly noted here that feminist commentators have suggested that there is a danger that by focusing primarily on the impact of social context on domestic abuse, individual violent men can be absolved of responsibility for their behaviour (Berns, 2004).

Safeguarding children

The concept of 'safeguarding' children has been defined as:

> The process of protecting children from abuse or neglect, preventing impairment of their health and development, and ensuring they are growing up in circumstances consistent with the provision of safe and effective care that enables children to have optimum life chances and enter adulthood successfully. (Ofsted, 2008, p. 3)

Traditionally, within children's services, safeguarding was commensurate with child protection. The job of practitioners coming into contact with children was to protect them from a range of potential harms. As this definition makes clear, the concept of safeguarding has since broadened out, and it now has this wider, more holistic meaning. Safeguarding is more than just the protection of children, it is about positively promoting child welfare to achieve the longer term aim of successful transition to adulthood.

Safeguarding, in its broadest sense, can be seen as the duty of members of a child's family, neighbours and the wider community, including *all* practitioners who come into contact with children. Some health and social care practitioners also have specific professional responsibilities to assess and coordinate responses where safeguarding concerns are raised. The statutory basis for this responsibility is enshrined primarily in the various forms of the Children Act

2004. The latter led to the establishment of Local Safeguarding Children Boards in England and Wales. In addition, the Safeguarding Vulnerable Groups Act (SVGA) 2006 stipulated the creation of the Independent Safeguarding Authority (ISA), which has powers in England, Wales and Northern Ireland. Scotland has its own version of the ISA as decreed in the Protecting Vulnerable Groups (Scotland) Act 2007. The ISA (2009) makes decisions about who should be barred from working with children and vulnerable adults. The SVGA 2006 grew out of the Bichard Inquiry established to examine child protection intelligence systems after two 10-year-olds, Holly Wells and Jessica Chapman, died at the hands of a school caretaker who had been vetted before taking up employment but whom, it subsequently emerged, had been investigated (without conviction) in relation to a number of sexual assaults against young girls.

The UK is not alone in treating children's exposure to domestic abuse as a safeguarding matter. In some US states – where more than 15 million children are believed to be living with some form of domestic abuse (McDonald et al., 2006) – children exposed to domestic abuse are automatically regarded as maltreated (Edleson, 2000). In Canada, 28% of substantiated child maltreatment cases involve exposure to domestic abuse as the primary form of maltreatment (Black et al., 2008). Yet, until fairly recently in the UK and elsewhere, children's experience of domestic abuse was not regarded as a safeguarding matter and was given relatively little prominence in research or policy. A number of developments are flagged up here as significantly leading to, or influencing, this change in approach to children's experience of domestic abuse:

1 The definition of 'harm' in the Children Act 1989 was amended in the Adoption and Children Act 2002 to include harm which might arise from witnessing the abuse of another (HMCS, 2006), thus providing a statutory basis for treatment of children's exposure to domestic abuse as a safeguarding issue in England and Wales.
2 There has been a growth in research on the harmful effects of domestic abuse on children (this is discussed further below).
3 Domestic abuse has been shown to coexist with child abuse, although estimates on this vary (Laing, 2003). In one analysis of 31 studies, 30–66% of children suffering physical abuse were also living with domestic abuse (Edleson, 1999), demonstrating that many of the factors that correlate with domestic abuse also correlate with child abuse; a fact that has obvious implications for the professional assessment of families where domestic abuse is an issue.
4 The move towards treating domestic abuse as a safeguarding issue may also be related to the more vigorous prosecution of perpetrators. This has led to greater awareness of the pervasiveness of domestic abuse as well as greater appreciation of the numbers of children who might be at risk. Domestic abuse

cases prosecuted by the Crown Prosecution Service (CPS) in England and Wales increased from 36,957 in 2006/7 to 52, 418 in 2008/9 (CPS, 2009).

Importantly, while domestic abuse is usually regarded as an adult issue that children have to deal with, this does not mean that children are passive bystanders in situations where domestic abuse is occurring (Mullender et al., 2002). Children may respond to domestic abuse when it is happening in a variety of ways: pretending not to hear; fleeing; defending a parent; or even behaving abusively towards the victimised parent (Edleson, 2000). The move towards treating domestic abuse as a safeguarding issue perhaps reflects wider social changes in perceptions of children's agency. Social constructions of the child as passive and dependent had previously meant that children's responses to domestic abuse were peripheralised (Mullender et al., 2002). Yet some children, even very young ones, can (alone or in combination with support and advocacy) exercise agency and exert control in situations where they might be presumed to be powerless and mere onlookers. Their responses to domestic abuse, when it is occurring and in its aftermath, can be active, reactive and complex.

Although domestic abuse is given prominence within policy to protect and support children in need, it does raise a number of tensions. For one, there can be a clash between approaches that are child centred (and which necessarily follow from the treatment of domestic abuse as a safeguarding issue) and those that are women centred. Child-centred approaches, focused primarily on the protection of children, emphasise the need for a child to avoid exposure to domestic abuse above other considerations. From this perspective, women can be blamed for not leaving abusive men and for not protecting their children (Laing, 2003). Women-centred approaches, conversely, are where the mother's needs are the focus of intervention. Laing (2003, p. 5) stated that:

> Those who caution against automatically defining exposure to violence as child abuse argue that this fails to take into account the efforts which women are making to protect their children ... and that insensitive child protection intervention may place the woman and her children at greater risk.

There are good reasons for this anxiety: women and their children are at significant risk when attempting to leave an abusive situation (DH, 2005) and many women and their children endure abuse and harassment in the post-separation stage (Hester and Radford, 1996). The ways in which a woman leaves a dangerous situation, the skills and strengths she is able to draw on to effectively manage her exit – as well as the services and resources she is able to access and utilise – all affect the degree of risk that she and her children are exposed to. Where social workers and other care professionals are castigated for failing to take children away from (apparently) abusive situations, there is a danger that child protection issues will dominate at the expense of abused women's needs. There is also the possibility that women will not access services when considering leaving a dangerous situation but needing help to do so, fearful that, if they do approach care professionals, their children will swiftly become the focus of intrusive child protection procedures (Sawer, 2008). Clearly, child protection procedures need to be alert to this risk and there is a need to develop practice that can steer a sensitive course between the needs of women and their children.

Another tension relates to the tendency to see children who have been exposed to domestic abuse as 'victims' by failing to recognise diversity in the effects of domestic abuse on children or their capacity for resilience. While a number of studies have found that children exposed to domestic abuse have suffered adverse effects, many of these did not control for background factors, or were limited by the use of small sample sizes or by only sampling children who lived in shelters (Edleson, 2000). More sophisticated analyses have produced mixed findings. Evidence from systematic reviews of the literature, for example, have demonstrated that children living with domestic abuse do not necessarily always have poor outcomes. A systematic review of the physical health outcomes of domestic abuse on children that examined use of health services, general health, immunisation, breastfeeding and failure to thrive did not produce firm conclusions. Two thousand studies were screened, with just 22 making it into the final review. Apart from the chance of being underimmunised and a greater chance of risk-taking, domestic abuse was not significantly associated with adverse child physical health outcomes. Similarly, in another systematic review of 41 studies, children's exposure to domestic abuse was related to emotional and behavioural problems, although the impact of domestic abuse on children was small. The co-occurrence of child abuse as well as exposure to domestic abuse increased the level of problems experienced by children (Wolfe et al., 2003).

It is worth pointing out here that, as Mullender and colleagues observed, the themes that dominate children's accounts of the impacts of domestic abuse are not about psychological or other effects, but are about safety and the loss of the familiar: 'He made me leave my home. He made me leave all my best friends. He made me leave all my things behind' (9-year-old girl, in Mullender et al., 2002, p. 108). These negative social effects of children's exposure to domestic abuse can be minimised or overlooked by those intervening to help children.

Importantly, some children appear to be better able to withstand the effects of domestic abuse than others. Edleson (2000) provided an overview of the literature of the effects of domestic abuse on children that highlights the variability in children's experiences and outcomes. He also described several studies where few or no impacts on children have been found and asked:

> How does one explain these findings? ... it may be that our measures are just not sensitive enough to observe the entire range of harm done to these children through exposure to violence. It may also be that we have not followed children long enough to

determine the true impact … it is also highly likely that children's experiences vary greatly in a number of ways:
■ The level of violence in each family.
■ The degree to which each child is exposed to that violence.
■ Other stressors to which a child may be exposed.
■ The harm it produces for each child.
■ How resilient a child and his or her environment is to violence exposure. (Edleson, 2004, p. 12)

Importantly, even though the research on the effects of domestic abuse on children shows that these vary and that not all children who witness such abuse will be irretrievably damaged, it is not being argued here that these are not children in need. They are in need, and are vulnerable, but practice responses to such children need to be alert to the fact that children vary in their response to domestic abuse.

Another tension revolves around the (highly pertinent) issue of managing workload where domestic abuse is treated as a child protection issue. In the USA, the state of Minnesota amended its legislation to include exposure to domestic abuse as a form of child maltreatment but the burden on the child welfare system became so onerous that the legislation was revoked just months later. Edleson et al. (2006, p. 169) noted that:

> By adding a large new category of children to those who were neglected, the legislators had unknowingly increased the number of children … subject to mandatory reporting … Although the legislators thought that the language change would merely clarify existing practices … agencies suddenly faced huge numbers of newly defined neglected children being reported to them.

Humphreys et al. (2008) reported that similar problems were seen in Scotland where domestic abuse involving children is also seen as an automatic safeguarding issue. In 2006/7, the Scottish Children's Reporters Association received 66,785 non-offence referrals, of which at least 18,004 were for domestic abuse (an increase of 5,000 domestic abuse referrals from 2004/5).

Practice solutions

In this relatively brief overview of domestic abuse as a safeguarding issue, it is impossible to explore all the possible implications for practice. However, three practice-relevant points are flagged up here. These apply as much to practitioners working in early years settings as those working with older children.

First, the recognition that children vary in their responses to domestic abuse is a reminder that it should not be assumed that domestic abuse will have long-term consequences for all children. Children should not treated as victims when they do not feel like victims, or we risk returning to a past where children were regarded as passive, dependent and incapable of agency or of demonstrating resilience (see, for example, Edleson et al., 2004). Even very young children can demonstrate resilience in the face of adversity.

Second, practitioners should attempt to draw on children's perspectives on domestic abuse. In part, this is because practice would benefit by it in terms of being more relevant and appropriate, but it is also because it is commensurate with children's rights to have their experiences heard and to be consulted as citizens. Children's experiences of domestic abuse are well summarised by Humphreys et al. (2008). Synthesis of research evidence discussed in this work showed that one of the key issues for children revolved around children's continuing fear of their fathers (especially in relation to contact at the post-separation stage). Children were also highly skilled at describing the factors that made a positive difference (support from mothers, peers and so on). One of the implications for practice made by Humphreys et al. (2008, p. 78) is that: 'Findings from children's perspectives literature should be centrally available and accessible to all working to improve things for children, and updated regularly with new research and evaluation.' Again, this advice is relevant for practitioners working with children of all ages.

One way forward is to develop and implement more community-level, multi-agency and culturally sensitive interventions, where women's and children's needs are addressed equally. One such approach, the Duluth model, has been intensively evaluated and found to be effective. It comprises several elements and is founded on key principles including placing the primary responsibility for domestic abuse with the community and the individual abuser, not the victim. The Duluth model stipulates four basic principles of 'interagency intervention':

1 'change will be required at the basic infrastructure levels of the multiple agencies involved in case processing' (DAIP, 2008)
2 the overall strategy must be victim safety centred
3 agencies must participate as collaborating partners
4 abusers must be held accountable for their violence.

The Duluth model, or variants of it, are one possible way forward, although because they involve multiple agencies and work across sectors, they are expensive to implement and do require consistency of implementation. Importantly, within this type of intervention, broader social context is important. Children exposed to domestic abuse may be living in communities where this and other forms of abuse are commonplace and not condemned, and domestic abuse has become normalised. Education may be needed to challenge community norms, although these may be ineffective if structural inequality is present.

Interventions aimed at particular communities can be helpful in raising awareness, although police and service response can be hampered by a lack of understanding, or, in some instances, fear of appearing to be discriminatory (Burman et al., 2002). This sometimes means that it can be easier to 'overlook' domestic abuse in some communities:

> While women in all cultures and classes have been positioned as representatives of cultural identity and as responsible for its reproduction through household and child-rearing responsibilities ... women leaving contexts of domestic violence challenge cultural norms held by both culturally mainstream and specialist services. These challenges are perhaps easier to avoid than address. (Burman et al., 2004, p. 337)

Final thoughts

Campaigns to raise awareness of domestic abuse have achieved some degree of success. In the UK and many other countries, it is now recognised that domestic abuse is widespread, can affect all sections of the community (including men) and can have profound health, emotional and social consequences. While domestic abuse can be related to individual pathology, social conditions such as structural inequality and neighbourhood norms that are accepting of violence are important in explaining variation in domestic abuse.

Earlier approaches to domestic abuse were focused primarily on women's needs, and children's responses to domestic abuse (at the time of exposure and post-exposure) were regarded as peripheral. Children were seen largely as silent or passive victims of domestic abuse. A number of developments led to, or influenced, the treatment of domestic abuse as a safeguarding issue. Children living in homes where domestic abuse takes place are now considered to be in need of additional help and protection. In some countries, including the UK, domestic abuse is now an automatic safeguarding issue. This change, introduced with the best of intentions, is not unproblematic, and some commentators have criticised the situation whereby children exposed to domestic abuse are now automatically considered to be maltreated. They have also observed that children vary in their responses to domestic abuse and many display resilience to its effects. Also important, especially in communities where services are already stretched, is the burden on practitioners of an increase in workload brought about by changes in policy on safeguarding. Practitioners may also struggle to equally meet the needs of abused women as well as those of their children.

More work needs to be done if the needs of children living with domestic abuse are to be met – but to be met without compromising abused women. This is likely to remain a significant issue for children living in societies where their exposure to domestic abuse is automatically treated as a support and safeguarding issue but where services are stretched and practitioners cannot cope with the demands placed on them.

References

Bacchus, L., Mezey, G., Bewley, S. and Haworth, A. (2005) 'Prevalence of domestic violence when midwives routinely enquire in pregnancy', *Obstetrical and Gynecological Survey*, **60**(1): 11–13.

Berns, N. (2004) *Framing the Victim: Domestic Violence, Media, and Social Problems*, Hawthorne, NY, Aldine de Gruyter.

Black, T., Trocmé, N., Fallon, B. and MacLaurin, B. (2008) 'The Canadian child welfare system response to exposure to domestic violence investigations', *Child Abuse and Neglect*, **32**(3): 393–404.

Bronfrenbrenner, U. (1979) *The Ecology of Human Development: Experiments by Nature and Design*, Cambridge, MA, Harvard University Press.

Burman, E. and Chantler, K. (2005) 'Domestic violence and minoritisation: Legal and policy barriers facing minoritized women leaving violent relationships', *International Journal of Law and Psychiatry*, **28**(1): 59–74.

Burman, E., Chantler, K. and Batsleer, J. (2002) 'Service responses to South Asian women who attempt suicide or self-harm: Challenges for service commissioning and delivery', *Critical Social Policy*, **22**(4): 641–8.

Burman, E., Smailes, S.L. and Chantler, K. (2004) '"Culture" as a barrier to service provision and delivery: Domestic violence services for minoritized women', *Critical Social Policy*, **24**(3): 332–7.

CPS (Crown Prosecution Service) (2009) *CPS Violence against Women Crime Report 2008–2009*, London, CPS.

DAIP (Domestic Abuse Intervention Programs) (2008) *Duluth Model on Public Intervention*, available online at <http://www.theduluthmodel.org/duluthmodelonpublic.php> [Accessed 31 March 2010].

DH (Department of Health) (2005) *Responding to Domestic Abuse: A Handbook for Health Professionals*, London, TSO.

Edleson, J.L. (1999) 'Children's witnessing of adult domestic violence', *Journal of Interpersonal Violence*, **14**(8): 839–70.

Edleson, J.L. (2004) 'Should childhood exposure to adult domestic violence be defined as child maltreatment under the law?', in P.G. Jaffe, L.L. Baker and A. Cunningham (eds) *Protecting Children from Domestic Violence: Strategies for Community Intervention*, New York, Guilford Press, pp. 8–29.

Edleson, J.L., Gassman-Pines, J. and Hill, M.B. (2006) 'Defining child exposure to domestic violence as neglect: Minnesota's difficult experience', *Social Work*, **51**(2): 167–74.

Hearn, J. and Whitehead, A. (2006) 'Collateral domestic abuse: Men's "domestic" violence to women seen through men's relations with men', *Probation Journal*, **53**(1): 38–56.

Hester, M. and Radford, L. (1996) *Domestic Violence and Child Contact Arrangements in England and Denmark*, Bristol, Policy Press.

HMCS (Her Majesty's Court Service) (2006) *A Quick Guide to the Adoption and Children Act 2002*, London, HMCS.

Humphreys, C. and Stanley, N. (2006) *Domestic Violence and Child Protection: Directions for Good Practice*, London, Jessica Kingsley.

Humphreys, C., Houghton, C. and Ellis, J. (2008) *Literature Review: Better Outcomes for Children and Young People Experiencing Domestic Abuse – Directions for Good Practice*, Edinburgh, Scottish Government.

ISA (Independent Safeguarding Authority) (2009) *The Safeguarding Vulnerable Groups Act 2006*, factsheet, available online at <http://www.isa-gov.org.uk/pdf/TheSVGAct2006.pdf > [Accessed 31 March 2010].

Johnson, M.P. (1995) 'Patriarchal terrorism and common couple violence: Two forms of violence against women', *Journal of Marriage and Family*, **57**(2): 283–94.

Laing, L. (2003) *Domestic Violence in the Context of Child Abuse and Neglect*, paper no 9, University of New South Wales, Sydney NSW, Australian Domestic and Family Violence Clearinghouse.

McDonald, R., Jouriles, E.N., Ramisetty-Mikler, S. et al. (2006) 'Estimating the number of American children living in partner-violent families', *Journal of Family Psychology*, **20**(10): 137–42.

MacMillan, H.L., Wathen, C.N., Jamieson, E. et al., Violence Against Women Research Group (2009) 'Screening for intimate partner violence in health care settings: A randomized trial', *Journal of the American Medical Association*, **302**(5): 493–501.

Mankind Initiative (2009) *Male Victims of Domestic Abuse: Key Statistics*, Taunton, Mankind Initiative.

Ministry of Justice (2009) 'Domestic violence: 18 new special courts announced', 26 March, available online at <http://www.justice.gov.uk/news/newsrelease260309a.htm> [Accessed 31 March 2010].

Mullender, A., Hague, G., Imam, U.F. et al. (2002) *Children's Perspectives on Domestic Violence*, London, Sage.

Ofsted (Office for Standards in Education) (2008) *Safeguarding Children: The Third Joint Chief Inspectors' Report on Arrangements to Safeguard Children*, London, Ofsted.

Raghavan, C., Gentile, K. and Rajah, V. (2009) A Feminist-community Model of Intimate Partner Violence, paper presented at the annual meeting of the American Society of Criminology, 24 May.

Sawer, P. (2008) 'British social services tried to kidnap my son', *Daily Telegraph*, 28 December.

Scottish Executive (2003) *Responding to Domestic Abuse: Guidelines for Health Care Workers in NHS Scotland*, Edinburgh, Scottish Executive.

Walby, S. (2004) *The Cost of Domestic Violence*, London, Women and Equality Unit.

Whitaker, D.J., Hall, D.M. and Coker, A.L. (2009) 'Primary prevention of intimate partner violence: Towards a developmental, social-ecological model', in C. Mitchell and D. Anglin (eds) *Intimate Partner Violence: A Health-based Perspective*, New York, Oxford University Press.

Wolfe, D.A., Crooks, C.V., Lee, V. et al. (2003) 'The effects of children's exposure to domestic violence: A meta-analysis and critique', *Clinical Child and Family Psychology*, **6**(3): 171–87.

Zolotor, A.J. and Runyan, D.K. (2006) 'Social capital, family violence, and neglect', *Pediatrics*, **117**(6): e1124–31.

9

Sons and daughters of foster carers: invisible, vulnerable or valued?

Gail Jackson and Peter Unwin

This chapter has been written from the perspectives of Gail, who worked as a foster carer in a household with her two young sons, between 2001 and 2008, and Peter who has worked as a social worker, manager and lecturer for over 30 years and has been a foster carer for a local authority since 2008. The chapter is about some of the different ways in which the sons and daughters of foster carers are constructed through the frameworks of research, policy and practice. The term 'sons and daughters' will be used throughout this chapter in reference to dependent children in a household that fosters children from the Looked After system. These could include birth, adopted, otherwise related or stepchildren as well as children under special guardianship.

The unique and complex position of these children and young people might most usefully be analysed from a social constructionist paradigm that variously represents them as invisible, vulnerable or valued:

- *Constructed as invisible*: the majority of research and practice rarely gives voice to sons and daughters of foster carers. Despite some recent initiatives within individual fostering agencies, there remains little focus on the effect of fostering on the childhoods of the sons and daughters of foster carers.
- *Constructed as vulnerable*: where research and policy does include these children, it is usually pertaining to child protection concerns, for example the degree to which the placement of certain foster children may pose a risk to the sons and daughters already in the household. The wider vulnerabilities of these children and the effects of fostering dynamics in the constructions of their childhoods have not been considered in any depth.

■ *Constructed as valued*: the sons and daughters of foster carers are viewed as a positive resource in fostering, for example they can give support to foster children and support to their parents. Again, there is little recognition of this in either policy or research.

The chapter concludes with recommendations for raising the profile of sons and daughters in policy, practice and research.

Fostering in the UK

Fostering is the public care of children conducted in private homes. It therefore constitutes a balance between professionally monitored, accountable care and family models of parenting that combine in attempting to provide the opportunity for fostered children and young people to experience family life, whether this is for short-term or more permanent living arrangements. The UK is actually one of the countries leading the way in using foster care as its main form of placement for Looked After children. There are approximately 74,000 children and young people being looked after by local authorities, over 53,000 (73%) of whom live with the 43,000 families who foster (Fostering Network, 2009a).

Contemporary foster care in the UK is influenced by the provisions of the UN Convention on the Rights of the Child (1989), the three main categories of articles of which are provision, protection and participation. The four main principles are based on the four articles of survival and development (Article 6), non-discrimination (Article 2), best interest (Article 3) and the right to be heard/participation (Article 12). Article 20 states:

> A child temporarily or permanently deprived of his or her family environment, or in whose own best interests cannot be allowed to remain in that environment, shall be entitled to special protection and assistance provided by the State. (United Nations, 1989)

These principles have been incorporated into legislation, such as the Children Act 1989 (in England and Wales) and the Children (Scotland) Act 1995, which make clear the responsibilities of the state for ensuring provision, protection and a voice for children placed in foster care. These issues are further developed in policy such as England's Fostering Services Regulations (DH, 2002), which comprise a series of minimum standards applying to both local authority and independent sector foster care provision. Also in England, *Every Child Matters* (DfES, 2003) states, as part of its commitment to supporting parents and carers, that there is a need to provide foster carers with the training and support they require to meet the increasingly complex needs of children and/or young people in their care. Current thinking with regard to the training of foster carers is that enhanced training opportunities and recognition for developing skills to care for children with particular difficulties should reflect the increasingly professional ways in which foster carers are now being asked to operate (Children's Workforce Development Council, 2007). Sons and daughters of foster carers generally remain invisible within most of these policies.

Although fostering is considered a socially valued role, foster children are rarely constructed in positive terms, creating implications for the way sons and daughters of foster carers are in turn constructed. The Fostering Network (2009b), a UK campaigning foster care charity, defines fostering, rather gently, as a way of offering children and young people a home while their own family is unable to look after them. However, given that government policy is that 'it is in the children's best interests to be brought up in their own families wherever possible' (DH, 2000, p. 1.13), it is generally as a last resort that children enter the 'Looked After' system. Thus foster carers look after some of the most vulnerable children in our society, yet fostered children are constructed, particularly by the media, as dangerous and a threat to others. Typically negative headlines include 'Name the devil boys: We must not let them hide' (MacFarlane, 2010) and 'Another horrific attack – so just how do we deal with damaged children' (McVeigh, 2009). Such media representations produce distorted concerns that people (including the sons and daughters of foster carers) who come into contact with foster children are necessarily vulnerable or at risk from their behaviour. There is, indeed, very little literature that promotes foster children and their possible contributions to families and the wider society. Holland (2009) is one of the few writers who reminds us that children and young people who are looked after can be both carers as well as care receivers and as such are part of the interdependency of human relationships.

What is known about the sons and daughters of foster carers?

Over half of all fostering families in England and Scotland have their own sons and daughters living in the same household (Triseliotis et al., 2000; Sinclair et al., 2004), yet there has been a lack of research attention focused on the needs of these children. This gap in knowledge is particularly significant for fostering, as research indicates that placement success, measured by placement stability and the absence of breakdown, is influenced by the existence of sons and daughters in the family and the age of these children relative to the fostered child (Wilson et al., 2000, 2003). Accessing the private worlds of foster families is a logistical and ethical challenge for researchers, much established knowledge about the construction of the childhoods of Looked After children being disproportionately based on residential settings (for example Green, 2005; Kendrick, 2008; Ofsted,

2010), such settings being easier to access although they look after far smaller numbers of children.

Partly due to such challenges of access, there have been only a few large-scale studies of foster carers in the UK over the past 20 years (for example Bebbington and Miles, 1990; Triseliotis et al., 2000; Sinclair et al., 2004). These studies, variously carried out with large sample groups across England and Scotland, examined a range of logistical and qualitative issues in foster care, but did not give serious consideration to the views of sons and daughters of foster families who remain invisible in the majority of this research. Other research studies (for example Kaplan, 1988; Part, 1993; Pugh, 1996; Höjer, 2007) have provided some insight into the ways that the sons and daughters of foster carers might construct their childhoods, although the majority of views represented across this research area come from the perspective of foster carers rather than their sons and daughters. It should be noted that Höjer's (2007) study was conducted in Sweden where, like the UK, fostering is the principal form of looking after children away from their families. Kaplan's (1988) study was based on research in the US where, although the providers of foster care are all independent of the state, the experiences within families who foster closely parallel those of the UK (Sargent, 2003). The UK research base is located firmly within the state sector of foster care, there being a limited number of studies within the growing independent sector of foster care (for example Sellick and Connolly, 2002; Spears and Cross, 2003; Sellick and Howell, 2004). Interestingly, the limited amount of available research into this sector is positive in its overall evaluation of services, and the one study (Spears and Cross, 2003) that focuses on sons and daughters in the independent sector largely presents a valued construction of their role. Spears and Cross (2003) interviewed 20 sons and daughters from within their own independent sector agency about their perceptions of the effects of fostering and found that, although sons and daughters acknowledged considerable stress, in many cases they appeared to have valued, and largely benefited from, the fostering experience.

Pugh (1996) also presented some valued constructions of the childhoods of the sons and daughters of foster carers: being a positive role model to the fostered child; acting as a go-between for the child and the carers; and giving support to their parents (both practically and emotionally). Part (1993) recognised that the sons and daughters of foster carers were a separate and important part of the fostering dynamic and, as noted by Pollock (2007), there is an encouraging, ongoing debate within parts of the British fostering community about the impact of fostering on the sons and daughters of foster carers. The weight of this debate (for example Fostering Network, 2008a) has tended to highlight the vulnerabilities of sons and daughters due to their exposure to the range of traumas and background experiences that characterise the histories of most foster children. This is not to argue that foster children are themselves 'bad' children but that the reality of most foster children's situations will be that their previous traumas and unsettled behaviours are likely to manifest themselves within the foster home; indeed, a good foster home would be one in which foster children are facilitated to express themselves. The challenge for foster carers is how to cope with such realities in ways that are constructive for the foster child but also not damaging to their own sons and daughters. Spears and Cross (2003) and Watson and Jones (2002) drew attention to the fact that placing a foster child in a family that already has their own sons and daughters could expose those children to an additional range of vulnerabilities. Watson and Jones (2002) carried out a questionnaire survey that involved over 100 sons and daughters of foster carers and found that, while there were certainly positives reported, some child protection concerns were highlighted. These concerns were particularly around keeping the sons and daughters of foster carers safe from issues such as being physically abused by fostered children in their home:

> These children suffer discrimination, in that they lose something of their parent/s' attention, daily support and care, feel that their voice is lost in the vast majority of cases, experience invasion of their personal space and suffer damage and loss of their personal possessions. Had similar treatment been suffered/experienced by a child/ young person looked after by the local authority, it could be subject to a planning meeting, review or a child protection conference. (Watson and Jones, 2002, p. 54)

Difficulties such as those detailed above have been found to be played down by foster carers, both Höjer (2004) and Kaplan (1988) having reported that foster carers perceived fostering differently to their sons and daughters. Höjer (2004) stated that foster carers rarely pointed out the consequences for their own children when describing a serious incident, whereas Kaplan (1988) asserted that foster carers often minimised their sons' and daughters' experiences and views. Perhaps these findings should not be viewed as surprising, given that placements are constantly monitored by social workers and continued engagement as a foster carer/continuation of a placement could be threatened if foster carers reported that their sons and daughters were experiencing problems.

It is instructive to reflect that, while there is a myriad of laws and policies that serve to protect all children in the UK and fostered children in particular, there is little that directly relates to enhancing the welfare and securing the protection of the sons and daughters of foster carers.

In summary, the actual views of sons and daughters themselves are largely unknown and little is known about how they construct themselves or how they are constructed by the foster children with whom they live. The changes that fostering brings to the sons and daughters within their families are, however, very real and visible and will be discussed below.

What changes does a fostered child bring to a family?

Fostering is a role that encroaches into every aspect of family life, and children who are fostered will share space, time and the possessions of the fostering family (Watson and Jones, 2002). Sinclair et al. (2004) found that only 10% of foster carers thought that fostering had had a negative effect on their family, although 41% said it was mixed, depending on the particular child they were thinking of when considering the question. Triseliotis et al. (2000), in their Scottish study, produced evidence that foster carers rated their own children highly in regards to their satisfaction levels regarding sharing. Overall, 63% of sons and daughters were viewed by their parents in this study as never, or hardly ever, having objected to sharing their bedroom, belongings, pets and parents. However, sharing facilities, possessions and family time was reported by children (rather than their parents) in the Watson and Jones (2002) study as some of the hardest aspects of fostering for sons and daughters. Ames (1997) had previously reported that many sons and daughters lose aspects of privacy as well as having to share other resources, including items they previously considered as their own. Martin (1993) found that the sons and daughters of foster carers were being expected to have the emotional intelligence to tolerate and understand the indiscretions of a foster child, such as when, for example, they damaged or destroyed property.

Höjer's (2007, p. 78) study included a focus group with sons and daughters that reported what were described as 'abnormal' levels of conflict between foster siblings and the sons and daughters of foster families. Such behaviours included hitting, pulling hair out, destroying prized possessions and name calling, behaviours that Höjer analysed as largely resultant from the fostered children's previous experiences. However, Hojer did express the reservation that the predominantly negative examples given by the focus groups in her study were perhaps biased by group dynamics, which led to an emphasis on talking about the more troubling aspects, rather than the more positive experiences, of having a foster sibling.

Triseliotis et al. (2000, p. 109) stated that there was scope for 'company, closeness and friendships as well as for rivalry and rejection' within foster sibling dynamics, an ambivalence found in other research. Attention given to the foster child (for example by the foster carers and social workers) was seen in Part's (1993) study as the second most difficult aspect of fostering for sons and daughters after having to deal with difficult behaviour. This study also commented that the sons and daughters seemed invisible at times besides their fostered peers. Adjusting to sharing their parents' time is not easy for sons and daughters or for the foster carers themselves. Höjer's (2004, p. 44) study found that 24% of foster carers felt that they 'often or quite often neglected their children' due to their fostering commitments and that this produced feelings of guilt and ambivalence.

On a more positive note, nearly half of all the children studied by Höjer (2007, p. 76) agreed with the statement 'My foster sibling feels just like a "real" sibling' and many felt that sharing their lives with a fostered child had a positive effect on their family lives. Triseliotis et al. (2000) also found that some carers claimed fostering built character in their children and Höjer (2004) found foster carers reported that fostering gave their sons and daughters more empathy. Triseliotis et al. (2000) reported that the behavioural and emotional problems presented by some fostered children that disturbed their sons and daughters the most were verbal and physical attacks, moodiness, destructiveness, stealing and lying. However, in the research carried out by Sinclair et al. (2004), some foster carers espoused a belief that witnessing and experiencing such behaviours had taught their own children important lessons in how not to behave and how to exercise tolerance:

> I sometimes wonder if my natural born children would be different if they hadn't seen and experienced some of the negative stuff ... but on the whole I think it's given them a sense of caring for others and a greater understanding. (foster carer) (Sinclair et al., 2004, p. 55)

The research of Pugh (1996) and Höjer (2004) recognised the vulnerability of the sons and daughters of foster carers in respect of exposure to areas of life from which most parents would ideally shield their children. These areas might include substance abuse, violent behaviours and extremes of emotional pain and loss. Kaplan's (1988) small-scale study into the psychological impact on sons and daughters in the US found many of the (mainly younger) sons and daughters believed that the children placed in their families had been moved from their birth families because they had been 'bad' and that the same might happen to them if they misbehaved. Using a Freudian hypothesis regarding loss, Kaplan (1988) found that the sons and daughters she studied exhibited signs of separation anxiety and were more likely to suffer from problems of attachment and loss. Pugh (1996) corroborated this view, particularly if a foster family experienced many short-term placements. Kaplan (1988) also found that the sons and daughters in her sample reported feeling guilty about their negative feelings towards some of the children their parents fostered. Mothers in this study tended to minimise the feelings and concerns that their own children had about fostering.

The above section can be seen to reflect the contradictions, ambivalence and tensions noted by Goldson (2001), as characterising adult constructions of childhood in general. It is of note that the constructions of the childhoods of sons and daughters of foster carers discussed so far are largely made from the perspectives of adults. Only recently there has been an interest in reflecting the direct views of sons and daughters of foster carers themselves (for example Fostering Network, 2008a, 2010).

What roles do sons and daughters play in the family that fosters and how might they be supported by parenting models and policy?

Many sons and daughters of foster carers take part in fostering in a direct way, as active participants rather than as passive observers (Höjer, 2004). Ames (1997) saw such active participation as ranging from watching a child while the carer is not in the room through to assisting in the primary care of younger children or children with disabilities. Such participation comprised what Watson and Jones (2002, p. 54) termed 'physical and intimate contact', such sensitive roles being potentially valued but also bringing with them exposure to vulnerability, for example the risk of allegations arising where a son or daughter is involved in elements of personal care. Little research has specifically examined this subject to date, despite the findings of a large-scale postal survey carried out by Swain (2006), on behalf of the Fostering Network, which found that the sons and daughters of foster carers received 12% of the total of allegations against fostering families. Although this survey did not differentiate between the type of allegations made against foster carers or their sons and daughters, by far the biggest category of allegations reported overall was that of physical abuse. The Fostering Network (2007) stated that most allegations are unfounded; however, allegations are always treated seriously, and represent an anxious time for all concerned. Sinclair and Wilson (2003) and the Fostering Network (2008b) acknowledge that allegations made by foster children can adversely affect sons and daughters, in both direct and indirect ways, and also note that many families cease to foster after an allegation, regardless of the outcome.

The above considerations illustrate the complexity of negotiating and maintaining family boundaries within fostering families and it is illuminative to reflect on the effect that a foster family's parenting style is likely to have on both their sons and daughters and their fostered siblings. A small-scale Canadian study by Heidbuurt (1995) used a social ecological perspective that produced three models of family boundary approaches to the fostering task, each of which raised different constructions for the roles of sons and daughters:

1 The *open boundary* model was characterised by foster carers promoting a caring culture that fully accepted and integrated all foster children into their family. This approach, however, presented problems for some sons and daughters who were unable to make such an unconditional acceptance and adopted behaviours described as 'partial seclusion', whereby they separated themselves emotionally from both their parents and the foster children.

2 The *solid nucleus* model might alternatively be termed the 'guest house' model, wherein a foster child is welcomed into the household but not into the family dynamics, effectively constructing the foster child as a guest in the

house. The hypothesis is that certain families adopt this model in order to protect and value their own sons and daughters physically and psychologically. Furthermore, this model was seen as offering benefits to sons and daughters, in that their own emotional security within their own family does not become invisible (even though the fostered child becomes more so).

3 The *selective integration* model was seen as one that incorporated elements of the open boundary and solid nucleus models, in that certain foster children were welcomed into the core family dynamics, whereas others were not. The suggestion is that this model acknowledges some degree of agency on behalf of sons and daughters, although the extent to which this agency is 'allowed' by the foster carers remains unclear.

Triseliotis et al. (2000) also utilised systems theory in their analysis of foster care. Fostering was seen as necessitating a family to constantly change its power and relationship dynamics as new foster children brought with them new challenges. Kaplan (1988) also recognised similar changes in family dynamics within foster families. A successful foster family would seem to require boundaries that are permeable and able to adapt to the comings and goings of fostered children, their own sons and daughters and social work/other professional staff. Inability to find a balance within these complex sets of dynamic processes can leave families struggling to re-establish stability at critical times of readjustment and loss (Triseliotis et al., 2000).

Achieving an appropriate balance within the dynamics of foster families is crucial if foster placements are to be valued experiences for both fostered children and the sons and daughters of foster families. The final section in this chapter suggests ways in which changes in support, training, practice and policy could help to recognise the value and contribution of sons and daughters.

Towards a valued construction of the sons and daughters of foster carers

In reflecting upon the social construction of the sons and daughters of foster carers, parallels might be drawn with the social construction of young carers that existed a decade ago, a once invisible group now supported and valued in much practice, policy and research. For example, Dearden and Becker (2004), who conducted the third national survey of young carers in contact with dedicated support projects (the previous ones being in 1995 and 1997), stated that the improvements seen in the lives of young carers in recent times could be attributable to 'the work of young carers' projects and the increased awareness of young carers' issues' (p. 16). The encouragement of similar projects and awareness raising could hopefully lead to similar outcomes for the sons and daughters of foster carers.

The sons and daughters of foster carers are not considered to have the same training and support needs as their parents, as they do not bear the same responsibilities (Watson and Jones, 2002). However, routinely giving sons and daughters opportunities to take part in training would prepare them to take on the challenges that will come their way. One of the few resources available that supports such a view is *Forgotten Voices: Sons and Daughters* (Fostering Network, 2008a), a DVD resource in which the direct views of sons and daughters provide a summary of the topics debated in this chapter. It illustrates the complexity of negotiating and maintaining family boundaries within fostering families. Its core message is that despite the problematic nature of being part of a fostering household, there is commitment and enthusiasm to continue fostering, albeit with the expressed desire for improved levels of support. This support might take the form of support groups, having their own support worker, training on dealing with some of the traumas and behaviours that foster children often bring with them, and a desire for regular respite in order that time can be spent alone with their parents. At the time of writing, it has been reported that there are 59 sons and daughters groups in England (Fostering Network, 2010), the majority of these seeming to operate on an activities basis, although others are involved in offering training and producing newsletters and DVDs about the contributions that sons and daughters make to foster care. Such groups can increasingly operate in ways that are attractive to sons and daughters, for example online forums and email, in addition to the more traditional face-to-face meetings and awaydays. Further research into these groups is strongly recommended.

At present, best practice (for example Children's Workforce Development Council 2007; Chapman, 2009; Fostering Network, 2010) suggests that sons and daughters should be intrinsically involved in the whole process of fostering from initial assessments through to reviews, but in practice, it has been our experience that such involvement is largely tokenistic and not valued by foster families or foster agencies. Routine, meaningful inclusion of sons and daughters from the first point in assessment of a potential foster family through to involving them in subsequent training, both as participants and trainers, could directly benefit both sons and daughters and the children their families look after, as well as help to raise general awareness about their role. Specific training for foster carers on their parenting styles and the effects that these styles have on the fostered child and their own sons and daughters is seen as another way forward for helping to raise the profile of sons and daughters, lessen their vulnerabilities, and afford them more recognition for the role they play. Foster agencies have introduced a wide range of training and competency-based development in response to recent government initiatives (for example DH, 2002; Children's Workforce Development Council, 2007), but parenting styles and their consequences do not feature highly on any of these agendas.

Final thoughts

Tightening up policy and practice in these above areas would increase visibility and reduce the ways in which the sons and daughters of foster carers are constructed as vulnerable. These actions would go some way towards beginning to construct a child-centred view, rather than an adult-derived view, of what should be a valued role for sons and daughters in foster care. Such inclusive practices should help to ensure that the childhoods of these children are fully valued; both as carers and care receivers, and that the potential irony of them being made vulnerable as a consequence of being part of families that safeguard other vulnerable children and young people is avoided.

References

Ames, J. (1997) 'Fostering children and young people with learning disabilities: The perspectives of birth children and carers', *Adoption and Fostering*, **20**(4): 36–41.

Bebbington, A. and Miles, J. (1990) 'The supply of foster families for children in care', *British Journal of Social Work*, **20**(4): 283–307.

Chapman, R. (2009) *Undertaking a Fostering Assessment: A Guide to Collecting and Analysing Information for Form F Fostering*, London, BAAF.

Children's Workforce Development Council (2007) *Ordinary People Doing Extraordinary Things: Training, Support and Development Standards for Foster Carers*, London, CWDC.

Dearden, C. and Becker, S. (2004) *Young Carers in the UK: The 2004 Report*, London, Carers UK.

DfES (Department for Education and Skills) (2003) *Every Child Matters*, London, TSO.

DH (Department of Health) (2000) *Framework for the Assessment of Children in Need and their Families*, Norwich, TSO.

DH (Department of Health) (2002) *Fostering Services: National Minimum Standards, Fostering Services Regulations*, London, HMSO.

Fostering Network (2007) *Allegations Against Foster Carers: Information for Foster Carers*, London, Fostering Network.

Fostering Network (2008a) *Forgotten Voices: Sons and Daughters*, available online at <http://www.fostering.net/events/sons-daughters-week/forgotten-voices-sons-daughters> [Accessed 27 January 2009].

Fostering Network (2008b) *Responding to Allegations Against Foster Carers*, available online at <http://www.fostering.net/resources/policy-and-position-statements/responding-allegations-against-foster-carers> [Accessed 1 February 2010].

Fostering Network (2009a) *Could you Foster? What is Fostering?*, available online at <http://www.couldyoufoster.org.uk/what> [Accessed 21 November 2009].

Fostering Network (2009b) *Statistics on Looked After Children*, available online at <http://www.fostering.net/about-fostering/statistics-looked-after-children> [Accessed 21 November 2009].

Fostering Network (2010) *Leading Our Lives*, available online at <http://www.fostering.net/leading-our-lives> [Accessed 21 January 2010].

Goldson, B. (2001) 'The demonization of children: From the symbolic to the institutional', in P. Foley, J. Roche and S. Tucker (eds) *Children in Society; Contemporary Theory, Policy and Practice*, Basingstoke, Palgrave/Open University, pp. 34–42.

Green, L (2005) 'Theorizing sexuality, sexual abuse and residential children's homes: Adding gender to the equation', *British Journal of Social Work*, **35**(4): 453–81.

Heidbuurt, J. (1995) All in the family home: The biological children of parents who foster, unpublished masters thesis, Faculty of Social Work, Wilfred Laurier University, Waterloo, Ontario, Canada, in R. Twigg and T. Swan (2003) 'What about the kids? Looking at the effects of fostering on foster parents' children', research abstract, Foster Family-based Treatment Association's 17th Annual Conference on Treatment Foster Care, available online at <http://www.ffta.org/research_outcomes/abstracts_twigg.pdf> [Accessed 12 December 2007].

Höjer, I. (2004) 'What happens in the foster family? A study of fostering relationships in Sweden', *Adoption and Fostering*, **28**(1): 38–48.

Höjer, I. (2007) 'Sons and daughters and the impact of fostering on their everyday life', *Child and Family Social Work*, **12**(1): 73–83.

Holland, S. (2009) 'Looked after children and the ethic of care', Advance Access published online on 10 August, *British Journal of Social Work*, doi:10.1093/bjsw/bcp086 [Accessed 23 October 2009].

Kaplan, C. (1988) 'The biological children of foster parents in the foster family', *Child and Adolescent Social Work*, **5**(4): 281–99.

Kendrick, A. (ed.) (2008) *Residential Child Care: Prospects and Challenges*, Research Highlights in Social Work Series, London, Jessica Kingsley.

MacFarlane, J. (2010) 'Name the devil boys: We must not let them hide', available online at <http://www.dailymail.co.uk/news/article-1245601/Name-Devil-Boys-We-let-hide.html> [Accessed 28 January 2010].

McVeigh, T. (2009) 'Another horrific attack: So just how do we deal with damaged children?', available online at <http://www.guardian.co.uk/society/2009/sep/06/edlington-attack-children-social-workers> [Accessed 12 November 2009].

Martin, G. (1993) 'Foster care: The protection and training of carers' children', *Child Abuse Review*, 2: 15–22, in A. Watson and D. Jones (2002) 'The impact of fostering on foster carers' own children', *Adoption and Fostering*, **26**(1): 49–55.

Ofsted (2010) *Keeping in Touch: A Report of Children's Experience*, Manchester, Ofsted.

Part, D. (1993) 'Fostering as seen by the carer's children', *Adoption and Fostering*, **17**(1): 26–31.

Pollock, L. (2007) 'Sharing is good for you', *Foster Care*, 128: 16.

Pugh, G. (1996) 'Seen but not heard? Addressing the needs of children who foster', *Adoption and Fostering*, **19**(1): 35–41.

Sargent, S. (2003) 'Adoption and looked after children: A comparison of legal initiatives in the UK and the USA', *Adoption and Fostering*, **27**(2): 44–52.

Scllick, C. and Connolly, J. (2002) 'Independent fostering agencies uncovered: The findings of a national study', *Child and Family Social Work*, **7**(1): 107–20.

Sellick, C. and Howell, D. (2004) 'A description and analysis of multi-sectoral fostering practice in the United Kingdom', *British Journal of Social Work*, **34**(4): 481–99.

Sinclair, I. and Wilson, K. (2003) 'Matches and mismatches: The contribution of carers and children to the success of foster placements', *British Journal of Social Work*, **33**(7): 871–84.

Sinclair, I., Wilson, K. and Gibbs, I. (2004) *Foster Carers: Why They Stay and Why They Leave*, London, Jessica Kingsley.

Spears, W. and Cross. M. (2003) 'How do "children who foster" perceive fostering?', *Adoption and Fostering*, **27**(4): 38–45.

Swain, V. (2006) *Allegations in Foster Care: A UK Study of Foster Carers' Experiences of Allegations*, London, Fostering Network.

Triseliotis, J., Borland, M. and Hill. M. (2000) *Delivering Foster Care*, London, BAAF.

United Nations (1989) *Convention on the Rights of the Child*, Geneva, United Nations.

Watson, A. and Jones, D. (2002) 'The impact of fostering on foster carers' own children', *Adoption and Fostering*, **26**(1): 49–55.

Wilson, K., Sinclair, I. and Gibbs, I. (2000) 'The trouble with foster care: The impact of stressful "events" on foster carers', *British Journal of Social Work*, **30**(2): 193–209.

Wilson, K., Sinclair, I., Petrie, S. and Gibbs, I. (2003) 'A kind of loving', *British Journal of Social Work*, **35**(8): 991–1003.

10

The social construction of home and school learning in multicultural communities

Sarah Crafter

Formal schooling takes up a major part of a child's everyday life and, second only to the home community, is a major socialising agent. This chapter will argue that formal schooling socially organises children in particular ways and that in culturally diverse settings, schools can operate to distance children from the varied values and identities of their home cultures to one which reflects the opinions of the wider society (Valsiner, 2005). My interest in this topic stems from my work as a developmental and cultural psychologist and focuses particularly on home and school mathematics learning in multicultural communities. Formal schooling is such a taken-for-granted activity within many societies that questions around what school means, outside those who focus on critical pedagogy, are rarely posed. What is education and who decides what children should or should not learn? How do we decide what are the best or appropriate forms of knowledge? What happens when knowledge developed for formal schooling is sent into culturally diverse home settings?

This chapter will explore how meanings and identities are co-constructed in culturally diverse home and school settings. It will be argued that school as an institution promotes particular pathways of child development through the reconstruction of socio-cultural practice. In some instances, these particular pathways are at odds or conflict with the socio-cultural practices of home communities (Hedegaard, 2005). These conflicts have sometimes led certain families and communities to be conceptualised as deficient (Cole, 1998; González et al., 2005), which can be resisted when diverse forms of knowledge are recognised and communities are not 'normalised'. In this instance, normalisation refers to the standardisation of communities and the people within them, whereby it is assumed that they share the same values and practices of mainstream society.

Learning in culturally diverse settings will be theorised using the social ecological approach (Bronfenbrenner, 1979; Wright and Smith, 1998), alongside the communities of practice framework (Wenger, 1998). These two theoretical approaches offer two units of analysis for study:

1 They position the learner as part of the relationship between the individual, the community and society.
2 They provide the mechanism by which meanings and identities are (re) constructed in socio-cultural practice.

In the context of this chapter, socio-cultural practice refers to:

> actions that are repeated, shared with others in a social group, and invested with normative expectations and with meanings or significances that go beyond the immediate goals of the action. (Miller and Goodnow, 1995, p. 6)

These practices are socio-cultural because our actions, what we do, are bound up with our belonging to communities (like school), which come with normative expectations, values and identities. In contexts like the classroom, practices are bound up with our relationships with others but may become (re)constructed (changed or altered) through new relationships and experiences.

Home and school learning as socially and culturally constructed

Formal schooling relies on age-related milestones to determine whether children are 'ahead' or 'behind' in their learning. In order to establish what children should learn at particular times, normative expectations need to be set up so 'batches' of children can learn the same work within the same age period (Rogoff, 2003). As such, institutional systems like school reflect a dominating and particular way of looking at children's learning where singular pathways to development, often age related, are considered 'appropriate' (Burman, 2008). Latterly, there has been a divergence of ideas about 'appropriate' development across the UK in terms of curriculum provision. However, dominant social and cultural constructions remain fairly stable with regards to assumptions about the role of education and the construction of the child. For this reason, formal schooling centres on the homogenisation of children, or the pursuit of sameness you could say, within its school practices (Valsiner, 2005). These conceptualisations influence what we think children should learn and what achievement outcomes are necessary by certain stages of development. Therefore, expectations for children's achievement are 'normed' against particular developmental milestones (Fleer, 2006). A good deal of this normalising of children within the school setting has come about as a consequence of standardised tests, which attempt to put swathes of children into set categories of competence.

Added to this, shifting patterns of migrancy and the geographical dispersal of the extended family mean that home cultures do not always reflect or share the normative expectations of formal school. In culturally diverse home settings, there may be differences in the practices, values, meanings and identities that are dominant in school. Despite this, there is still a strong political drive, across the UK, to have parents involved as a partner in their children's learning (Crozier, 2000), although the expectation is that knowledge constructed in school will go home but that knowledge from home has little place in the school (González et al., 2005). It could be argued that schools in contexts like England are largely representative of white middle-class groups (Rogoff, 2003) and others have argued that school, as we know it now, was developed in the late eighteenth century as a reformation of the working classes and, in turn, their families (Burman, 2008). As such, the imposing of these school norms, values and practices on the home has been viewed as a form of 'colonization' (Edwards and Warin, 1999, p. 337), meaning that emphasis is placed on changing or 'teaching' parents home practices rather than encouraging a shared collaboration. This approach leaves little space for more culturally diverse and marginalised family practices to be explored in schools. Other aspects of 'difference' can also be problematised in a similar way, such as gender (MacKinnon et al., 1998), disability and special educational needs (Frederickson and Cline, 2009) and race (Wright and Smith, 1998).

Across the UK, governments maintain that home/school partnerships, and parental involvement in school learning in particular, are a powerful force in raising achievement standards (for example Scottish Executive, 2006; CCEA in Northern Ireland, 2006; DCSF, 2008; Estyn, 2009). To be allies with the school institution, however, parents must reproduce the values, practices and discourses of the school. This raises questions around which parents most advantageously gain from having a home community aligned so closely with school. Reay and Lucey (2000, cited in Street et al., 2008) argued that the middle classes have aligned their discourses with the school to create an advantage. In other words, the middle classes quickly learn to utilise the language and practices that come from the school.

In a review of minority parental involvement in formal schooling, Kim (2009) found considerable evidence that schools viewed minority parents' involvement in learning to be limited. This perspective can sometimes lead to a model of parents as deficient or unwilling to cooperate with their children's home learning (Edwards and Warin, 1999). However, the propensity for parents in marginalised positions to be seen as deficient has been steadfastly resisted by those who take a more critical approach when focusing on culturally diverse home/school settings (Wright and Smith, 1998; Cole, 1998). A study by Gallimore and Goldenberg (2001) with Latino parents in the US found that parents who were not considered to be 'involved' by the school were deeply interested in their child's success but did not understand that the school expected them to contribute to formal subject teaching. Instead, these parents felt that their role as 'teacher' was the transmission of moral and behavioural knowledge.

Recognising that home communities are rich with learning practices would also strengthen connections between home and school. There are a number of examples from practitioner-based research where knowledge from home communities has been brought into the school. González et al. (2005) avoid seeing home communities as deficient by drawing on 'funds of knowledge' from the household which can contribute to children's learning. These authors work with Hispanic (mainly Mexican) families in the US, although similar studies within the 'funds of knowledge' framework have been taken up in the UK. For example, funds of knowledge work in Cardiff and Bristol is helping to shed new light on home mathematics learning in culturally diverse communities (Andrews and Yee, 2006; Hughes and Pollard, 2006). There is flexibility within the curriculum to explore diverse home practices within the classroom but the culturally diverse complexities of home need to be foreground in political and educational policy rhetoric. Individual schools and their staff need time and politically driven support to draw on these kinds of funds of knowledge.

The narrow focus of curriculum subjects like literacy and numeracy can have a damaging effect in culturally diverse learning settings. Street (2003) wrote about a model of literacy that views literacy learning as a socially and culturally sensitive practice. For example, Hughes and Greenhough (1998) conducted a study in which they analysed the level of conversing on behalf of teachers and parents while reading with children. While the prevailing view from educational policy was that reading at home raised attainment (Dearing, 1994), there was less consensus among academics researching in the area. This led to a focus on the behaviour of parents during home reading, with the suggestion that when parents entered into a discussion about the story, the reading activity was more stimulating and enjoyable for the child. Schools also promote the act of conversing as a way to improve reading standards. However, Hughes and Greenhough (1998) found class gaps in the level of conversing among parents, with high-conversing parents more likely to have higher levels of formal education. Low-conversing parents were more likely to construct reading as an activity that is instrumental or a means to an end, rather than an enjoyable activity in and of itself.

Numeracy, perhaps even more than literacy, suffers from a prevailing view that mathematics is not a socially and culturally constructed practice. However, when using socio-cultural theorising of mathematical activity, links can be made between both social and cultural contexts with cognition (Abreu et al., 2002) and thus mathematical learning is not a neutral or culture-free subject (Abreu and Cline, 2003; Swanson, 2005). Hale and Abreu (in press) report on one example from a Portuguese student who had immigrated to the UK:

> Liliana: Maths was one of my biggest problems because I was a really good student in Maths in Portugal. I was an 'A' [standard] student and when I came over here because they did everything so different, I couldn't understand. I felt completely lost and that was the worst thing because I thought, oh at least I can do good in Maths because it's just numbers, but no.

Viewing parents as 'deficient' can be avoided by examining how knowledge is constructed within communities where the schools are situated. For example, the Scottish Executive (2006) recognised that parents can also make positive contributions to the teaching and learning within the classroom. They recommend that schools encourage active participation in schools through various avenues like parent helpers, parent teacher associations, parent governors and so on, although the emphasis still lies in the parents being active in the school rather than the school seeking resources from the home. The social construction of home and school practices should not be viewed in isolation but as part of wider community, political, policy and societal discourses. The next section will use the social ecological approach alongside communities of practice to theorise how educational practice can be inclusive of practices and meanings of culturally diverse homes and schools.

Theorising home and school learning in culturally diverse settings

The social ecological approach suggests that the individual child should never been viewed in isolation, but as part of the relationship between the individual, the community and society (Wright and Smith, 1998). The social ecological approach proposes looking at the individual child as embedded in multiple contexts. Within the home, educational practices can vary and the experiences we have and how these shape us is culturally, historically and contextually embedded (Vygotksy, 1978). The work of Bronfenbrenner (1979) is perhaps the most well-known ecological approach and is particularly useful for focusing on educational contexts. The microsystem and macrosystem are the most widely used concepts; the former relating to face-to-face contexts (for example home and school) and the latter to overarching forces or systems (for example political forces or institutional systems). Bronfenbrenner (1979) also wrote of the mesosystem, which refers to the relationship between microsystems (for example how relationships within the home might influence the child at school), and the exosystem, which are settings the child is not directly part of but may be influenced by (for example parents' difficulties at work affecting home life).

Learning within multiple contexts does not just take place at the cognitive level in the form of skills and strategies (for example learning long division) but also at the level of meanings, practices and identities (for example learning long division at home may be different from school because of the parents cultural upbringing). Wenger's (1998) communities of practice framework becomes useful for understanding learning as socially constructed and part of everyday lived experience. The communities of practice framework proposes four key components – community, practice, meaning and identity (Wenger, 1998, p. 5):

- *Practice:* practice suggests the act of 'doing' or the engagement in activity – it could include what is talked about, the roles taken, the documents created and so on. It is important that practice is seen as being part of a historical and social context.
- *Community:* community refers to our 'social configurations' (p. 5) and connotes a sense of learning as belonging. Communities and practice should not be viewed separately but as part of one unit. They could be home, school, work, the church, our hobbies – as such, we can belong to any number of different communities of practice.
- *Meaning:* through communities of practice, meaning is constructed as an experience of everyday life. Wenger uses the notion of meaning in a very general way; when we talk to friends, read a book, discuss a new work contract, or settle an argument, we are always in the process of negotiating meaning.
- *Identity:* how these meanings are negotiated and experienced will influence how we define who we are, in other words, construct our identity. However, for Wenger (1998, p. 145): 'The concept of identity serves as a pivot between the social and the individual, so that each can be talked about in terms of the other.'

The following interview extract will help to provide an example of the way communities of practice can be used to theorise about children's learning experiences in culturally diverse settings. The extract is from a study looking at representations of home mathematics learning. The interviewee is Monifa (a pseudonym), a high-achieving daughter (aged 10 years old) of a Black African (Nigerian) family. She belonged to a multicultural school in a fairly large industrial town in southeast England. Monifa initially began by talking about differences in mathematical practice between home and school, but as the narrative progressed, issues on cultural identity were raised (Crafter and Abreu, 2010, p. 14):

Sarah: Does your dad explain it [mathematics] in the same way your teacher does? Are there any differences?

Monifa: My dad explains it very differently actually. Like the teacher explains it so everybody can understand but because my dad knows me, cos we're father and daughter, he explains it to me so I can understand it properly, so it's better for my dad to do it.

Sarah: Are the differences in the way he explains it, in the words he uses, or in the strategies he uses, or both?

Monifa: Yeah, because I figured that out one day when Miss Durham and my dad, I don't know why, but I don't think Miss Durham is too keen on my dad anymore because once when I took my homework to my dad I told him that Miss Durham said this, and that this is how you do it, and then my dad said 'no, that is completely wrong' so when he told me it, then I understood more. But then when I took it to Miss Durham, Miss Durham said 'no, your daddy's wrong, that isn't how you do it. You can go and ask my husband in the high school.' And I wasn't too keen but I understand my dad's more so I went with my dad. But she's my schoolteacher in school, so.

Sarah: Which do you think is the proper way, the way your dad does it or the way the teacher does it?

Monifa: I don't know. Sometimes they just explain it differently but it's the same because, well I think it's the different ages. Because my dad would have done it differently and it's where we come from because my dad was taught in Nigeria, and he taught in Nigeria. And Miss Durham has been here so … they do it in different ways. But my dad teaches it so I can understand even though, sometimes I don't understand him because he's been taught in Nigeria.

Two communities, home and school, are the focus of this discussion between Monifa and I. Within these two contexts, there are many different learning practices but in this instance Monifa has been asked to focus on mathematics learning. Monifa is trying to make meaning of the interaction between her father and teacher, which she has inferred is 'tense'. She draws upon cultural identifications to make sense of the different mathematical strategies by talking about her father's upbringing in a different country from where she goes to school. We might surmise that her own identity alignment more closely fits with her home community through the use of the subjective personal pronoun 'we' in relation to her father.

Transitions between home and school are not the only ways in which communities of practice can be theorised. Migration to a new country is another instance where the transition between communities of practice in the home country to a new community of practice in another country requires the reconstruction of meanings and identities (Abreu and Hale, 2009). From the ecological viewpoint, migration places the individual in new community and societal contexts which must be negotiated. School becomes a key force in the new settlement of young people, and interactions with teachers and peers can be fundemental in constructing cultural identities. Abreu et al. (2004) undertook a study with Portuguese pupils in British schools. In these next quotes from their project, issues around ethnicity, culture and language intersect in the negotiation of meaning and identity:

Nadia: I like being different because I am not ashamed of being Portuguese. And, I like this because I feel lucky to be able to speak three or four languages, I like being this way but ... however, sometimes I also ... If I were more like them, they would not point us out as being different. And, we are different! (Abreu et al., 2004, p. 124)

Nela: At lunch and break time I used to stay quiet. They used to talk and I would stay quiet because I did not know any English.

Interviewer: And did they try to speak to you?

Nela: They did try a lot. In fact, it was with them that I learned nearly all the English. Because they pushed me. The teachers also. But basically the teachers did not play a very important part in my learning to speak the English language. Thus, it was more with other students. (Abreu and Hale, 2009, p. 100)

The authors talk about a process whereby for some of these students, a lack of mastery in the English language led to a self-imposed withdrawing from the school community, which in the case of Nela was recovered through the support of friends. With Nadia's quote, there is a sense that her Portuguese identity was strongly maintained, while acknowledging that this identity set her as different from the mainstream English peer group.

The social ecological and communities of practice approaches to learning not only seek to situate the connectedness of the individual, community and society, but also to view these within a historical frame (Bronfenbrenner, 1979; Wenger, 1998). Organised schooling in industrialised countries like the UK is a practice that has developed over the past 250 years (Rogoff, 2003). Similarly, the stratification of children by age has led to an age-related curriculum being developed. Practitioner-based politics and policy are also subject to historical change, which can sometimes make it difficult for parents to understand what their children are learning in school. The introduction of a new national curriculum in 1988 meant that many parents' past educational histories were quite different from those of their children, particularly for parents who were not educated in the UK (O'Toole and Abreu, 2005). Even parents who have been part of the English educational system face challenges in understanding major educational reform following the introduction of the national curriculum (McMullen and Abreu, 2009).

Using these theoretical frameworks has shown that the learner, as an individual, operates with reference to the family, the wider community and society more generally. When the individual is placed at the centre of learning communities (like home and school), then what the individual does (practice), what they understand (meanings) and who they are (identities) are all at a point of constant renegotiation and (re)construction. By focusing on socio-cultural practice, it is possible to avoid looking at only one aspect of potential diversity and view the child as situated within a number of, sometimes conflicting, identities in relation to school; for example the young person who truants from school to help translate for a parent who can't speak English may hold an identity that going to school and helping the family is equally important (see Crafter et al. 2009).

Final thoughts

The late 1990s and early turn of the twenty-first century saw a decisive shift in focus on behalf of the government across the UK to focus on learning in culturally diverse settings. There was, for example, a focus on minority ethnic pupils in particular sociogeographical locations like cities (Kendall et al., 2005) or mainly white settings (Cline et al., 2002). Others focused on the overrepresentation or underrepresentation of minority ethnic pupils with special educational needs (Lindsay et al., 2006). Other research focused on the broad experiences of minority ethnic pupils in schools (Insight 16, 2005). Much of this research recognised that learning has a great deal to do with cultural identity and that some facets of identity, such as language, are linked to feelings of academic competence and emotional wellbeing (DfES, 2004).

Other research work commissioned by the English government has tended to take a more homogenised view of home/school communities, particularly when focusing on parental involvement. Cultural forces, such as social economic status (SES), ethnicity, poverty, disability, sociogeographical location and so on, are not singular aspects of a whole person but may be experienced in complex ways. Instead, research has focused almost solely on attainment in relation to parental values and what constitutes 'good parenting in the home' (Desforges and Abouchaar, 2003, p. 4). This serves to move the focus within education to the individual and away from the community. What is not properly addressed nor fully questioned is what kinds of parental values are considered the best. Those most likely to share the same values as school are also most likely to be in white, middle-class, non-marginalised positions (Hedegaard, 2005).

It is important to take notice of practitioner-based issues and approaches to working within a school situated in culturally diverse communities. Carpentier and Lall (2005) provide some positive solutions for studying parental involvement without neglecting the many rich and divergent facets that home communities have to offer the learning situation. For example, schools, those who work in them and policy makers should avoid homogenising parents under an assumption that a 'one size fits all' approach is feasible. Policies that govern the focus on parental involvement should have enough flexibility in them to take into account ranging community contexts so that the concept of the 'family norm' can be widened (Edwards and Alldred, 2000). This would be greatly improved if practitioners were given greater support during training regarding working in culturally diverse settings. Schools that have staff from the local community who can speak the first language of the parents may be an asset to both the school and home communities. Schools can recognise the multiple languages represented by their pupils and try to incorporate these into the curriculum. Carpentier and Lall (2005) proposed having an open-door policy supported through inclusive practice between parents and teachers. Examples can include inviting parents into school to volunteer in helping raise funds, join in school trips or listen to children read.

The social ecological approach and communities of practice framework have provided the means by which culturally diverse community settings are not viewed as homogenised or normed against dominant representations around children's learning. Diversity should be acknowledged beyond a focus on race and ethnicity to include issues such as gender, age, disability, sociogeographical locations and SES. But diversity should also be viewed as relating to social practices, meanings, histories and identities so that too much is not taken for granted.

References

Abreu, G. de and Cline, T. (2003) 'Schooled mathematics and cultural knowledge', *Pedagogy, Culture and Society*, **11**(1): 11–30.

Abreu, G. de and Hale, H. (2009) '"Self" and "other" imposed withdrawing in social interactions at school', in M. Cesar and K. Kumpulainen (eds) *Social Interactions in Multicultural Settings*, Rotterdam, Sense, pp. 91–116.

Abreu, G. de, Bishop, A. and Presmeg, N. (2002) *Transitions Between Contexts of Mathematical Practices*, Dordrecht, Kluwer.

Abreu, G. de, Silva, T. and Lambert, H. (2004) 'From crying to controlling: How Portuguese girls adapted to their secondary school in England', in G. de Abreu, T. Clines and H. Lambert (now Hale), *The Education of Portuguese Children in Britain: Insights from Research and Practice in England and Overseas*, London, Portuguese Education Department/Calouste Gulbenkian Foundation, pp. 103–27.

Andrews, J. and Yee, W.C. (2006) 'Children's "funds of knowledge" and their real life activities: Two minority ethnic children learning in out-of-school contexts in the UK', *Educational Review*, **58**(4): 435–49.

Bronfenbrenner, U. (1979) *The Ecology of Human Development: Experiements by Nature and Design*, Cambridge, MA, Havard University Press.

Burman, E. (2008) *Deconstructing Developmental Psychology*, Abingdon, Routledge.

Carpentier, V. and Lall, M. (2005) *Review of Successful Parental Involvement Practice for 'Hard to Reach' Parents*, University of London, Institute of Education.

Cline, T. Abreu, G. de, Fihosy, C. et al. (2002) *Minority Ethnic Pupils in Mainly White Schools*, Research Report No. 365, Norwich, HMSO.

Cole, M. (1998) 'Can cultural psychology help us think about diversity?', *Mind, Culture, and Activity*, **5**(4): 291–304.

CCEA (Council for the Curriculum, Examinations and Assessments) in Northern Ireland (2006) *The Power of Teachers in a Young Persons World: The Rationale for Teaching Personal Development in Post Primary Schools in Northern Ireland*, Northern Ireland, CCEA.

Crafter, S. and Abreu, G. de (2010) 'Constructing identities in multicultural learning contexts', *Mind, Culture, and Activity*, **17**(2): 1–17.

Crafter, S., O'Dell, L., Abreu, G. de and Cline, T. (2009) 'Young people's representations of "atypical" work in English society', *Children and Society*, 23: 176–88.

Crozier, G. (2000) *Parents and Schools: Partners or Protagonists?*, Stoke-on-Trent, Trentham Books.

DCSF (Department for Children, Schools and Families) (2008) *Independent Review of Mathematical Teaching in Early Years Settings and Primary Schools*, Williams Report, London, DCSF.

Dearing, R. (1994) *The National Curriculum and its Assessment: Final Report*, London, School Curriculum and Assessment Authority.

Desforges, C. and Abouchaar, A. (2003) *The Impact of Parental Involvement, Parental Support and Family Education on Pupil Achievement and Adjustments: A Literature Review*, Nottingham, HMSO.

DfES (Department for Education and Skills) (2004) *Aiming Higher: Understanding the Educational Needs of Minority Ethnic Pupils*, Nottingham, HMSO.

Edwards, A. and Warin, J. (1999) 'Parental involvement in raising the achievement of primary school pupils: Why bother?', *Oxford Review of Education*, **25**(3): 325–42.

Edwards, R. and Alldred, P. (2000) 'A typology of parental involvement in education centring on children and young people: Negotiating familiarisation, institutionalisation and individualisation', *British Journal of the Sociology of Education*, **21**(3): 435–55.

Estyn (2009) *Good Practice in Parental Involvement in Primary Schools*, Cardiff, Estyn.

Fleer, M. (2006) 'The cultural construction of child development: Creating institutional and cultural intersubjectivity', *International Journal of Early Years Education*, **14**(2): 127–40.

Frederickson, N. and Cline, T. (2009) *Special Educational Needs, Inclusion and Diversity*, Maidenhead, McGraw-Hill/Open University Press.

Gallimore, R. and Goldenberg, C. (2001) 'Analysing cultural models and settings to connect minority achievement and school improvement research', *Educational Psychologist*, **36**(1): 45–56.

González, N., Moll, L. and Amanti, C. (2005) *Funds of Knowledge: Theorizing Practices in Households, Communities, and Classrooms*, Mahwah, NJ, Lawrence Erlbaum.

Hale, H. and Abreu, G. de (in press) 'Drawing on the notion of symbolic resources in exploring the development of cultural identities in immigrant transitions', *Culture and Psychology*.

Hedegaard, M. (2005) 'Strategies for dealing with conflicts in value positions between home and school: Influences on ethnic minority students' development of motives and identity', *Culture and Psychology*, **11**(2): 187–205.

Hughes, M. and Greenhough, P. (1998) 'Parents' and teachers' interventions in children's reading', *British Educational Research Journal*, **24**(4): 383–98.

Hughes, M. and Pollard, A. (2006) 'Home-school knowledge exchange in context', *Educational Review*, **58**(4): 385–95.

Insight 16 (2005) *Minority Ethnic Pupils' Experiences of School in Scotland (MEPESS)*, Edinburgh, Scottish Executive.

Kendall, L., Rutt, S. and Schagen, I. (2005) *Minority Ethnic Pupils and Excellence in Cities: Final Report*, Nottingham, HMSO.

Kim, Y. (2009) 'Minority parental involvement and school barriers: Moving the focus away from deficiencies of parents', *Educational Research Review*, **4**(2): 80–102.

Lindsay, G., Pather, S. and Strand, S. (2006) *Special Educational Needs and Ethnicity: Issues of Over- and Under-Representation*, Nottingham, HMSO.

MacKinnon, A., Elgqvist-Saltzman, I. and Prentice, A. (1998) *Education into the 21st Century: Dangerous Terrain for Women?*, London, Falmer Press.

McMullen, R. and Abreu, G. de (2009) Parents' experiences as mediators of their children's learning: the impact of being a parent-teacher, Proceedings from the 6th Conference of the European Society for Research in Mathematics Education, (pp. 53–63), Lyon, France, available online at <http://cerme6.univ-lyon1.fr/information.php> [Accessed 1 April 2010].

Miller, P. and Goodnow, J. (1995) 'Cultural practices: Toward an integration of culture and development', in J. Goodnow, P. Miller and F. Kessel (eds) *Cultural Practices as Contexts for Development*, San Francisco, Jossey-Bass, pp. 5–15.

O'Toole (now Crafter), S. and Abreu, G. de (2005) 'Parents' past experiences as resources for mediation in the child's current mathematical learning', *European Journal of Psychology of Education*, **20**(1): 75–89.

Rogoff, B. (2003) *The Cultural Nature of Human Development*, Oxford, OUP.

Scottish Executive (2006) *Scottish Schools (Parental Involvement) Act 2006*, Edinburgh, Scottish Executive.

Street, B. (2003) 'What's "new" in new literacy studies? Critical approaches to literacy in theory and practice', *Current Issues in Comparative Education*, **5**(2): 77–91.

Street, B., Baker, D. and Tomlin, A. (2008) *Navigating Numeracies: Home/School Numeracy Practices*, Heidelberg, Springer.

Swanson, D.M. (2005) 'Schooled mathematics: Discourse and the politics of context', in A. Chronaki and I.M. Christiansen (eds) *Challenging Perspectives on Mathematics Classroom Communication*, Greenwich, CT, Information Age, pp. 261–94.

Valsiner, J. (2005) *Culture and Humand Development*, London, Sage.

Vygotksy, L. (1978) *Mind in Society: The Development of Higher Psychological Processes*, Cambridge MA, Harvard University Press.

Wenger, E. (1998) *Communities of Practice: Learning, Meaning, and Identity*, Cambridge, Cambridge University Press.

Wright, G. and Smith, E.P. (1998) 'Home, school, and community partnerships: Integrating issues of race, culture, and social class', *Clinical Child and Family Psychology Review*, **1**(3): 145–62.

11

Children's welfare and children's rights

Gerison Lansdown

Traditionally, children, as minors in law, have had neither full autonomy nor the right to make choices or decisions on their own behalf. Instead, responsibility for such decisions and for the welfare of children has been vested with those adults who care for them. It has always been presumed not only that adults are better placed than children to exercise responsibility for decision making, but also that in so doing they will act in children's best interests. This presumption has also been established as a legal obligation in the courts, which for many years have been required to give paramountcy to the welfare of the child in making decisions concerning their day-to-day lives (Children Act 1989, s.1). It does require that children's wishes and feelings are given consideration, but as a model of adult/child relationships, it does construct children as the passive recipients of adult protection and goodwill, lacking the competence to exercise responsibility for their own lives. However, over the past 20 years, we have witnessed a growing body of evidence concerning children's lives that challenges any capacity for complacency that children's welfare is being adequately protected by adults. This leads to a need to re-examine the assumptions underpinning adult responsibilities towards children:

1 that adults can be relied on to act in children's best interests
2 that children lack the competence to act as agents in their own lives
3 that adults have the monopoly of expertise in determining outcomes in children's lives.

The traditional perception of children as passive recipients of adult protection is now challenged by a recognition that children are subjects of rights, a concept that has gradually developed during the course of the twentieth century, culminating in the adoption by the UN General Assembly in 1989 of the UN Convention on the Rights of the Child. This is a comprehensive human rights treaty encompassing social, economic and cultural as well as civil and political rights. It has almost universal acceptance, having been ratified by 193 countries throughout the world. Only the US and Somalia have not yet made the full commitment under international law to comply with the principles and standards it embodies. Its framework of rights and principles provides the goals that societies must aspire to for every child, as well as a set of standards against which to measure progress, and to be held to account.

The limitations of a welfare approach

In this section I argue that a welfare approach, which relies predominantly on a presumption of adult capacity and goodwill in promoting children's welfare, runs the risk of failing to provide adequate accountability to children in the realisation of their rights.

Adults in positions of power over children can exploit and abuse that power, to the detriment of children's wellbeing. During the 1970s, there was a reawakening of awareness of the extent to which children are vulnerable to physical abuse within their own families. The extent and scale of violence that parents were capable of perpetrating on their own children emerged through the work of Henry Kempe in the US and was brought home forcefully in this country with the case of Maria Colwell, a young girl who was returned from care to live with her parents, who subsequently beat her to death (Howells, 1974). It was not, however, until the 1980s that the phenomenon of sexual abuse within families, as a day-to-day reality for many thousands of children, hit the public consciousness in this country with the Cleveland child sexual abuse scandal (DHSS, 1988). There was, initially, considerable resistance to the recognition that parents and other adult relatives could, and do, rape and assault their children. It challenges the very notion of family life that we wish to believe exists for all children – the view that children are safest within their families. It also challenges the legitimacy of the powerful cultural desire for protecting the privacy of family life, undermining the comfortable assumption that parents can always be relied on to promote the welfare of their children.

However, it was not only in families that children were vulnerable. It took until the 1990s to uncover the next scandal in the catalogue of failure on the part of responsible adults to protect and promote the welfare of children. In a series of public inquiries, it became apparent not only that children in public care in a number of local authorities had been subjected to systematic physical and sexual abuse by staff in children's homes, but also that these practices had been surrounded by a culture of collusion, neglect, indifference and silence on the part of the officers and elected members within those authorities. It is now acknowledged that this experience of abuse was not simply the consequence of a few paedophiles entering the public care system (DH/Welsh Office, 2000). Rather, it was an endemic problem, affecting children in authorities across the country and symptomatic of a fundamental failure to provide effective protective care towards vulnerable children. One of the most forceful lessons to emerge from these public inquiries was the extent to which the children involved were denied any opportunity to challenge what was happening to them (Levy and Kahan, 1991; Kirkwood, 1993; DH/Welsh Office, 2000). They were systematically disbelieved in favour of adult versions of events. They were denied access to any advocacy to help them articulate their concerns. Indeed, if and when they did complain, they risked further abuse. In other words, the adults involved could, with impunity, behave in ways entirely contrary to the children's welfare. These findings were influential and have begun to change attitudes. There is now a recognition that social workers should act on the presumption that children are telling the truth, backed up by statutory duties to consult with children.

Nevertheless, the pattern of abuse of children by adults has continued in the new millennium. The internet and new forms of electronic communication have resulted in an increased demand for child pornography, which has also become a significant contributor to child-sex tourism. The online environment has created new opportunities to abuse children, including the production, distribution and use of materials depicting child sexual abuse, online solicitation or 'grooming' for sexual activity with children, exposure to inappropriate materials, which can lead to psychological distress for young people themselves, and harassment and intimidation, including bullying (ECPAT International, 2009). In 2009 in the UK, this problem was exemplified in the case of a nursery nurse photographing young children while abusing them, and then distributing the images through the internet. The last decade has also borne witness to a growing pattern of trafficking of children into the UK for purposes of sexual exploitation, domestic servitude, servile marriages and other forms of criminal activity (CEOP, 2007).

We can, then, no longer disregard the fact that children can be and are both physically and sexually abused by the very adults who are responsible for their care, within families, in state institutions and beyond. And in confronting that reality, it becomes necessary to move beyond the assumption that simple reliance on adults to promote the wellbeing of children, because of their biological or professional relationship with the child, is an adequate approach to caring for children.

Actions detrimental to the wellbeing of children do not merely occur when adults deliberately abuse or neglect children. During the course of the twentieth century, adults with responsibility for children across the professional spectrum have been responsible for decisions, policies and actions that have been inappropriate for, if not actively harmful to, children, while believing that they were acting to promote their welfare. One does not have to look far for the evidence:

- We separated children from parents in the war evacuations.
- We excluded mothers from hospital when their children were sick, in pain and frightened.
- We failed to acknowledge that small babies experience pain and denied them analgesics.
- We undertook routine tonsillectomies that were unnecessary and often distressing to children.
- We promoted adoptions for the babies of unmarried mothers with no possibility of future contact.
- We placed children in care and cut them off from their birth families.
- We looked after them in large, unloving institutions that stigmatised them and denied them opportunities for emotional and psychological wellbeing.
- We removed disabled children from their families and placed them in long-term institutional care.

In all these examples, there is now public recognition that children were more harmed than helped by these practices. In other words, judgements as to the best interests of the child are often highly subjective, can and do change over time, and differ widely between professionals. While an important principle, it is clear that without reference to a holistic analysis of how a particular decision will impact on the realisation of the child's rights, or to the perspectives of children themselves, the concept of best interests is an inadequate benchmark on which to rely for decision making in children's lives.

However, the existence of public policy that serves to act against the best interests of children is not simply a matter of history. Current examples are all too frequent. We continue to place disabled children in special schools on grounds of the 'efficient use of resources' rather than the promotion of the child's best interests (Education Act 1996, s.316). The Sexual Offences Act 2003 makes any form of sexual activity, including sexual touching, an offence if one or both people are aged under 16 years, irrespective of whether there is close proximity in age and understanding, and the behaviour was mutually agreed. This legislation runs counter to the best interests of children: not only does it effectively criminalise huge numbers of young people for forms of commonly accepted sexual behaviour, but could also have the impact of deterring them from seeking sexual health advice and services. The British government has refused to remove legal provisions that criminalise child prostitutes, refusing to accept the arguments that they are victims of abuse rather than perpetrators of an offence. Children do not choose prostitution as a career option: many have run away from abusive homes, while others are brought into the UK for the sole purpose of prostitution. However, as long as there remains any risk of criminal prosecution, young prostitutes are likely to fear asking for the help they so desperately need, or to give the police the details of the pimps who have exploited and abused them.

Public policy often supports the rights and interests of parents ahead of those of children, even when the consequences of so doing are detrimental to the welfare of children. Corporal punishment of children, for example, remains legal in England despite the fact that it represents a clear breach of children's human rights. In 2004, the UK government supported legislation that continues to allow parents to justify common assault on their children as 'reasonable punishment'. It resisted campaigns by an alliance of over 400 organisations, including all the major children's organisations, and refused to allow its MPs a free vote on an alternative proposal, which would have resulted in compliance with international human rights standards by removing the defence completely to give children the same protection from assault as that enjoyed by adults.

The Committee on the Rights of the Child (CRC), the international body established to monitor compliance by governments with their obligations under the UN Convention on the Rights of the Child, has now expressed concern in all three of its examinations of the UK government over its determination to retain the defence of 'reasonable chastisement' (UN Committee on the Rights of the Child, 1995, 2002, 2008). It has expressed 'deep regret' at its persistence in prioritising the rights of parents to use such punishments over the rights of children to appropriate protection. The CRC has emphasised that proposals to limit rather than remove the defence do not comply with the provisions of the Convention on the Rights of the Child, constitute a violation of the dignity of the child and suggest that some forms of corporal punishment are acceptable, thereby undermining educational measures to promote positive and non-violent discipline. The Committee on Economic, Social and Cultural Rights (2002) has also made similar recommendations and the European Committee on Social Rights has stated that the UK is not in compliance with the European Social Charter because of its failure to prohibit corporal punishment.

There is considerable evidence that physical punishment of children is not an effective form of discipline, that it can and does cause harm, and that as a form of punishment it can and does escalate. A 2002 meta-analysis of available research demonstrated that, almost without exception, this approach to managing children's behaviour predicts negative outcomes (Gerschoff, 2002). While physical punishment can induce short-term compliance, this apparent immediate gain can come at a high, long-term cost. Physical punishment has been consistently associated with poorer child mental health, including depression, unhappiness and anxiety, and feelings of hopelessness (Strauss and Donnelly, 2001). And while some parents might believe that physical punishment teaches children right from wrong, most studies in this area have shown that the opposite is more likely the case. Children who are physically punished are actually less likely to internalise moral values, such as empathy, altruism and resistance to temptation, than those who are not physically punished (Durrant and Ensom, 2006). It can also be seen from the experience of the 23 countries that have banned it that it does not lead to a rise in prosecutions of parents (see, for example, www.endcorporalpunishment.org), it does change parental behaviour in favour of more positive forms of discipline, and it does not lead to worse behaved or ill-disciplined children.

Accordingly, I would conclude that the continued position of the UK government appears to be based on a desire to assuage adult public opinion rather than the rights and welfare of children.

Children's interests are frequently disregarded in the public policy sphere in favour of those of more powerful interest groups. It is not necessarily the case that children's welfare is deliberately disregarded, but rather that children, and the impact of public policy on their lives, are often not visible in decision-making forums and, accordingly, never reach the top of the political agenda. Just consider, for example, the impact of public policy on children during the 1980s and 90s. In 1979, 1 in 10 children were living in poverty. By 1991, the proportion had increased to 1 in 3 (DSS, 1993). This alone is sufficient indictment of our neglect of children. Even more significantly, however, it is children who bore the disproportionate burden of the increase in poverty during that period: no other group in society experienced a growth in poverty on a comparable scale (DSS, 1993). The consequences of that poverty on children's life chances are profound, impacting on educational attainment, physical and mental health, emotional wellbeing, and employment opportunities (Bradshaw et al., 2007). At a collective level, then, our society failed to promote and protect the welfare of children over two decades.

Since 1998, there has been a political commitment to halve child poverty by 2010 and end it by 2020. However, despite some significant policies such as Sure Start, increased investment in education, and child tax allowances designed to support that objective, gross inequalities remain. Government data from 2006 reveals that 33% of children were still living in poverty (DWP, 2006). Current projections suggest that by 2010, under existing policies, about 1.1 million fewer children will be in poverty than in 1998 when the target was set. Despite this progress, it will achieve only two-thirds of the targeted 2010 reduction. This will make it more difficult to meet the more ambitious goal of eradicating child poverty by 2020. Without any new policies to help low-income families, such as redistributing wealth to poor families, providing better support for working parents, improving childcare, and promoting equal pay for women, child poverty could rise again to 3.1 million by 2020 (Hirsch, 2009). The failure to build a 'child-friendly' society in the UK, in which public policy is directed at promoting the wellbeing of children, was powerfully illustrated in the recent comparative analysis of child wellbeing in rich countries undertaken by UNICEF. The study reviewed data relating to six broad indicators of wellbeing: material wellbeing and poverty; health and safety; education; relationships with family and friends; behaviours and risks; and children's own views on their lives. The UK was placed bottom out of 21 countries in the overall rankings (UNICEF, 2007).

Despite a repeated recommendation from the CRC that the government should conduct regular child rights' impact assessments to evaluate whether the allocation of budget is proportionate to the realisation of policy developments and the implementation of legislation to implement its obligations to children under the CRC, no action has been taken (UN Committee on the Rights of the Child, 2009). Yet we know from the few analyses that have been undertaken that children are often marginalised in public expenditure. For example, in 1999, a review of expenditure in health authorities found that they spend 5% of their mental health budgets on children and adolescent mental health services, even though this age group represents 25% of the population (Audit Commission, 1999).

We have also grown increasingly intolerant of children in the public arena. Far from developing towns and cities that are designed with children in mind, that are child friendly, as befits a society with the welfare of children at its heart, we view children as undesirable unless accompanied by an adult. A new strategy for dispersing young people, known as the 'mosquito anti-social device', has been widely employed by commercial outlets across England. It works by emitting a high pitched noise only heard by under-25s. The government has introduced powers that allow police and local authorities to designate an area a 'dispersal zone' simply on the grounds that a member of the public has been alarmed, distressed or harassed by a group of two or more people, and the police also have new blanket powers to impose a curfew on children in designated areas and to take any under 16-year-olds home between the hours of 9 p.m. and 6 a.m., purely on grounds of age. In other words, a curfew can be imposed on children, the vast majority of whom have not committed any offence. These policies take no account of the wellbeing and wishes of children.

Overall, public spaces are seen to be 'owned' by adults, with young people's presence in those spaces representing an unwanted intrusion. Yet these are the adults on whom children rely to promote their best interests. These are the adults who are responsible for protecting children's welfare. Public policy has adopted a 'deficit' model towards children and young people, which is damaging to their wellbeing and in breach of their human rights. It identifies specific behaviours of a minority as a problem and targets punitive measures to address them, rather than investing in a more holistic approach, which would focus on the strengths and assets of young people and build strategies in partnership with them to produce more positive outcomes. These negative approaches are widely reinforced in the media, which all too frequently represents children and young people only as thugs, 'hoodies', drunks or slappers.

The welfare model of childcare constructs a view of protection as a process determined and provided by adults for children, largely without reference to children themselves. However, as illustrated above, it is a highly flawed model. One of the weaknesses in a welfare approach is the failure to involve children in decisions that affect their own lives: their lack of direct engagement can be argued to have contributed to many of the mistakes and poor judgements exercised by adults when acting on children's behalf. There is now a growing body of evidence that children, both in respect of individual decisions that affect their lives and as a body in the broader public policy arena, have a considerable contribution to make to decision making (UNICEF, 2008; Percy-Smith and Thomas, 2009). Children, even when very young, can act, for example, as peer counsellors, mediators or mentors for other children. Local and health authorities have successfully involved children in the development of new hospitals, anti-poverty strategies and advice services. Children have been involved in conducting their own research, as advocates for policy change, and as partners in developing government policies and legislation (for example UNICEF, 2008). Many children are organising their own local parliaments, school councils, youth councils, or are sitting on the boards of local and national organisations. In other words, far from being 'in waiting' until they acquire adult competencies, children can, when empowered to do so, act as a source of expertise, skill and information for adults and contribute towards realising and advocating for their own rights.

Moving beyond a welfare approach

Once it is acknowledged not only that adults are capable of abusing children, but also that children's welfare can be undermined by conflicting interests, neglect, indifference and even hostility on the part of adults, it becomes clear that it is not sufficient to rely exclusively on adults to define children's needs, and be responsible for meeting them, without any form of accountability, and without reference to their rights. Indeed, the welfare model has failed children. However, the Convention on the Rights of the Child does provide an alternative framework. It requires all legislation, policy and practice affecting children to adhere to a comprehensive framework of principles and standards, which are elaborated and monitored in the international sphere by the Committee on the Rights of the Child.

Central to the CRC is Article 3, which states that the best interests of the child must be a primary consideration in all actions concerning the child. The CRC has emphasised that this principle must be applied in the implementation of all other rights. It also emphasised that the application of this principle 'must prevail in all cases where there is a direct relation between the state and those subject to its jurisdiction', and that it applies to children both as individuals and as a constituency (OHCHR, 1997). Such an approach, however, does not take us back to a welfare model: a commitment to respecting the human rights of children requires more than the personal judgement of the best interests of the child by adults. The determination of children's best interests must be understood through the lens of the CRC as a whole. Not only does this necessitate that any assessment of children's welfare must be assessed with reference to the extent to which any proposed action, decision and policy of law protects or promotes children's rights, but it also requires that children are recognised as active participants when decisions affecting them are being made. Two key articles establish the principles that must guide decisions affecting children. Article 5 emphasises that although parents have rights and responsibilities to guide and direct children, this must be undertaken in accordance with the evolving capacities of the child: in other words, as the child acquires the necessary capacities, they are entitled to exercise those rights for themselves. Article 12 demands that children are provided with the opportunity to express their views on all matters of concern to them and to have those views taken seriously in accordance with age and maturity. This recognition of children's evolving capacities or emerging maturity can serve as an enabling principle through which to analyse legislation, policies, services and practice in terms of their impact on children's wellbeing. It also provides a useful framework through which to approach the obligations to realise the human rights of children (Lansdown, 2005).

Children's welfare can best be understood in terms of their overall optimal development. Governments have obligations under the convention to *fulfil* children's rights through the provision of environments in which they can achieve that potential. It includes, for example, articles which address the right to maximum development of the child, to an adequate standard of living for proper development, to provision of healthcare, to education directed to fulfilling children's potential, to play, and to the fullest possible development for disabled children.

While children carry within themselves the potential for their own development, this can only be realised through the creation by adults of the necessary environments in which children will thrive (Petren and Hart, 2000). The convention constructs development as a continuing process of interaction between the individual child with their inherent characteristics and the immediate and wider environment, leading to the evolving capacities and maturity of the child. It has been argued that children have four basic needs: for love and security, for new experiences, for praise and recognition, and for responsibility (Kellmer-Pringle, 1980). These needs must be met by creating environments for children that provide support for families, quality education, opportunities for play, and for active participation in decision making. However, action is needed beyond the provision of services, supports and opportunities to individual children. It is also necessary to remove the barriers to optimal development. This means creating child-friendly environments in towns, cities and rural communities where children are included, safe and involved. It also means addressing social inequities.

The recent study on the social determinants of health provides powerful testimony to the importance of tackling social injustice as the primary cause of poor life chances and wellbeing (WHO, 2008). It points to the fact that health inequities are caused primarily by the unequal distribution of power, income, goods and services, and the consequent unfairness in the immediate, visible circumstances of children's lives. However, none of these policies should be developed without the active engagement of children themselves. They will have a key role to play in identifying the nature of the challenges they face, the impact of existing or inadequate legislation, policies and services, and potential strategies for change. They need to be engaged as partners in the creation of environments designed to promote their welfare and ultimate optimum development.

The convention also includes provisions that assert the civil rights of children to exercise their own rights in accordance with their evolving capacities. In addition to the right to express views and have them taken seriously, it includes the right to freedom of expression, conscience and religion, association, the right to privacy and to information. It imposes obligations on governments to *respect* these rights that acknowledge the child as a social actor in actions and decisions that affect them. In other words, children must be afforded the opportunity to influence decisions and actions that will impact on their welfare. Given the prevailing culture in which children are not widely recognised as competent actors in their own lives, the challenge is how to support and enable children to take responsibility to exercise those rights for which they have the competence.

In reality, our knowledge, to date, as to children's capacities for informed and rational decision making in their own lives remains limited. There is evidence (Woodhead, 1999) to suggest the need for extreme caution in drawing conclusions on age-related competencies, arguing instead that a wide range of other factors influence how children function, including, for example, levels of support and information, cultural and social expectations, opportunities and experience, and individual personality and strengths. Furthermore, recent research into children's own perspectives and experiences indicates that adults do consistently underestimate children's capacities (Lansdown, 2005). Obviously, many children's physical immaturity, relative inexperience and lack of knowledge do render them vulnerable and necessitate specific protections. However, it seems clear that children are widely denied opportunities for decision making in accordance with their evolving capacities. Neither legal frameworks, nor policy and practice give sufficient consideration to the importance of recognising and respecting the real capacities of children. The lack of coherence in acknowledging children's evolving capacities can be seen, for example, in the conflicting constructions of competence in civil and criminal law. In England, the age of criminal responsibility is currently 10 years: in other words, children are deemed to be competent to both understand the full consequences of their actions and to take responsibility for them from that age. However, in civil law, adults retain responsibility for making decisions on behalf of children, for example in care proceedings or matters relating to where children live, until they are 16 years old. There is a requirement to take account of children's wishes and feeling, but they are not, nevertheless, deemed competent to take full responsibility themselves for those decisions.

Listening to children and taking them seriously is important, not only as a human right, but also because children have a body of experience and views that is relevant to the development of public policy, improving the quality of decision making and rendering it more accountable. Beyond this, it is an essential element in their protection. Children who experience respect for their views and are encouraged to take responsibility for those decisions they are competent to make will acquire the confidence to challenge any abuse of their rights. The right to be heard is also a vital means of ensuring accountability to children: only if children have access to the courts and to complaints and appeals procedures, coupled with access to independent advocacy, will they be empowered to claim their rights and challenge violations. In other words, respect for the right to be heard, and to exercise rights in accordance with evolving capacities, is integral to the obligation to promote children's best interests.

Throughout childhood, children's capacities are still evolving, and they have rights to protection on the part of both parents and the state from engagement in or exposure to activities likely to cause them harm. In other words, they are not afforded full autonomy. The convention contains a range of provisions that acknowledge the specific obligations on governments to *protect* children – the right to protection from all forms of violence, to sexual, economic and all other forms of exploitation, armed conflict, and discrimination. Perhaps most fundamentally, the obligation to give primary consideration to the best interests of the child reflects the view that childhood is a period of relative vulnerability, limiting children's capacity either to engage in certain activities or to take the necessary action to protect themselves from any consequent harm. This obligation to have regard to the best interests of children is also acknowledged in articles in the convention relating to non-separation from parents, support for parents to enable them to protect their children, and obligations to ensure alternative care or adoption of children when necessary.

Governments must introduce the appropriate legislation, polices and services to ensure the protection of children in accordance with their best interests. However, in so doing, they need to balance children's rights to adequate and appropriate protection with their right to take responsibility for the exercise of those decisions and actions they are competent to take for themselves. Protection itself is not synonymous with the best interests of the child. Indeed, overprotection can be as harmful as underprotection. Traditionally, it has been seen as a one-way process, with adults as agents and children as recipients. The reality is more complex: legislation, strategies, policies and programmes designed to protect children need to recognise and support children's capacities to contribute towards their own protection, and allow them to build on those strengths. Adults need to listen to children in order to gain their insights into the nature of the dangers they face and the type of protection they need. In practice, much of the vulnerability of children derives not from their lack of capacity, but rather from their lack of power and status with which to exercise their rights and challenge abuses.

Final thoughts

All societies want to do the best for their children. The UK is no exception. And realisation of their human rights through the holistic implementation of the Convention on the Rights of the Child is the most effective means of promoting their best interests and ensuring their optimum development and wellbeing. It is important to overcome the continuing resistance to the concept of rights in this country, particularly when applied to children. It is a resistance shared by many parents, politicians, policy makers and the media. It derives, at least in part, from a fear that children represent a threat to stability and order if they are not kept under control. Furthermore, it reflects the strong cultural tradition that children are 'owned' by their parents and that the state should play as minimal a role as possible in their care. Attempts by the state to act to protect children are thus viewed with suspicion and hostility.

However, promoting the rights of children is not about giving a licence to children to take complete control of their lives irrespective of their levels of competence. It is not about allowing children to ride roughshod over the rights of others, any more than adult rights permit such abuses. Rather, it is about moving away from the discredited assumption that adults alone can determine what happens in children's lives without regard for children's own views, experiences and aspirations. It means accepting that children, even very small children, are entitled to be listened to and taken seriously. It means acknowledging that, as children grow older, they can take greater responsibility for exercising their own rights. It involves recognising that the state has explicit obligations towards children, for which it should be held accountable. A commitment to respecting children's rights does not mean abandoning their welfare: it means promoting their welfare by adherence to the human rights standards defined by international law.

References

Audit Commission (1999) *Children in Need*, London, Audit Commission.
Bradshaw, J., Hoelscher, P. and Richardson, D. (2007) 'An index of child well-being in the European Union', *Social Indicators Research*, 80: 133–77.

CEOP (Child Exploitation and Online Protection Centre) (2007) *A Scoping Project on Child Trafficking in the UK*, London, CEOP.

DH (Department of Health)/Welsh Office (2000) *Lost in Care: The Report of the Tribunal of Inquiry into the Abuse of Children in Care in the Former County Council Areas of Gwynedd and Clwyd since 1974*, Waterhouse Report, London, TSO.

DHSS (Department of Health and Social Security) (1988) *Report of the Inquiry into Child Abuse in Cleveland*, London, HMSO.

DSS (Department of Social Security) (1993) *Households Below Average Income 1979–1990/1*, London, HMSO.

Durrant, J. and Ensom, R. (2006) 'Physical punishment and children's health', *Newsletter of Infant Mental Health Promotion (IMP)*, 45, Spring.

DWP (Department for Work and Pensions) (2006) *Households Below Average Income (HBAI) 1994/5–2005/6*, London, HMSO.

ECPAT International (2009) *Report of the World Congress III Against Sexual Exploitation of Children and Adolescents*, Bangkok, ECPAT International.

Gershoff, E.T. (2002) 'Corporal punishment by parents and associated child behaviors and experiences: A meta-analytic and theoretical review', *Psychological Bulletin*, **128**(4): 539–79.

Hirsch, D. (2009) *Ending Child Poverty in a Changing Economy*, York, Joseph Rowntree Foundation.

Howells, J.H. (1974) *Remember Maria*, London, John H. Butterworth.

Kellmer-Pringle, M. (1980) *The Needs of Children*, London, Hutchinson.

Kirkwood, A. (1993) *The Leicestershire Inquiry 1992*, Leicester, Leicestershire County Council.

Lansdown, G. (2005) *The Evolving Capacities of the Child*, Florence, UNICEF Innocenti Research Centre.

Levy, A. and Kahan, B. (1991) *The Pindown Experience and the Protection of Children: The Report of the Staffordshire Child Care Inquiry 1990*, Stafford, Staffordshire County Council.

OHCHR (Office of the High Commissioner of Human Rights) (1997) *The Convention on the Rights of the Child*, in M. Santos Pais, *Manual on Human Rights Reporting*, Geneva, UN.

Percy-Smith, B. and Thomas, N. (2009) *A Handbook of Children and Young People's Participation: Perspectives from Theory and Practice*, London, Routledge.

Petren, A. and Hart, R. (2000) 'The right to development', in A. Petren and J. Himes (eds) *Children's Rights: Turning Principles into Practice*, Stockholm, Radda Barnen/UNICEF, pp. 43–60.

Strauss, M.A. and Donnelly, D.A. (2001) *Beating the Devil out of Them: Corporal Punishment in American Families and its Effect on Children*, New Brunswick, Transaction.

UN Committee on Economic, Social and Cultural Rights (2002) *Concluding Observations*, UK, E/C.12/1/Add.79.

UN Committee on the Rights of the Child (1995) *Concluding Observations of the Committee on the Rights of the Child: United Kingdom of Great Britain and Northern Ireland*, 15/02/95, CRC/C/15/Add.34.

UN Committee on the Rights of the Child (2002) *Concluding Observations: United Kingdom of Great Britain and Northern Ireland*, 9/10/02, CRC/C/15/Add.188.

UN Committee on the Rights of the Child (2008) *Concluding Observations: United Kingdom of Great Britain and Northern Ireland*, 20/10/08, CRC/C/GBR/CO/4.

UN Committee on the Rights of the Child (2009) *UN Committee on the Rights of the Children, Concluding Observations*, UK CRC/C/GBR/CO/4, CRC/C/15/Add.188, CRC/C/15/Add.34.

UNICEF (2007) *Child Poverty in Perspective: An Overview of Child Wellbeing in Rich Countries*, Innocenti Report Card No.7, Florence, UNICEF Innocenti Research Centre.

UNICEF (2008) *Child and Youth Participation Resource Guide*, New York, UNICEF.

WHO/Commission on the Social Determinants of Health (2008) *Closing the Gap in a Generation: Health Equity through Action on the Social Determinants of Health*, London.

Woodhead, M. (1999) 'Reconstructing developmental psychology: Some first steps', *Children and Society*, 13: 3–19.

12

Between the rocks and hard places: young people negotiating fear and criminalisation

Peter Squires

'Beware of the kids'

As a critical criminologist I have been researching youth and criminalisation for many years and New Labour's 'anti-social behaviour' agenda was of particular interest, especially when this began to merge with growing concerns about youth violence, weapon use and gangs. During the summer of 2009, the 10-year anniversary of the Anti-Social Behaviour Order (ASBO) (introduced by Section 1 of the 1998 Crime and Disorder Act, available to the courts from 1999) was reached in England and Wales, prompting questions about how effective this controversial measure had been.

The decade had begun with rising concerns about 'youth nuisance' and social exclusion but ended with concerns about youth gangs, street violence, knives and guns (Squires, 2009; CCJS, 2009). A new youth justice system had been launched in 1998, whereas 2008 saw the implementation of *Tackling Gangs* and the Tackling Knives Action Programme (Home Office, 2008a, 2008b) associated with a seeming 'gangsterisation' of youth crime, the deployment of specialist police operations piloting area-based stop and search exercises for weapons (Operations Blunt 1 and 2), culminating in a new Home Office strategy for tackling violence (Home Office, 2008c). Such developments cast a shadow over any evaluation of the government's youth justice strategy. Arguably, we need to look at the issues in a rather broader time frame.

In this chapter I argue that a deeper understanding of these issues will not be found in some simple, rational, evidence-based policy evaluation but rather in a more searching cultural politics, in which fear and alarm, moral panic (Cohen, 1973) and political calculation have all played their parts (Goldson, 1999; Muncie, 1999; Pitts, 2003). This story begins significantly before 1998 and illustrates the changing tides of opinion surrounding youth crime and disorder. To illustrate this argument, it is helpful to refer to a case that coincided closely with the 10-year anniversary of the ASBO and which recalls an earlier cause célèbre of British youth justice.

Two boys aged 10 and 11 were in court in August 2009 following their horrific attack on two other boys of similar ages in woodlands near Doncaster. The victims had been subjected to a terrifying beating, in which they were battered, burned, stabbed and wrapped in barbed wire. The older victim was finally thrown to the floor while rocks were dropped onto his head. The tabloid media had a field day reporting the incident, dredging up a vocabulary that had first seen the light of day in the wake of the murder of James Bulger in 1992. The attackers were described by journalists as 'devil brothers', 'hell boys' and 'savage' and 'evil' (Taylor, 2009).

The changing politics of youth crime

The James Bulger case in 1992, in which two boys aged 10 and 11 abducted and subsequently murdered a 2-year-old boy, had been a critical turning point in the politics of late modern youth crime (Haydon and Scraton, 2000). The close identification of youth with anti-social behaviour management appeared to license an especially hostile set of attitudes and language to refer to young people. Perpetrators of anti-social behaviour (ASB) came to be described as 'yobs', 'scum' or 'neighbours from hell' (see Squires and Stephen, 2005). In November 2008, Barnardo's released survey findings suggesting that such attitudes were having a much wider impact across the youth justice system as a whole. Roughly half of a sample of over 2,000 adults felt that it was appropriate to use words like 'animal', 'feral' or 'vermin' to describe young people, and over a third believed that their residential streets were increasingly 'infested' with young people. Furthermore, the adults surveyed overestimated the amount of crime attributable to young people by a factor of four (Barnardo's, 2008). Evidence of this nature suggests that cultural attitudes, regularly sustained by immoderate reporting of youth crime incidents, continue to play a vital role in sustaining a punitive politics of youth justice strongly favouring supposed law and order 'solutions' for youth problems while neglecting a wider analysis of those problems.

Reflecting upon these persisting themes during the tenth anniversary of the ASBO encourages one to reflect briefly on just what a watershed the Bulger case really was and how it has set the pattern for the ensuing years, even moving beyond recent preoccupations with ASB. The rhetorics of 'evil' and 'irresponsible' youth implied that young people were part of an official culture of impunity and irresponsibility (Squires and Stephen, 2005, p. 26), where youth justice professionals supposedly 'conspired' to proffer a series of excuses, collectively rationalised as a policy of 'diversion', which failed to tackle the unacceptable behaviour. *No More Excuses* (Home Office, 1997), the White Paper published by New Labour shortly after its election in 1997, makes explicit the cultural shift being sought in British youth justice.

Unfortunately, however, the methods and procedures of ASB management (ASBOs, Acceptable Behaviour Contracts, Parenting Orders, Dispersal Orders, curfews, electronic tagging, naming and shaming, penalty notices for disorder) did not so much break a link between nuisance behaviour and crime as disperse discipline (Cohen, 1985) and the power to criminalise over yet wider groups of young people. ASB became the Pandora's box, which opened up an entirely new range of fears and concerns about youth, in the process facilitating a paradigm shift in the seriousness with which these behaviours were viewed. Discussing New Labour's prioritisation of ASB, Michael Tonry argued that the government had merely succeeded in making a small problem much worse (Tonry, 2004, p. 57).

Yet Tonry's point related not just to the *scale* of ASB problems, but also to their nature. Here the evidence of a cluster of social problems – chronic urban deprivation, social exclusion, high rates of ASB, victimisation and violence, the prevalence of illegal economies, collectively what Hope (2000) has referred to as 'communities of fate' – exposed the fallacy that lay behind the promise of 'breaking the link' between ASB and crime. ASB was generally worst where other social and criminal problems were also at their worst. Furthermore, the distribution of criminal victimisation had become more uneven over the two decades since the mid-1980s (Hope, 2001) and some communities had clearly not shared in the general reduction in recorded crime that the Home Office was keen to celebrate (Finney, 2004). Looked at in this light, ASB was not a separate, still less a 'pre-criminal', phenomenon – it was rather that aggressive and disorderly 'kids who show no respect [were] merely symbols of a world falling apart' (Lea and Young, 1984, p. 55).

Over there

By contrast with the UK, American research into youth violence and disorder has for some time been significantly dominated by the spectre of 'the gang'. Zimring (1998), for instance, has noted how the 'group context' is essential to the understanding of youth offending. Most youth offending is undertaken in group contexts and/or with co-offenders. Reflecting this, in the US, gang research is characterised by two principal traditions, on the one hand, a more convention-ally criminological perspective allied to enforcement priorities, which studies the gang with a view to understanding how gangs accelerate the offending behav-iour of their members (Reed and Decker, 2002). On the other hand, there is a more sociological tradition seeking to understand gangs and young people's reasons for forming them, as arising out of the difficult contexts and experiences encountered by young people living in dangerous and contested urban areas (Klein, 1995). This more 'ecological' approach to gang formation dates back to some of the earliest Chicago school sociology in the 1920s (Thrasher, 1927).

At the heart of Thrasher's account of gang development is the sense of an 'interstitial' social and geographical 'no-mans-land' (sometimes he referred to this directly as 'gangland'), where gangs form and where youth behaviour devel-ops according to distinctive logics of its own. Young people occupy interstitial spaces: vacant, public areas claimed by no one else. In life course terms, they also exist in limbo, no longer children, but not yet adults. As Thrasher (1927, p. 35) explained:

> Gangs represent the spontaneous efforts of boys to create a society for themselves where none adequate to their needs exists ... Gangs provide for the 'thrill' and 'zest' of participating in common interests.

While the dominant perspective on young people socialising in gangs has stressed their allegedly 'anti-social' character, another view of youth behaviour in gangs has seen it as ecologically produced, meeting a number fundamental social needs. A recent commentator has written of how:

> Gangs ... mint power for the otherwise powerless from their control of small urban spaces: street corners, slums, playgrounds, parks ... these informal spatial monopo-lies provide some measure of entrepreneurial opportunity as well as local prestige and warrior glamour ...some gangs are vampire-like parasites, others play Robin Hood or employer of last resort; most combine elements of both. (Davis, 2008, p. xi)

Even when concerns about young people forming gangs began to surface in the UK in the late 1990s (Pitts, 2007, 2008), amid a rising preoccupation with disrespectful, violent and anti-social youth behaviour, no similarly 'ecological' perspective surfaced this side of the Atlantic. On the contrary, most discussions were given over to the question about whether street gangs were really present at all on the streets of the UK's inner cities (Sharp et al., 2006; Alexander, 2008; Hallsworth and Young, 2008). What this discussion rather neglected was any deeper examination of the changing contexts of young people's lives, influencing both their behaviour *and* official reactions to them.

Over here

Following the 'gang-related', 'drive-by' shooting of two young girls in Birmingham on New Year's Eve 2003 and the murder of Rhys Jones in Liverpool during 2007, fresh concern came to centre upon the gang question. First, the use of guns and later, during the first part of 2008, a spate of vicious stabbings prominently reported in the media seemed to suggest a new level of street brutalism affecting some young people. Weapon carrying appeared to run contrary to a generally falling trend for violent crime. Victims and perpetrators were disproportionately Black or of mixed race and the problem was often highly localised. A Home Affairs Select Committee Report on *Young Black People and the Criminal Justice System* made explicit reference to the continuing negative influence of discrimination, inequality and social exclusion in Black communities today:

> Social exclusion is a key underlying cause of young black people's overrepresentation as both victims and suspects. Not only does it fuel involvement in crime directly, it makes young people vulnerable to a host of other risk factors, such as living in neighbourhoods where crime is high, underachieving at school and frequent contacts with the police. (House of Commons, 2007, p. 29)

Governmental responses emphasised police enforcement and tougher sentencing, although research findings began to present another side to the UK 'street weapons crisis' (CCJS, 2008).

Behind this apparent 'crisis' in some inner-urban communities lay broader questions about social and economic inequality and youth exclusion. A 2007 UNICEF report placed the UK firmly at the bottom of a list of the 21 most affluent countries, judged in terms of the social, material and emotional wellbeing of children and young people. The analysis drew upon 40 separate indicators relevant to children's lives and children's rights. Government commentators questioned the reliability of some of the data but there was little disputing the central conclusion regarding the cumulative social impact of these problems. The issues related directly to the risk factors that strongly predict juvenile involvement in delinquency, gang activity and interpersonal violence (Loeber and Farrington, 1998; Pitts, 2003). According to UNICEF (2007, p. 39), a disadvantaged social background

> particularly when prolonged ... has been shown to be likely to have an effect on children's health, cognitive development, achievement at school, aspirations, self-perceptions, relationships, risk behaviours and employment prospects.

This toxic mix of deprivation and social exclusion directly frames the social relations of adolescence in the poorest areas.

This analysis was complemented by an important report from the Institute for Public Policy Research entitled *Make me a Criminal* (Margo and Stevens, 2008), which examined the criminal influences permeating the social relations of contemporary urban adolescence. The report recounted the ways in which social and policy changes had undermined 'the capacity of communities, including families, local community, schools, early years education and youth [services] to socialize norms of behaviour and respect' (Margo and Stevens, 2008, p. 4). Furthermore, despite nearly 10 years of policy specifically addressing the needs of the country's poorest communities, 'the capacity of social services, health services and specialist programmes to both reach and improve the behaviour of the most at-risk groups, such as those committing anti-social behaviour, showing emotional problems, or having problems at school' (ibid.) had, they claimed, been undermined.

An important finding of this work was that, compared to a range of 23 European societies, teenagers under 16 in the UK spent more evenings a week in the company of peers rather than with their families: 'The combination of less time with parents plus few affordable or easily accessible alternatives of adult-led activities has resulted in some of the most at-risk groups of young people being "freer" to socialize unsupervised with peers in public areas than in the past' (Margo and Stevens, 2008, p. 20). This finding, combined with Zimring's observation about the 'group context' of juvenile offending, suggests a potent cocktail of social exclusion and youth withdrawal, a combination all the more acute for the estimated 12% of British 14- to 16-year-olds who claimed to be members of a gang (Sharp et al., 2006).

Constructing defensible spaces and dangerous identities

Such findings were echoed in work published by the Joseph Rowntree Foundation in 2008. 'Street socialising' and strong territorial identities were reported to be key aspects of young people's lives in six 'disadvantaged' inner-urban locations in the UK (Kintrea et al., 2008). Territoriality was said to be a 'cultural expectation' and a source of respect emerging 'where young people's identity was closely associated with their neighbourhoods' (ibid., p. 4). Furthermore, while 'young people often had positive motivations, such as developing their identity and friendships, for becoming involved in territorial behaviour ... territorial identities were frequently expressed in violent conflict with territorial groups from other areas. [Territoriality could also be] ... associated with gangs and criminality', anti-social behaviour, weapon ownership and violence (Kintrea et al., 2008, pp. 4–6). Although the level and frequency of the violence varied, conflict was said to be a characteristic of all the areas studied, and such conflicts were 'heavily overlain or paralleled by other divisions between groups. By far the most important division was ethnic origin' (ibid., p. 5).

Few more potent testimonies as to the bleak, dangerous and confining existence that such territorial conflicts condemned young people can be offered than the remark of one young Black man, when giving evidence to the Home Affairs Select Committee hearings on knife crime in November 2008. Struggling to get his point across when pressed by the MPs about why young people adopted such strong territorial – even postcode identifications – and why they carried weapons, ostensibly for personal protection, he exclaimed: 'these estates are like cages, man'. Many young people apparently felt unable or deeply reluctant to cross territorial boundaries and this could place severe limits on their freedom of movement: 'Simply crossing a boundary into a neighbouring territory was regarded as an insult and could lead to conflict' (Kintrea et al., 2008, pp. 4–5). Finally, as the researchers noted, territoriality could also have a much wider impact upon communities, in that the anti-social or territorial behaviour of some young people 'often led the wider community to demonise all of them, with any group of young men viewed with particular suspicion' (ibid., p. 9). In turn, such suspicions led to the increasing involvement of the authorities, one direct consequence of which could be a higher level of police presence, increased rates of stop and search and, where community safety teams were proactive, the establishment of 'dispersal areas' to effectively banish groups of young people from public spaces.

Since the late 1990s, there is convincing evidence (Squires and Stephen, 2005; Hughes and Follett, 2006; Goldsmith, 2008; Sadler, 2008) that the more that young people have become the targets of community safety and, especially, anti-social behaviour legislation, the more they have been thrust back onto their own resources. This process has taken on two primary dimensions: first, as we have seen, facing more pronounced adult criticism (ASB complaints about young people 'hanging around') and encountering a far more explicit police targeting, young people have taken more obvious refuge in peer groups, a process rendered all the more attractive to them by the effective globalisation of gang cultures, identities, fashion, style and even language (Pitts, 2007; Hagedorn, 2009). Second, as a result of their de facto exclusion from the protections of the adult community, young people have been increasingly forced to find their own protections in a world that they perceive to be dangerous and threatening. Throughout the recent decade, rates of knife carrying appeared to have been increasing. The first indications of this may have been utterances from a few chief constables in the 1990s. They spoke of weapons (often firearms, both real and imitation) carried as supposed 'fashion accessories' by wannabe gangsters. Such calls may have been premature, or sensational – or the tip of an iceberg.

Yet statistics on 'blade possession' taken alone are an unreliable source; like most police statistics, they are evidence of police performance; the harder the police look for knives, the more they are likely to find. However, taken together with hospital admissions for stabbings, the data provides evidence of an underlying trend. A hospital A&E study published in 2007 also confirmed that, during the period 1997–2005, the number of people admitted as a result of stab or sharp object injuries rose by 30% (Maxwell et al., 2007).

Such evidence regarding the apparent scale of weapon carrying by young people – especially in certain areas – and the increase in serious weapon-related victimisation of young people certainly pointed to a number of changes affecting the lives of some young people in some of our inner-urban areas. The numbers of young people (aged under 18) stabbed may have been dwarfed by the numbers of older victims (although all the trends were rising) but the percentage increases were significant: over five years there was an 88% increase in stab victims aged under 16 and a 75% increase in victims aged 16–18. Above all, however, it was the increase in teenage knife murders, which lay at the centre of the most acute concerns. During the first months of 2008, a series of particularly brutal stabbings grabbed the newspaper headlines. Marfleet (2008) identified 36 teenagers fatally stabbed in London during 2007 and 2008.

The rise of knife-related violence has certainly played its part in a developing discourse on the depravity of modern youth. For although the use of a knife involves a more rudimentary and inefficient means of inflicting injury, it might be construed as immeasurably worse precisely because of the meanings associated with – and the motives attributed to – the unambiguous, up close and personal, visceral brutality of stabbing a blade into a fellow human being. Carrying and using knives suggested a new brutalism at street level. The media focused upon the relative youth of the victims and perpetrators; they were not the most numerous but their deaths certainly appeared the more tragic and pointless.

Although evidence about the frequency of teenage knife carrying was often rather ambiguous (Eades et al., 2007), teenage motives for carrying knives were reported in a series of surveys. Some 26% of young people living in 'high-risk' areas perceived knife crime to be either a big or fairly big problem in their area (11 Million/YouGov, 2009). Most of the knife carriers claimed to do so only rarely, but 85% of these said that they did so in order to protect themselves, while 7% said they had used their knives to threaten and 2% said they had used knives to cause injury (Wilson et al., 2006).

A report in 2004 concluded that fear of crime and experiences of victimisation 'played the most significant role in a young person's decision to carry a knife or weapon' (Lemos, 2004, p. 9). It also drew attention to a range of more diffuse cultural pressures influencing young people's choices, including a desire to assert strong gender identities, and aspirations towards street credibility and 'respect'. Marfleet (2008, p. 84) has referred to knife carrying having a 'replicative externality': 'knife carrying by [some] teenagers who are seen as a threat, appears to directly influence the likelihood that others will carry in response'.

Other surveys have questioned young people directly about their knife and weapon-carrying behaviours. A study by Broadhurst et al. (2008) found evidence of the protective and self-defensive practices followed by some young people – even on the way to school:

- It's not a bad thing to bring a weapon into school. You might get attacked on the way to school, on the way back. It's protection.
- I can protect myself with a knife or a gun. I would rather be arrested than dead.
- It's not a bad thing to bring weapons into school because of the area you are going to on the way to school. (Broadhurst et al., 2008, pp. 15–16)

Such notions of protection and self-defence appear to predominate in young people's accounts of weapon carrying, however dangerous this may be.

Although the problems of social and (in some cases) 'racial' exclusion (House of Commons, 2007), gang formation and ghettoisation are far removed from the scale reported in US cities where gang violence problems have been reported (Wacquant, 2007), the young people experiencing dangerous lives on some British streets tell a not dissimilar story. The Chicago sociology, which provided the first analyses of youth 'street gangs' (Thrasher, 1927), has more recently come to describe the 'violence ecologies' of inner-urban life (Fagan and Wilkinson, 1998), in which young people have to adapt and survive. But it is not young Black Londoners who have created the environments in which they now live, on the contrary, as Sandberg (2008) has argued, their 'street' identities are simply the resources they employ to negotiate their challenging contexts. Heale's (2008) discussion of 'gangland rules' helps bring these issues to life; how young people must live, feel, dress, think, walk, talk and respond – and the consequences. 'Gangland' sustains this way of being and young people translate these rules into their other social relations in a truly vicious circle. In 'gangland', violence is always an option, sometimes a *necessary* first response. Cultivating a violent identity and carrying a weapon may seem like a sensible precaution.

Final thoughts

Far from being merely outside the protections and social capital offered by adult community and its forms of authority (in the first instance, the police), young people are increasingly the objects of local systems of crime and disorder governance. Criminal justice processes have become increasingly implicated in the predicament of marginalised youth, as their socially excluded status and identity is reinforced and recycled through increasingly frequent encounters with the police, a wider cadre of new community safety agents and a hostile climate of public fear and alarm.

Accordingly, the most lasting legacy of our 10 years' experience of the new system of youth justice established in 1998, and the policy reviews of 2008–09 which followed, may well be a return to more robust street policing including widespread stop and search and a counterproductive reliance on increased rates of custodial sentencing for young people – quite contrary to the original aspirations of the Youth Justice Board. As an indication of what is to come, the Home Office's evaluation of the first phase of the implementation of the Tackling Knives Action Programme (TKAP) (Ward and Diamond, 2009) pointed to stop and search numbers rising in all areas and tougher and longer sentences handed down (especially in the TKAP project areas) for knife possession – including more custodial sentences. As the predicaments of socially excluded young people, lacking opportunities to access work, training or rejoin mainstream education, have become more acute, their situations have come to approximate more closely the crimogenic and violence prone 'advanced marginality' described by Wacquant (2007). While Wacquant is careful to caution against drawing his ideas beyond their primary context, it is possible to recognise the ebbing of 'welfare principles' in the new youth justice policies and their replacement by rather more disciplinary measures (Wacquant, 2009). In the process, many young people have been left in some very difficult – even impossible – circumstances to negotiate their transitions to adulthood.

That this recourse to further criminalisation is *not* an inevitable development can be gauged from the ASB 'regimes' adopted, first in Scotland, where an early decision was taken to avoid using the ASBO for young people aged under 16 (Scottish Executive, 2005), and also in Wales, where the measure is only to be implemented as a 'last resort' (Edwards and Hughes, 2008). By 2007, in England too, there was also some indication that a hitherto very 'top-down' ASB strategy had begun to moderate, following the influence of experienced youth justice practitioners, a group that had, in large part, been overlooked when the original policies had been developed (Mayfield and Mills, 2008). There are, undoubtedly, important differences between policy development and policy implementation and different kinds of opportunities for influence to be brought to bear at different times.

References

11 Million/YouGov (2009) *Solutions to Gun and Knife Crime: Final Report*, London, YouGov, available online at <http://www.childrenscommissioner.gov.uk/content/publications/content_371> [Accessed 14 June 2010].

Alexander, C. (2008) *Rethinking Gangs*, London, Runnymede Trust.

Barnado's (2008) The shame of Britain's intolerance of children, press release, 17 November, available online at <http://www.barnardos.org.uk/news_and_events/media_centre/press_releases.htm?ref=42088> [Accessed 7 April 2010].

Broadhurst, K., Duffin, M. and Taylor, E. (2008) *Gangs and Schools: Interim Report: An Interim Report for NASUWT*, Birmingham, Perpetuity Group/NASUWT.

CCJS (Centre for Crime and Justice Studies) (2008) *Street Weapons Commission Evidence: Guns, Knives and Street Violence*, King's College London, CCJS.

Cohen, S. (1973) *Folk Devils and Moral Panics*, St Albans, Paladin.

Cohen, S. (1985) *Visions of Social Control*, Cambridge, Polity Press.

Davis, M. (2008) 'Foreword: Reading John Hagedorn', in J.M. Hagedorn (ed.) *A World of Gangs: Armed Young Men and Gangsta Culture*, Minneapolis, MN, University of Minnesota Press, pp. xi–xvii.

Eades, C., Grimshaw, R., Silvestri, A. and Solomon, E. (2007) *'Knife Crime': A Review of Evidence and Policy* (2nd edn), King's College London, CCJS.

Edwards, A. and Hughes, G. (2008) 'Resilient Fabians: Anti-social behaviour and community safety work in Wales', in P. Squires (ed.) *ASBO Nation*, Bristol, Policy Press, pp. 57–72.

Fagan, J. and Wilkinson, D. (1998) 'Guns, youth violence and social identity in inner cities', *Crime and Justice: Annual Review of Research*, 24: 105–88

Finney, A. (2004) 'Perceptions of changing crime levels', in S. Nicholas and A. Walker (eds) *Crime in England and Wales 2002/2003*, supplementary vol 2: *Crime, Disorder and the Criminal Justice System: Public Attitudes and Perceptions*, London, Home Office Research and Statistics Directorate.

Goldsmith, C. (2008) 'Cameras, cops and contracts: What anti-social behaviour management feels like to young people', in P. Squires (ed.) *ASBO Nation*, Bristol, Policy Press, pp. 223–38.

Goldson, B. (1999) 'Youth (in)justice: Contemporary developments in policy and practice', in B. Goldson (ed.) *Youth Justice: Contemporary Policy and Practice*, Aldershot, Ashgate, pp. 1–27.

Hagedorn, J.M. (1988) *People and Folks: Gangs, Crime and the Underclass in a Rustbelt City*, Chicago, Lakeview Press.

Hagedorn, J.M. (2009) *A World of Gangs: Armed Young Men and Gangsta Culture*, Minneapolis, MN, University of Minnesota Press.

Hallsworth, S. and Young, T. (2008) 'Gang talk and gang talkers: A critique', *Crime, Media, Culture*, 4(2): 175–95.

Haydon, D. and Scraton, P. (2000) 'Condemn a little more, understand a little less: The political context and rights' implications of the domestic and European rulings in the Venables-Thompson case', *Journal of Law and Society*, **27**(3): 416–48.

Heale, J. (2008) *One Blood: Inside Britain's New Street Gangs*, London, Simon & Schuster.

Home Office (1997) *No More Excuses*, Cm 3809, London, HMSO.

Home Office (2008a) *Tackling Gangs: A Practical Guide for Local Authorities, CDRPs and Other Local Partners*, London, Home Office.

Home Office (2008b) *Tough New Sanctions to Tackle Knife Crime*, press release, 5 June, available online at <http://www.direct.gov.uk/en/Nl1/Newsroom/DG_078582> [Accessed 14 June 2010].

Home Office (2008c) *Saving Lives. Reducing Harm. Protecting the Public: An Action Plan for Tackling Violence 2008–11*, London, Home Office.

Hope, T. (2000) 'Inequality and the clubbing of private security', in T. Hope and R. Sparks (eds) *Crime, Risk and Insecurity*, London, Routledge, pp. 83–106.

Hope, T. (2001) 'Crime victimisation and inequality in risk society', in R. Matthews and J. Pitts (eds) *Crime, Disorder and Community Safety*, London, Routledge, pp. 193–218.

House of Commons, Home Affairs Select Committee (2007) *Young Black People and the Criminal Justice System*, HC 181, 1 and 2, London, TSO.

Hughes, G. and Follett, M. (2006) 'Community safety, youth and the "anti-social"', in B. Goldson and J. Muncie (eds) *Youth Crime and Justice*, London, Sage, pp. 157–71.

Kintrea, K., Bannister, J., Pickering, J. et al. (2008) *Young People and Territoriality in British Cities*, York, Joseph Rowntree Foundation.

Klein, M. (1995) *The American Street Gang: Its Nature, Prevalence and Control*, Oxford, Oxford University Press.

Lea, J. and Young, J. (1984) *What is to be Done About Law and Order*, Harmondsworth, Penguin.

Lemos, G. (2004) *Fear and Fashion: The Use of Knives and Other Weapons by Young People*, London, Lemos & Crane.

Loeber, R. and Farrington, D. (eds) (1998) *Serious and Violent Juvenile Offenders: Risk Factors and Successful Interventions*, Thousand Oaks, CA, Sage.

Margo, J. and Stevens, A. (2008) *Make me a Criminal: Preventing Youth Crime*, London, Institute for Public Policy Research.

Marfleet, N. (2008) *Why Carry a Weapon? A Study of Knife Crime Amongst 15–17 Year Old Males in London*, London, Howard League for Penal Reform.

Maxwell, R., Trotter, C., Verne, J. et al. (2007) 'Trends in admissions to hospital involving an assault using a knife or other sharp instrument, England, 1997–2005', *Journal of Public Health*, **29**(2): 186–90.

Mayfield, G. and Mills, A. (2008) 'Towards a balanced and practical approach to anti-social behaviour management', in P. Squires (ed.) *ASBO Nation*, Bristol, Policy Press, pp. 73–86.

Muncie, J. (1999) 'Institutionalised intolerance: Youth crime and the 1998 Crime and Disorder Act', *Critical Social Policy*, **19**(2): 147–75.

Pitts, J. (2003) *The New Politics of Youth Crime*, Lyme Regis, Russell House.

Pitts, J. (2007) 'Americanization, the third way and the racialization of youth crime and disorder', in J. Hagedorn (ed.) *Gangs in the Global City: Alternatives to Traditional Criminology*, Chicago, University of Illinois Press, pp. 273–92.

Pitts, J. (2008) *Reluctant Gangsters*, Cullompton, Willan.

Reed, W.L. and Decker, S. (ed.) (2002) *Responding to Gangs: Evaluation and Research*, Washington DC, National Institute of Justice, US Department of Justice, Office of Justice Programs.

Sadler, J. (2008) 'Implementing the youth anti-social behaviour agenda: Policing the Ashton Estate', *Youth Justice*, 8: 57–73.

Sandberg, S. (2008) 'Street capital: Ethnicity and violence on the streets of Oslo', *Theoretical Criminology*, **12**(2): 153–71.

Scottish Executive (2005) *Use of Anti-social Behaviour Orders in Scotland*, DTZ Pieda Consulting/Heriot Watt University, available online at <http://www.scotland.gov.uk/Resource/Doc/1101/0010249.pdf> [Accessed 7 April 2010].

Sharp, C., Aldridge, J. and Medina, J. (2006) *Delinquent Youth Groups and Offending*

Behaviour: Findings from the 2004 Offending, Crime and Justice Survey, Home Office online report 14/06, London, TSO, available online at <www.homeoffice.gov.uk/rds/pdfs06/rdsolr1406.pdf> [Accessed 7 April 2010].

Squires, P. (2009) 'The knife crime "epidemic" and British politics', *British Politics*, 4: 127–57.

Squires, P. and Stephen, D.E. (2005) *Rougher Justice: Anti-social Behaviour and Young People*, Cullompton, Willan.

Taylor, A. (2009) 'Brothers beat and burned boys', *The Sun*, 3 September.

Thrasher, F. (1927) *The Gang: A Study of 1,313 Gangs in Chicago*, Chicago, University of Chicago Press.

Tonry, M. (2004) *Punishment and Politics: Evidence and Emulation in the Making of English Crime Control Policy*, Cullompton, Willan.

UNICEF (2007) *An Overview of Child Well-Being in Rich Countries*, Florence, UNICEF.

Wacquant, L. (2007) *Urban Outcasts: A Comparative Sociology of Advanced Marginality*, Cambridge, Polity Press.

Wacquant, L. (2009) *Punishing the Poor: The Neoliberal Governance of Social Insecurity*, London, Duke University Press.

Ward, L. and Diamond, A. (2009) *Tackling Knives Action Programme (TKAP) Phase 1: Overview of Key Trends from a Monitoring Programme*, Research Report 18, Home Office Research and Statistics Directorate.

Wilson, D., Sharp, C. and Patterson, A. (2006) *Young People and Crime: Findings from the 2005 Offending, Crime and Justice Survey*, London, Home Office.

Zimring, F. (1998) *American Youth Violence*, Oxford, Oxford University Press.

13

Constructing practice within the parenting agenda: the case of Sure Start and Parenting Orders

Amanda Holt

This chapter outlines the different ways in which 'parenting practices' are constructed by structures, institutions, families and individuals in contemporary Britain. It begins by briefly outlining the ways in which the 'parenting agenda' has been at the heart of social policy developments in the early twenty-first century. This chapter then examines two particular high-profile parenting initiatives – Sure Start and Parenting Orders – and explores some of the ways in which service user experiences are shaped by particular discursive constructions and material realities. The chapter concludes by suggesting what could be done to challenge some of the more unhelpful practices that serve to reconfigure children and families in particular ways.

Contemporary constructions of parenting in twenty-first century Britain

A number of chapters in this book have conceptualised childhood and youth as a socially constructed phenomena. However, given that constructions of parenthood exist in relation to constructions of childhood (and vice versa) (Burman, 1995), then one must consider the socially constructed nature of parenthood, as well as societal and political responses to this construct. Thus, in contemporary Britain, the notion of a unified and uniform 'parent' is constructed as the unit of analysis, and policy initiatives have increasingly responded to 'parenting' in this way. As Overall (1987) explained, such constructions of parenting sit alongside the current western tradition of conceptualising children as a 'commodity', something which is possessed and owned. Such a model necessitates an 'owner' (that is, the parent) and consequently there is a need for each child to be assigned one or two specific 'owners' who are boundaried and can claim ownership rights in their entirety. Although, as Reece (2009) pointed out, the notion of 'parental rights' has been increasingly subsumed within a notion of 'parental responsibilities' over the past 20 years. Alongside this, there has also been a considerable increase in discourses of 'emotional investment' in children by their parents (Ambert, 1994). This is likely, at least in part, to be a product of the ways in which developmental psychology has reconstructed parenting as a labour of love, thus shaping contemporary parental subjectivities with an emotional hue which has not always been present (Rose, 1989).

Theorists who have recognised the problematic way in which contemporary forms of parenting have been socially constructed have tended to approach the problem from a feminist angle, with concern focusing on the construction of 'motherhood'. For example, Adrienne Rich (1976) has long suggested a model of the 'mothering continuum', which acknowledges the fluidity of the parenting role and avoids the westernised model of child-rearing, which promotes a strict 'either/or' distinction between parents and non-parents. Similarly, bell hooks (1984) promoted the term 'child-rearing' rather than 'mothering' (or 'parenting'), which, again, recognises the fluidity of parenting and the work of those, for example teachers, social workers, babysitters, who are not 'blood parents'.

Furthermore, the current western dominance of 'the parent' as a distinct unit of analysis has shaped – and been shaped by – scientific attempts to operationalise it and give it the status of 'psychological object'. Such scientific practices date back to the end of the nineteenth century with the advent of psychological models, most notably psychoanalysis and behaviourism, which attempted to explain an individual's current behaviour, and 'behavioural problems', through the lens of their childhood experiences – and consequently their parents' role in shaping such experiences. Attempts to further establish the status of parenting through the production of apparently objective 'good' and 'bad' parenting practices have been endemic, and the current dominance of 'risk factor research' (most notably Farrington's Cambridge Study in Delinquency Development 1961–81; see, for example, Farrington, 1995, 2003) has been particularly influential in shaping a number of social policies in twenty-first century Britain. In particular, the New Labour government's investment in the parenting agenda has been at the heart of its wider 'politics of (anti-social) behaviour', which can be seen in a number of policy areas: for example in the Department of Education's Parenting Early Intervention Pathfinders, in the Department of Health's Family Nurse Partnership Programme (both of which apply in England) and in the

Ministry of Justice's Parenting Contracts and Parenting Orders (which apply across the UK). This parenting agenda has been driven by the underlying principle that 'what matters is what works' (Davies et al., 2000) – a principle that formed a key tenet of New Labour's election manifesto in 1997. But however well meaning and rationalist this principle is, policy decision making is more complex than this, with political expediency, rather than sound evidence, frequently driving policy-making decisions. In addition, as Fergusson (2007) pointed out, policy rhetoric rarely reflects its codification, which in turn does not neatly translate into practice 'on the ground'. Furthermore, as this chapter will later discuss, professional practices on the ground are not necessarily read and experienced as intended by the service users themselves.

The parenting agenda: a new policy focus for a new century

Since the turn of the twenty-first century, a focus on parenting has been one of the key tenets of the UK government's social policy agenda. Furthermore, a very specific kind of 'parental determinism' has been produced by the specific governmental investment (both socially and economically) in the child as 'citizen-worker-of-the-future' (see Lister, 2003). 'Parental determinism' refers to a dominant discourse that frames parents as determining *all* aspects of their child's development.

This is evident in many of the government's policy documents, most notably in England with *Every Child Matters* (DfES, 2003), a Green Paper that placed parents at the centre of its agenda and which has enabled 'parent support' to seep into almost every aspect of public policy. This parenting focus was supported by the claim that parenting is *more important* than 'poverty, school environment and the influence of peers' (DfES, 2003, p. 18) in educational attainment, although the evidence base for this was provided by a single reference that was cited as 'in draft for DfES' (2003, p. 49).

With attempts to tackle everything from social exclusion to anti-social behaviour through parenting support (Goldson, 2002), this has led many to suggest that such policies have enabled the transformation from a 'social welfare state' to a 'therapeutic state' (Polsky, 1991; Nolan, 1998). A 'therapeutic state' defines what it is to be a 'good parent' in line with what makes a 'good child', which, as suggested above, is more about what the child will *become* than what the child *is*. Such fundamental changes in social policy have undoubtedly reconfigured relationships between the state, professionals, parents and children, and shifts towards more preventive interventions are likely to reconfigure these relationships further (Parton, 2006).

The problem, of course, is that with something as morally loaded as 'good/bad parenting', those who are defined as 'in need' of parenting support are likely to read such policy initiatives, and the interventions which they generate, in ways which may not necessarily be intended by either the policy makers who determine what support should look like, or the professional practitioners who shape how support manifests in practice. Wider social, political and moral discourses, which operate within a framework of 'parental determinism', are reproduced through a range of channels such as transformative television shows (for example *Supernanny*, *Driving Mum and Dad Mad*), popular and academic psychology (including Farrington's influential research) and policy documents and political debates. Such a framework, based on the dominant dyad of the 'vulnerable child' and the 'god-like' parent, enables the perceived problems of children and young people to be contained (and packaged) within a parent–child dynamic that ignores their structural and interactional context (Burman, 2008).

Furthermore, such representations of poor parent(ing) are continually framed through a social class lens, with middle-class nuclear family practices constructed as 'normal' and other forms of family formation (for example lone-parent families) and practices (for example working-class practices) continually framed as deviant. With such powerful representations being continually circulated in popular discourse, it is impossible to imagine that this would not shape how policy makers, institutions, practitioners and service users themselves construct and experience particular 'parenting support' initiatives. To analyse this issue in more detail, this chapter now turns to the ways in which policy and practice have been constructed in the cases of Sure Start and Parenting Orders. These two initiatives constituted perhaps the most high profile of New Labour's parenting agenda. However, while both operated within the policy discourse of parent support, Sure Start was designed as a service targeted towards particular communities and was taken up voluntarily by parents: Parenting Orders were designed to target individuals and were made enforceable through the judicial system. The analysis that follows suggests that such differences shape the way that parenting support initiatives are constructed and consequently experienced by service users themselves.

Constructing practice in Sure Start

Sure Start was launched in 1999 as a beacon in New Labour's action against social exclusion and child poverty, with the first round of Sure Start local programmes (SSLPs) located in the poorest 20% of wards in the UK. While the responsibility for early education and childcare lies with the devolved administrations, Sure Start is nevertheless a UK-wide initiative and, in general, the types of services and support on offer vary little. The initial aim of Sure Start was to provide an interagency support service for the parents of preschool children who were living in deprived neighbourhoods, but SSLPs soon developed into Sure Start children's centres, which offered services to children up to 14 years old (or 16 for children with disabilities) and their families. These services include links to JobCentre Plus, health support services, drop-in sessions for parents and children, and parenting and family advice. They also provided links to additional services for families experiencing particular problems in relation to mental health, disabilities and/or criminal activity (among others) (DfES, 2006). While Sure Start is a New Labour policy, the new coalition government, elected in May 2010, has committed itself to protecting funding for Sure Start for at least a further year. In *The Coalition: Our Programme for Government* (Cabinet Office, 2010, p. 19), it stated:

> We will take Sure Start back to its original purpose of early intervention, increase its focus on the neediest families, and better involve organisations with a track record ofsupporting families.

How this will manifest remains to be seen.

Sure Start itself operated within what Levitas (1998) termed a 'social integrationist' discourse, meaning that the policy solution to social disadvantage is framed in terms of the state's role in supporting individual opportunities through educational and skills provision (Clarke, 2006). Thus, the provision of childcare, education and information, skills and training – as well as opportunities for volunteer and paid work within the programme itself – enable social change by addressing the behaviour and development of individuals. Such an approach certainly aligns with commonsense understandings of childhood as a time of vulnerability and of a development shaped by early family experiences: indeed, the very term 'sure start' evokes the apparent truism that if the early groundwork is in place, a normative developmental pathway will surely follow.

One of the key aims of Sure Start was to make engagement in the programme 'non-stigmatising' (Rutter, 2006) and it was hoped that, by locating the programmes in geographically defined areas and then making them available to all, any potential stigma could be avoided. Although, as Power and Wilmott (2005) pointed out, targeted services such as Sure Start can nevertheless end up stigmatising all those families who live in areas defined as a 'problem'. However, as Clarke (2006) pointed out, while Sure Start aimed to be non-stigmatising through its 'universality', the objectives that were assessed as part of its evaluation appeared to operate within a pathologising discourse in relation to the parents who use the programme. For example, the first objective, which made reference to 'improving social and emotional development, in particular, by supporting early bonding between parents and their children, helping families to function' (Sure Start, 2002) implied that poor bonding and family functioning underlies problems in social and emotional development, and assumes that those families living in Sure Start areas are particularly prone to them (Clarke, 2006). Furthermore, by individualising the outcome targets in this way, Sure Start became less a community-based resource and more of a vehicle for disciplining particular kinds of parents by instilling in them the norms of white, middle-class families, which were implicitly advocated in their programmes and advice (Gillies, 2005).

Some evidence does indeed suggest that Sure Start has been experienced as stigmatising by those families who have used it. For example, a number of researchers have found that, at least in its initial stages, parents perceived Sure Start as stigmatising because the Sure Start centre was located in a former social services family centre (Chappell et al., 2002; Hayden, 2007) and because it was seen as being there 'for people who can't look after their kids properly' (Avis et al., 2007, p. 208). Hayden (2007) and Power and Wilmott (2005) also found that some users of Sure Start experienced resentment from those living nearby who did not live in the catchment area and could not benefit from the programme, which also produced a desire in parents to stay in the Sure Start 'problem area' despite its apparent social and economic disadvantages.

Nevertheless, the majority of the numerous local Sure Start evaluation projects that have taken place have found that parents gain much from engaging in Sure Start services across the UK. Qualitative studies have found that, in particular, the provision of childcare, training opportunities, social interaction and information sharing has been greatly valued by the parents who engage with Sure Start (Avis et al., 2007). However, it appears that such benefits may have been mediated by wider social forces, such as social class: in their evaluation of 150 SSLPs, Belsky et al. (2006) found that those parents who benefitted were relatively less socially deprived, perhaps because they had greater resources to draw on in accessing the Sure Start services on offer. In contrast, those parents most socially deprived appeared to experience the most adverse effects from living in SSLP areas, perhaps because they found the extra attention stressful and intrusive (Belsky et al., 2006). However, more recent evaluation findings suggested that such differences were diminishing as Sure Start became more established (Clarke, 2008).

Constructions of what engaging in Sure Start means to service users can also be understood in terms of gender, which is perhaps unsurprising given the gendered construction of parenting. For example, in their analysis of fathers' engagement with Sure Start, Lloyd et al. (2003) found that a combination of cultural discourses, institutional practices and material realities meant that fathers felt unable to engage with Sure Start services. For example, at the cultural level, fathers expressed feeling intimidated by what is traditionally a female arena, and were acutely aware of suspicions that they were there to 'pick up' women, suggestions that were reinforced by light-hearted teasing from the female participants. Similar findings have been reported by the government's own

National Evaluation of Sure Start (NESS), which found that fathers felt that the Sure Start centres were 'women's places' dominated by a feminine culture, making them feel uncomfortable and excluded. Such experiences were intensified by Sure Start services being delivered during what was perceived as 'women and children times' (DfES, 2007, p. 82). Furthermore, in terms of material realities, many of the fathers felt that the centres' 'office hours' produced a barrier to access, since many more fathers than mothers work full time, meaning that their own material circumstances limited their involvement with Sure Start.

Of course, the discursive and material practices that shape parents' experiences of Sure Start do not happen in a vacuum, and, as described above, both institutional and individual practitioner practices contribute to the shaping of such experiences. For example, in terms of the lack of fathers' uptake of Sure Start services, Lloyd et al. (2003) found that many of the Sure Start programmes were implicitly 'female-oriented', with practitioners encouraging attendance by offering 'supermarket-style reward points' to service users, redeemable against services such as massages and facials, for example. Similarly, the DfES (2007) NESS report found that practitioners justified fathers' exclusion from Sure Start centres by drawing on constructions of the local men as entrenched within 'macho ex-miner cultures'. The report also found that practitioners' perceptions of 'cultural constraints' operating within local Muslim communities (such as believing that fathers and mothers could not be mixed) enabled practitioners to justify the lack of fathers' access to Sure Start services (DfES, 2007).

Furthermore, since implementation is key to determining whether a particular support programme works, the role of different service agencies operating under different legislative frameworks is likely to have a powerful role in shaping outcomes. For example, Belsky et al. (2006) found that those programmes led by health services were more effective than those led by local authorities and voluntary organisations, perhaps because they already had frameworks in place to enable home visits and access birth records. Working professional cultures are also likely to shape implementation: for example, Pithouse (2008) highlighted the ways in which particular occupational professionals draw tight boundaries around their own occupational role in childcare services, preventing the policy rhetoric of 'a shared agenda' for early intervention from working out that way in practice.

Nevertheless, while it is too early to asses the long-term impact of Sure Start, short-term findings suggest that parents have been generally positive towards this particular policy initiative, and have appreciated the resources and effort that have gone into setting up and maintaining the Sure Start children's centres. However, a second parenting policy has produced some very different outcomes, and an analysis of the way it is constructed by the service users themselves may shed some light into why.

Constructing practice in Parenting Orders

Like Sure Start, Parenting Orders were the second of New Labour's flagship policy initiatives introduced in 1998, which aimed to provide 'parents in need' with support. Although Parenting Orders have their roots in the parental bind-over, introduced in 1991 by the Conservative government. However, unlike Sure Start, the support that was offered was enforced and took the form of a parenting support programme managed by the local Youth Offending Team (YOT). The Parenting Order itself is issued to parents through the courts, as a result of their child either committing an offence, or being at risk of doing so, or as a result of their child's non-attendance at school. It can last for up to 12 months, with the threat of a fine and/or summary conviction if parents fail to engage with such services (see the Crime and Disorder Act 1998). However, as I have argued elsewhere (see Holt, 2008), Parenting Orders tend to be issued to mothers, lone parents and those who are the most socially and economically disadvantaged. Furthermore, as in the case of Sure Start, there appears to be an implicit ideal of what 'normal' parents look like (that is, white, middle class, married), and there is evidence that both the practitioners who assess the parents (for the pre-sentence report) and the magistrates who ultimately issue the Parenting Order use such ideals to navigate their decision-making processes. For example, Longstaff (2004) found that it was how parents 'speak and act' in court that determined whether they were issued with a Parenting Order. As Hollingsworth (2007, p. 207) noted, 'those who parent in the way acceptable to the State, even if their child offends, are not subject to the same intervention as others'.

Despite the apparent punitiveness of Parenting Orders at the levels of policy rhetoric and implementation, there is a growing body of research that has explored the ways in which youth justice agents, such as magistrates (for example Longstaff, 2004) and practitioners (for example Field, 2007), have attempted to mediate how policy is played out through their own cultures of professional practice. This is particularly so in professionals' attempts to practise a more 'welfarist' agenda through the exercise of discretion: for example, Burnett and Appleton (2004) found in their study of one YOT that practitioners viewed Parenting Orders as stigmatising and unhelpful, and so rarely recommended them. Similarly, Longstaff (2004) found that some courts resisted the use of Parenting Orders by stating in open court that they did not think a Parenting Order was 'appropriate' in a particular case, enabling them to circumnavigate the legislation that prescribes that *all* courts must issue a Parenting Order in cases where the child is under 16 years old, and must state in open court the reasons why they have chosen not to. Longstaff (2004) also found evidence of different professional practices operating within different YOTs, with some teams less willing to recommend a Parenting Order in their pre-sentence report because of fears around the possible consequences of further disciplining already fragile families.

Such professional practices of resistance can also operate at a national level. For example, in Scotland, where professional practices operate within a different ideological and legislative framework than in England, local authorities have neither prepared for their use nor issued any Parenting Orders (Scottish Parliament, 2008), since they felt that they were inappropriate and essentially about punishment, rather than welfare (Walters and Woodward, 2007).

It is perhaps surprising that, compared to Sure Start, there has been very little evaluation of Parenting Orders, or research into parents' experiences of them. While New Labour used the same evidence-based 'what works' framework to justify Parenting Orders – utilising medical and psychological discourses to support the importance of early intervention – the government has only commissioned one evaluation survey, which tracked the effectiveness of YOT-based parenting support groups in its pilot stage. This report, by Ghate and Ramella (2002), found that many parents reported positive changes in their parenting skills and that the average number of offences per young person was reduced by over 50%. However, this report has a number of methodological flaws (including missing data, sampling biases and a lack of control group), not least that the majority of parents evaluated attended the parenting programme voluntarily, with only 16% attending through Parenting Orders.

Research that has examined parents' experiences of Parenting Orders found something very different: that the ways in which parents construct Parenting Orders shape the way they experience the parenting support that is a condition of the Parenting Order. Research by Holt (2010a, 2010b) has found that, for the parents who were the recipients of Parenting Orders, the parenting support that followed was almost universally experienced as a punishment. This is not to suggest that parents gained nothing from the support classes, but what some of the parents found helpful (that is, the space to talk about their problems) made little impact on their relationships with their families, nor on their child's level of offending (see Holt, 2010b). This is because the parenting support was one aspect of a longer process, whereby parents were first made to attend court and were made to feel, in the parents' own words, like a 'bad parent'. Thus, despite practitioners' best efforts to engage with parents on an equal and supportive footing, the very fact that Parenting Orders operate within a dominant framework of 'parental determinism' inevitably shapes parents' reading, and experiences, of this particular parenting support measure.

Final thoughts

This chapter has briefly outlined the ways in which the parenting agenda has been constructed and made central to social policy during the first decade of the twenty-first century. Such a policy focus has been supported by a particularly moralising and individualising discourse that has enabled the idea of a 'parenting deficit' to shape policy making. The idea that professional practice with parents is co-constructed has been explored through the analysis of two of the most high-profile social policy initiatives within the parenting agenda: Sure Start and Parenting Orders. While both policies operate within this wider parenting deficit discourse, this chapter has illustrated some of the ways in which this discourse interacts with particular structuring axes (such as gender and social class), particular institutions (such as family centres and criminal courts) and particular individuals (such as magistrates and family practitioners). Such complex interactions have resulted in some very different experiences for the parents who are in receipt of such alleged support. This suggests that all forms of parenting support are not – and should not be understood as – merely different means of achieving the same ends of supporting parents.

However, too little research has explored these interacting spheres and, given the complexities of the process from policy to legislature to practice to experience, it is unlikely that research could ever pin down a chain of causation in a way that would satisfy those who like explanations to come with flow charts and percentages. However, what this analysis does do is highlight what could be done to challenge some of the more unhelpful practices that serve to reconstruct children and families in particular ways. For example, it is clear that practice needs to focus on more community-based measures, rather than compensating for a supposed deficit in parenting skills. While Sure Start initially focused on the notion that local parents could be enabled to empower themselves at community level, this soon shifted as Sure Start came under local authority ownership and transformed into universal children's centres. A community-based focus would necessarily focus on economic and structural disadvantage, and Pitts (2008) described one example of how neighbourhood-capacity initiatives have been enabled to develop from family support programmes to positive effect.

Alongside this, for both Sure Start and Parenting Orders, there also needs to be wider acknowledgement of the context of disadvantage (such as race and gender). As Clarke (2008) suggested, this will prevent the 'objectives' of parenting support being assimilated into white middle-class norms. This also requires an awareness of practitioner language, and Cruddas (2009) has described how Waltham Forest local authority/children's services department trains practitioners to be aware of the language that informs their parenting work, such as ensuring that parenting practitioners are not presented as 'experts' but as 'parenting workers' to avoid any implicit hierarchising of power relations between worker and parent.

This is also a matter for policy makers: while recent government attempts to involve fathers, for example the Think Fathers campaign, is positive, such initiatives have nevertheless focused on fathers' engagement in the 'emotional' aspects, for example reading to their child, rather than the 'practical' aspects, for example cleaning, of parenting. Such initiatives leave wider inequalities untouched. Finally, academics and researchers need to accept responsibility for their role in perpetuating parental determinism: for example, McCaslin and Infanti (1998) found that, in 1,000 parenting articles and advice columns, 97% of parents were blamed for the problems encountered with their adolescent children, and 68% were advised to seek expert help. Such spurious conclusions only serve to unhelpfully blame parents (and not all parents are equally blamed) and deskill parents' own sense of competency.

References

Ambert, A. (1994) 'An international perspective on parenting: Social change and social constructs', *Journal of Marriage and the Family*, 56: 529–43.

Avis, M., Bulman, D. and Leighton, P. (2007) 'Factors affecting participation in Sure Start programmes: A qualitative investigation of parents' views', *Health and Social Care in the Community*, **15**(3): 203–11.

Belsky, J., Melhuish, E., Barnes, J. et al. (2006) 'Effects of Sure Start local programmes on children and families: Early findings from a quasi-experimental, cross sectional study', *British Medical Journal*, **332**(7556): 1476–9.

Burman, E. (1995) 'Who is it?', in S. Wilkinson and C. Kitzinger (eds) *Feminism and Discourse: Psychological Perspectives*, Thousand Oaks, CA, Sage, pp. 49–67.

Burman, E. (2008) *Deconstructing Developmental Psychology*, 2nd edn, London, Routledge.

Burnett, R. and Appleton, C. (2004) *Joined-up Youth Justice: Tackling Youth Crime in Partnership*, Lyme Regis, Russell House.

Cabinet Office (2010) *The Coalition: Our Programme for Government*, London, Cabinet Office.

Chappell, T., Schafer, J. and Stewert-Brown, S. (2002) *Rose Hill – Littlemore Sure Start: The First Two Years: A Report of the Local Evaluation*, Health Services Research Unit, University of Oxford, available online at <http://www.publichealth.ox.ac.uk/units/hsru/copy_of_reports/surestartrep> [Accessed 29 August 2009].

Clarke, C. (2008) 'Early intervention and prevention: Lessons from the Sure Start programme', in M. Blyth and E. Soloman (eds) *Prevention and Youth Crime: Is Early Intervention Working?*, Bristol, Policy Press, pp. 53–68.

Clarke, K. (2006) 'Childhood, parenting and early intervention: A critical examination of the Sure Start national programme', *Critical Social Policy*, 26: 699–721.

Cruddas, L. (2009) Does the policy agenda aim to transform all parents into middle-class parents? Paper presented at 'Is Parenting a Class Issue?', 2 July, London, National Family and Parenting Institute.

Davies, H.T., Nutley, S.M. and Smith, P.C. (2000) *What Works? Evidence-based Policy and Practice in Public Services*, Bristol, Polity Press.

DfES (Department for Education and Skills) (2003) *Every Child Matters: Change for Children*, London, HMSO.

DfES (Department for Education and Skills) (2006) *Sure Start Children's Centres Prac-*

tice Guidance, DfES, HMSO, available online at <www.dcsf.gov.uk/everychildmat-ters/research/publications/surestartpublications/1854/> [Accessed 29 August 2009].

DfES (Department for Education and Skills) (2007) *Understanding Variations in Effectiveness amongst Sure Start Local Programmes*, the National Evaluation of Sure Start, HMSO, available online at <www.dcsf.gov.uk/everychildmatters/publi-cations/0/1906/> [Accessed 29 August 2009].

Farrington, D.P. (1995) 'The development of offending and antisocial behaviour from childhood: Key findings from the Cambridge study in delinquent development', *Journal of Child Psychology and Psychiatry*, 36: 929–64.

Farrington, D.P. (2003) 'Key results from the first 40 years of the Cambridge study in delinquent development', in T.P. Thornberry and M.D. Krohn (eds) *Taking Stock of Delinquency: An Overview of Findings from Contemporary Longitudinal Studies*, New York, Kluwer/Plenum, pp. 137–83.

Fergusson, R. (2007) 'Making sense of the melting pot: Multiple discourses in youth justice policy', *Youth Justice*, **7**(3): 179–94.

Field, S. (2007) 'Practice cultures and the 'new' youth justice in England and Wales, *British Journal of Criminology*, **42**(2): 311–30.

Ghate, D. and Ramella, M. (2002) *Positive Parenting: The National Evaluation of the Youth Justice Board's Parenting Programme*, Policy Research Bureau, available online at <http://www.youth-justice-board.gov.uk> [Accessed 12 December 2005].

Gillies, V. (2005) Meeting parents' needs? Discourses of 'support' and 'inclusion' in family policy, *Critical Social Policy*, **25**(1): 70–90.

Goldson, B. (2002) 'New Labour, social justice and children: Political calculations and the deserving-undeserving schism', *British Journal of Social Work*, **32**(6): 683–95.

Hayden, C. (2007) *Children in Trouble: Reviewing the Role of Families, Schools and Communities*, Basingstoke, Palgrave Macmillan.

Hollingsworth, K. (2007) 'Responsibility and rights: Children and their parents in the youth justice system', *International Journal of Law, Policy and the Family*, 21: 190–219.

Holt, A. (2008) 'Room for resistance? Parenting orders, disciplinary power and the construction of the bad parent', in P. Squires (ed.) *ASBO Nation: The Criminalisa-tion of Nuisance*, Bristol, Policy Press, pp. 103–22.

Holt, A. (2010a) 'Disciplining 'problem parents' in the youth court: Between regula-tion and resistance', *Social Policy and Society*, **9**(1): 89–99.

Holt, A. (2010b) 'Managing 'spoiled identities': Parents' experiences of compulsory parenting support programmes', *Children and Society*, available online at <http://www3.interscience.wiley.com/journal/93519361/issue> [Accessed 15 January 2010].

hooks, b. (1984) *Feminist Theory: From Margin to Centre*, Boston, South End Press.

Levitas, R. (1998) *The Inclusive Society? Social Exclusion and New Labour*, Basing-stoke, Macmillan – now Palgrave Macmillan.

Lister, R. (2003) 'Investing in the citizen-workers of the future: Transformations in citizenship and the state under New Labour', *Social Policy and Administration*, **37**(5): 427–43.

Longstaff, E. (2004) Good Enough Parenting? Youth Crime and Parental Responsibility, unpublished PhD thesis, University of Cambridge, Cambridge.

Lloyd, N., O'Brien, M. and Lewis, C. (2003) *Fathers in Sure Start: The National Evaluation of Sure Start*, Birkbeck College, London.

McCaslin, M. and Infanti, H. (1998) 'The generativity crisis and the "scold war": What about those parents?', *Teachers College Record*, **100**(2): 282–4.

Nolan, J.L. (1998) *The Therapeutic State: Justifying Government at Century's End*, New York, New York University Press.

Overall, C. (1987) *Ethics and Human Reproduction: A Feminist Analysis*, Boston, Unwin Hyman.

Parton, N. (2006) '*Every Child Matters*: The shift to prevention whilst strengthening protection in children's services in England', *Children and Youth Services Review*, **28**(8): 976–92.

Pithouse, A. (2008) 'Early intervention in the round: A great idea but …', *British Journal of Social Work*, **38**(8): 1536–52.

Pitts, J. (2008) *Reluctant Gangsters: The Changing Face of Youth Crime*, Cullompton, Willan.

Polsky, A. (1991) *The Rise of the Therapeutic State*, Princeton, Princeton University Press.

Power, A. and Willmott, H. (2005) 'Bringing up families in poor neighbourhoods under New Labour', in J. Hills and K. Stewart (eds) *A More Equal Society? New Labour, Poverty, Inequality and Exclusion*, Bristol, Policy Press, pp. 277–96.

Reece, H. (2009) 'The degradation of parental responsibility', in R. Probert, S. Gilmore and J. Herring (eds) *Responsible Parents and Parental Responsibility*, Oxford, Hart, pp. 85–102.

Rich, A. (1976) *Of Woman Born: Motherhood as Experience and Institution*, New York, WW Norton.

Rose, N. (1989) *Governing the Soul*, London, Routledge.

Rutter, M. (2006) 'Is Sure Start an effective preventive intervention?', *Child and Adolescent Mental Health*, **11**(3): 135–41.

Scottish Parliament (2008) *Written Answers S3W-15964*, 10 September, available online at <http://www.scottish.parliament.uk/business/pqa/wa-08/wa0910.htm#14> [Accessed 16 October 2008].

Sure Starts (2002) *Sure Start: A Guide for Sixth Wave Programmes*, London, DfES Sure Start Unit.

Walters, R. and Woodward, R. (2007) 'Punishing "poor parents": "Respect", "responsibility" and parenting orders in Scotland', *Youth Justice*, **7**(1): 5–20.

14

Forest School

Tracy Kelly-Freer

Borradaile (2006, p. 16) describes Forest School as a

> useful tool that can be used to achieve many outcomes, relating to inclusive lifelong learning – knowledge and understanding, skills, and values and dispositions – in a different, stimulating, enjoyable, healthy and experiential way. The secret of its success is in the synergy between the physical woodland setting and the presentation and ethos behind the activities – the sum is more than the parts.

In this chapter I examine the extent to which Forest School contests or reproduces dominant constructions of learning and of childhood within the UK. My interest in Forest School has grown out of research into classroom practice and use of the outdoor learning environment in my role as a senior lecturer in education.

The origins and appropriation of Forest School within a UK context

The mid-1990s was a time of change in the educational domain in England: the impetus for change at this time can be partially attributed to the failure of the standards agenda in relation to numeracy and literacy (Brehony, 2005). As I discuss below, this was also an era when governments increasingly used schools as a focus for a range of other health and welfare policies. Ideas and models from around the world were imported into the UK. In this context, the development of Forest School began in England, based on the long established Scandinavian model that considers children's contact with nature to be extremely important, focuses on teaching children about the natural world, and views children as resilient and capable agents of their own learning. The concept was originally imported by nursery nursing students from Bridgwater College in Somerset following a visit to Denmark (Murray, 2004).

Currently across the UK, Forest School is used extensively with early years education and is expanding to include other groups, including adults with health problems, disaffected youths, parents and families. Forest School is becoming widespread and widely accepted: for example, there are 330 active Forest Schools in Hereford and Worcestershire, and in Oxfordshire it is a stipulation for new nurseries that they are located within 15 minutes' drive of a Forest School (Borradaile, 2006). Forest School Wales, Forestry Commission Wales and the Forest Education Initiative have all worked together to ensure that there are now Forest School projects within every county of Wales (Forest School Wales, 2009). In Scotland, the Forestry Commission has mapped schools within 1 kilometre of the national forest estate (Forestry Commission Scotland, 2005). This now provides a focus to help facilitate the use of the national forest resource by those identified schools and thus promotes an aim of the 'Woods for Learning' education strategy, which is to use local woods for learning.

Current societal trends and recent government initiatives have created the optimum environment for Forest School to flourish. In particular, there has been a strong emphasis on targeting childhood in pursuit of wider social and economic goals. This includes initiatives designed to ensure children leave school with specific skills and general good health suited for participation in the labour market. Investing in aspects of children's development and wellbeing is considered essential for the future development and wellbeing of society. Murray and O'Brien's (2005) evaluation of Forest School in England and Wales noted that the government has acknowledged that the reduction in the number of school trips in recent years due to concerns about safety and liability may have been detrimental to children's development. As a result, the government in England is now encouraging a greater emphasis on the use of the outdoors for learning, recognising that it brings depth to the curriculum and makes a significant contribution to physical, personal and social education (Ofsted, 2006). A decline in opportunities for children to play outside and a rise in problems such as increasingly sedentary children, obesity and diabetes and related stress have made outdoor education and experience topical issues (Brown et al., 2006). The government is targeting schools, families and children to initiate change, so the embracing of Forest School could be viewed as part of a series of developments in policy and government agendas to produce healthy citizens, such as the Healthy School Standard (promoting pupils' emotional and physical wellbeing).

Forest School also draws on some traditional views of good early childhood educational principles and more recent curriculum frameworks in England and Wales, for example Eco-schools (http://www.eco-schools.org.uk/), Manifesto for Learning Outside the Classroom (http://www.lotc.org.uk/) and the world class curriculum (Waters, 2006). Simultaneously, government policies and initiatives such as 'Excellence and Enjoyment' (DfES, 2003) require excitement and engagement in learning to raise standards. When launching its *Learning Outside the Classroom Manifesto* (DfES, 2006), the government expressed the belief that outside the classroom there is the opportunity to transform learning and raise achievement:

> Learning outside the classroom allows participants to learn in context, to learn by practical engagement, and to learn by personal discovery. They can master new skills, work collaboratively with others and develop a better sense of themselves and their potential. (DfES, 2006, p. 1)

The important role of the outdoors in learning is also recognised in the renewed Early Years Foundation Stage framework (DCSF, 2008) in England, which encourages daily purposeful outdoor activity, and in the foundation phase in Wales (Welsh Assembly Government, 2009), with its emphasis on outdoor activities promoting problem solving and learning about conservation and sustainability. In Scotland, the *Curriculum for Excellence* recognises that learning is embedded in experience. By taking learning outdoors, traditional classroom barriers between young people and first-hand, real-life experiences can be removed (Learning and Teaching Scotland, 2009). The Forest Education Initiative (www.foresteducation.org) has taken a lead in the development of Forest School in Scotland, and while delivery is mainly in primary schools, practice is spreading from nursery to adult groups.

Forest School in the UK appears to have embraced this wide range of government initiatives and policies while maintaining principles and approaches from its Scandinavian origins. There are also similarities between Forest School and other movements promoting outdoor learning such as the Scouts, Woodcraft Folk and the Forest Education Initiative. All advocate learning by doing, giving children responsibility, teamwork, taking acceptable risks and thinking for themselves. The Forest Education Initiative, like Forest School, also promotes the environmental, social and economic potential of trees, woodlands and forests. However, there are key differences, not least that Forest School takes place in the context of regular and prolonged contact for the children over a significant period of time, including all year round and in all weathers, within the school day.

Forest School is also linked to a set of aims and a value base that move beyond and reconstruct more traditional school-based pedagogy and interrelationships. Because adult–child relationships within Forest School are underpinned by the principles of mutual respect and shared agency, it allows for increased autonomy and initiation by children. There is an emphasis on sustained thinking with children, and their interests are closely monitored through observation. This is less about surveillance of behaviour than an opportunity for gathering ideas to inform general planning and the development of personalised learning opportunities. The sustained experience within the woodland setting, facilitated by a high ratio of adults to pupils, also opens up new possibilities for free play and the management of risk-taking. In the Forest School setting, children have opportunities to develop physical skills as they demonstrate the readiness and need to do so. These skills include those often considered too risky for young children in other contexts: sawing, drilling, fire-making, use of axes and knives, and tree-climbing. These activities challenge the current risk-averse attitudes to childhood, which hold sway in mainstream education and public opinion – they are a challenge to the current constructs of childhood in the UK. Forest School also aims to offer 'children, young people and adult's regular opportunities to achieve, and develop confidence and self-esteem through hands-on learning experiences' (Murray and O'Brien, 2005, p. 4). These, in turn, are designed to help those participating to develop awareness of their own and others feelings, sometimes described as 'emotional intelligence'.

Evaluating Forest School

Murray and O'Brien's (2005, p. 46) evaluation of Forest School in England and Wales suggested that:

> Forest School benefits many children and should be used on a wider basis as a vital part of children's outdoor learning experience, and to provide many more children with the opportunity to experience this as part of their overall education.

As I have outlined, the Forest School philosophy seeks to promote a range of benefits to children and society more generally. Although some of the wider social and health benefits are difficult to measure, some small-scale evaluations indicate that Forest Schools are having some success in changing behaviour and increasing opportunities for children and their families.

Several evaluations (Maynard, 2003; Murray, 2004; Murray and O'Brien, 2005; Massey, 2005; Borradaile, 2006) identify a range of principal benefits for children, including:

- increased self-esteem and self-confidence
- improved social skills
- the development of language and communication skills
- improved physical motor skills
- improved motivation and concentration
- increased knowledge and understanding of the environment
- raised levels of physical activity, observational skills and the use of imagination.

These authors concur that Forest School also enables children to discover their abilities without fear of failure or criticism. Maynard (2003) found that the children's expressive language skills increased and self-esteem and self-worth were raised. The research also highlights the correlation between self-esteem and academic achievement. Massey (2005) found that all the children show increased confidence and independence with the activities and in the care of the natural environment, leading to a sense of success and raised self-esteem.

Davis et al. (2006) reported that when parents were asked about how boisterous, confident or shy their children were before and after Forest School, in the majority of cases, the children were perceived to have moved towards becoming more confident. In the same study, children reported enjoying making dens, playing hide and seek games and cooking on an open fire. Massey (2005) recorded that parents expressed their wonder at the increased confidence and independence their children showed after Forest School. There is also evidence of the benefits of Forest School for children with additional needs. This has often been reported informally and was recorded by Maynard (2003): for example a child with Attention Deficit Hyperactivity Disorder who needed a full-time carer in the classroom found his energies were channelled in Forest School. He showed that he could be a successful team member, he made friends and gained respect from his peers.

These gains potentially can be transferred to other areas of children's lives as well as to their families and the communities in which they live. Evaluation of Forest School in Scotland (Borradaile, 2006) found that there were demonstrable and multiple impacts in terms of children's learning in the areas of personal, social and health education, including relationships with the natural world, sustainability, children's health and attitude to learning, lifestyle choices, and activity in the outdoors, their creativity and enterprise. Brown et al. (2006) cited most parents as expressing gratitude that their children got the opportunity to play outdoors at school because many of them had no access to a garden at home. All the parents felt that the Forest School experience would change the nature of their trips out in future, allowing their children more freedom. There is also evidence showing that following Forest School experiences, parents and children began to use the outdoor environment more frequently beyond school (Borradaile, 2006). It has also been suggested from the Scottish research that 'Forest School provides an excellent opportunity to pool resources and expertise across all Scottish Executive departments, agencies, and initiatives benefiting from the investment' (Borradaile, 2006, p. 42); for example those related to health, outdoor education, enterprise and lifelong learning, rural affairs, forestry and sustainable development (Borradaile, 2006).

Education, pedagogy and the construction of the child as an active learner

There are synergies between Forest School and early years education and the Early Years Foundation Stage (birth to five in England, birth to seven in Wales, three to five in Scotland). The early years tradition in England draws on theories proposed by pioneers such as Rousseau, Froebel, Montessori and Dewey, safeguarding the centrality of 'child-centred', progressive education, which views the child as intrinsically curious and capable. This approach also values free play and first-hand learning, which stem from individual children's interests and is not contained by subject boundaries, and views the teacher as a guide and facilitator (Bruce, 2005; Moyles, 2005; Maynard, 2007). Forest School pedagogy is also influenced by ideas on child-centred learning, behaviourism and emotional intelligence (Bronfenbrenner, 1979; Skinner, 1953; Weare, 2000), and the models of guided participation and communities of practice offered by Rogoff (1990) and Wenger (1998).

Rogoff (1990) describes child cognitive development from a social cultural perspective. Development is viewed as an apprenticeship: a guided participation in social activity with support from carers in developing children's understanding of and skills in using the tools of culture. For Rogoff (1990), guided participation means a collaborative process between children and carers to reach new understandings and learn new skills, with dynamic shifts in the development of children's responsibility. Wenger's theory of learning (1998) assumes that engagement in social practice is the fundamental process of self-discovery. This process is the informal 'communities of practice' that individuals develop as they work together over time. The theory explores the connection between issues of community, social practice, meaning and identity in a framework for considering learning as a process of social participation (Wenger, 1998).

Although it should be acknowledged that the dominant discourse in English primary education is in a state of flux, at the time of writing a new curriculum appears to be emerging, which claims to put skills for life at the centre of teaching and learning and moves away from the content-driven model of the national curriculum (Rose, 2009). The alternative to classroom-based, curriculum-led teaching that Forest School offers is a holistic approach to learning with a strong active child at its centre. Forest School celebrates the child as an active agent, eager to learn, actively constructing their own social world and their place in it. Forest School challenges the dominant discourse with a different philosophy regarding learner dependence, learning environments, safety and risk-taking, and models of teaching and learning that currently define practice in the (UK) education system as a whole.

Thus, based on mutual respect and respect for the environment, Forest School has firmly embedded emotional intelligence, self-esteem and child-led learning in its practice. Forest School pedagogy is explicit in expecting practitioners to actively, consciously and deliberately promote self-esteem, to be flexible, fair, definite, clear, consistent, sincere, kind, respectful and attentive. Emotional intelligence is a fundamental part of the Forest School leader's training as it is closely related to self-esteem and notions of the 'ideal self'. Weare (2004) defined emotional intelligence as the ability to understand, express and manage our own emotions and to be sensitive to those of others. The explicit acknowledgement of these fundamental features of human interaction makes Forest School unique in its chosen starting point for interaction with learners. The acknowledgement of the importance of emotional intelligence contributes to the redefinition of the teaching and learning relationship in Forest School. While this could be perceived as an additional pressure, the contribution it makes to improved relationships is valued by all those concerned.

Borradaile's (2006) study observed the conflict between the dominant educational discourse and that of Forest School. Forest School training highlights the need for a positive response to behaviour for leaders. Forest School can present a challenge to accepted practices in mainstream teaching and to the notion of instructors in outdoor education. Murray and O'Brien (2005) identified new perspectives for teachers as an important outcome of Forest School activity, for example child-led learning and minimal restrictions on children's choice of activity. Practitioners are expected to build trusting relationships with the children and to establish a better understanding of each individual child's particular learning style by working in small groups in the outdoor setting weekly over the entire school year. Forest School provides an opportunity for understanding the children more holistically. Teachers reported feeling honoured to have shared the Forest School experience with children (Murray and O'Brien, 2005). Brown et al. (2006) reported teachers embracing their role on the periphery of the children's activities, lending themselves to role play and extending, rather than leading, what the children are doing.

In Forest School, close observation is used to establish children's interests and to inform planning and resourcing for the next session. The children lead their own learning at their own pace, they are encouraged to reflect upon their performance and determine their own goals. Practitioners act as a resource bank for the children to draw upon, which results in child-led learning, rather than adult-directed, curriculum-based teaching. This established model of working in Forest School is becoming more widely evident in mainstream education, with the introduction of the new Early Years Foundation Stage documents (DCSF, 2008), and the world class curriculum (Waters, 2006), which also embrace these principles.

Reconstructing risk and childhood through Forest Schools?

As I have discussed, Forest School has its own distinct set of principles and aims and therefore the potential to reconstruct traditional aspects of educational pedagogy and the curriculum. There is also some evidence to suggest that Forest Schools are able to address and produce favourable outcomes in line with government health initiatives and social policies. In this section I consider the extent to which Forest School is related to the conceptualisation of childhood as socially constructed. Childhood can be viewed as a social construct in which societies describe their own versions of desirable and appropriate attributes, which vary with time and place (Corsaro, 2005). The new sociology of childhood (Prout and James, 1997; Fureudi, 2002; Louv, 2006) has helped identify how the dominant contemporary construction of childhood often sees children as vulnerable, passive learners and in need of adult protection/guidance. A key question to be answered is the extent to which the Forest School principles and activities reproduce or contest this dominant construction.

Cunningham (2006) noted that in British society we have become so fixated on creating long and happy childhoods that we underestimate children's abilities and resilience. Gill (2007) went on to argue that childhood itself is being undermined by adult and societal risk aversion. The claim that children are growing up faster in today's society is not new (Hillman et al., 1993) and yet current statistics show that their independence and freedom continue to be reduced (National Office for Statistics, 2010).

Constructing childhood as a time of dependency and passivity means that we view children as especially in need of protection. Here I consider the extent to which Forest School – with its emphasis on children being in a risky, natural environment – challenges this construction. The perception of risk and the associated feelings are significant influences on what children are encouraged to do and what they are prevented from trying to do in school and in wider society (Brown et al., 2006). Decreasing public spaces for play and a growing culture of fear have contributed to reduced outdoor experiences for children, leading to a consequent reduction in development of their confidence, decision making and independence (Lindon, 1999). Lindon (1999) also suggested that the objective of childhood is to emerge as a confident and capable adults and our responsibility as adults is to assist children to identify risk levels and deal effectively with dangers.

Forest School makes a positive case for engaging in managed risk with children. Children are involved in the process of assessing risk within the forest environment – this raised awareness of potential risks is combined with an understanding of how to manage, overcome or avoid the risks. As the children become part of this process, their ability to manage risk safely increases and equips them with transferable skills for other situations. A similar argument underpins other educational training, for example cycling proficiency and road safety awareness (Gill, 2007). It is also argued elsewhere that children's outdoor play will always involve risks but these are outweighed by health and developmental benefits (Lindon, 1999; Jones, 2007).

Gill's (2007) thoughts on risk aversion include a consideration of attitudes to children's playgrounds. Despite systematic research demonstrating comparatively low levels of injuries related to playground equipment (Ball, 1988, 2002, cited in Gill, 2007), safety surfaces and a restricted range of approved equipment are now omnipresent in our playgrounds. These changes often render the play space less useful, engaging or challenging for their intended users – children. Here the risk aversion of the authorities conflicts with the children's own agency, restricting opportunities for children to learn to manage their own safety. Such measures confirm that the view of children as incapable of learning to look after themselves or manage their own safety remains dominant. By contrast, in Forest School, children are engaged in the risk assessment process and learn to undertake it themselves. Decisions related to safety are not simply imposed on children by adults but rather considered in partnership between adult and child. Forest School practitioners have emphasised the necessity and importance of challenge and exploratory learning in order to enable children to become risk aware and competent (Brown et al., 2006).

Final thoughts

In presenting an overview of Forest School, I have discussed how its values and aims involve a reconstruction of more traditional educational practices and how these have been widely welcomed by children, parents, policy makers and practitioners. Forest School constructs children as active agents who, through inter-relationships with adults, manage aspects of their own learning, including the risks associated with outdoor activity. This suggests a departure from the dominant construction of children as passive and vulnerable and, potentially, offers itself as an alternative to the risk-averse attitudes and practices of adults. However, it is also evident that some of the Forest School outcomes are complementary to state policies associated with improving the health and wellbeing of the nation. This represents a continuity of another construction of childhood as 'the future'. In this construction, the emphasis is placed more on children as an asset for future collective wellbeing than on their present individual desires and wants. This might, for example, explain why Forest School is becoming more widely evident in mainstream provision. There is some evidence that children themselves benefit from and enjoy Forest Schools, although more research with children is needed, particularly to ascertain the extent to which Forest School is experienced as a departure from more traditional models of learning.

References

Borradaile, L. (2006) *Forest School Scotland: An Evaluation*, Edinburgh, Forestry Commission Scotland, available online at <http://www.forestresearch.gov.uk/pdf/ForestSchoolfinalreport.pdf/$FILE/ForestSchoolfinalreport.pdf> [Accessed 1 September 2009].

Brehony, K.J. (2005) 'Primary schooling under New Labour: The irresolvable contradiction of excellence and enjoyment', *Oxford Review of Education*, **3**(1): 29–46.

Bronfenbrenner, U. (1979) *The Ecology of Human Development: Experiments by Nature and Design*, Cambridge, MA, Harvard University Press.

Brown, K., Davis, B. and Waite, S. (2006) *Five Stories of Outdoor Learning from Settings for 2-11 Year Olds in Devon*, available online at <http://www.edu.plymouth.ac.uk/oelresnet/documents/Structure%20for%20case%20study%20report31.7.doc> [Accessed 21 November 2009].

Bruce, T. (2005) *Early Childhood Education*, London, Hodder Arnold.

Corsaro, W. (2005) *The Sociology of Childhood*, London, Sage.

Cunningham, H. (2006) *The Invention of Childhood*, London, BBC Books.

Davis, B. and Waite, S. (2005) *Forest School: Opportunities and Challenges in Early Years*, University of Plymouth, available online at <http://www.edu.plymouth.ac.uk/oelresnet/documents/Forestschoofinalreport2.doc?page=17736> [Accessed 17 November 2009].

Davis, B., Rea, T. and Waite, S. (2006) 'The special nature of the outdoors: Its contribution to the education of children aged 3–11', *Australian Journal of Outdoor Education*, **10**(2): 3–12, available online at <http://www.oric.org.au/Resources/AJOE_22.html> [Accessed 1 September 2009].

DCSF (Department for Children, Schools and Families) (2008) *The Early Years Foundation Stage (EYFS) Pack May 2008*, London, HMSO.

DfES (Department for Education and Skills) (2003) *Every Child Matters,* available online at <http://www.dcsf.gov.uk/everychildmatters/publications/outcomescyp/> [Accessed 17 November 2009].

DfES (Department for Education and Skills) (2006) *Learning Outside the Classroom Manifesto*, London, HMSO.

Forestry Commission Scotland (2005) *Woods for Learning Education Strategy*, Scottish Executive, available online at www.forestry.gov.uk/pdf/fcfc106.pdf/$FILE/fcfc106.pdf [Accessed 17 Feb 2010].

Forest School Wales (2009) *Forest School: Ethos and History*, available online at <http://www.forestschoolwales.org.uk/ysgol-goedwigforest-school/forest-school-ethos-history/> [Accessed 17 February 2010].

Furedi, F. (2002) *Culture of Fear*, London, Cassell.

Gill, T. (2007) *No Fear: Growing Up in a Risk Averse Society*, London, Calouste Gulbenkian Foundation.

Hillman, M., Adams, J. and Whitelegg, J. (1993) *One False Move: A Study of Children's Independent Mobility*, London, Policy Studies Institute.

Jones, D. (2007) *Cotton Wool Kids: Releasing the Potential for Children to Take Risks and Innovate*, Coventry, HTI.

Learning and Teaching Scotland (2009) *Curriculum for Excellence*, available online at <http://www.ltscotland.org.uk/curriculumforexcellence/index.asp> [Accessed 5 April 2010].

Lindon, J. (1999) *Too Safe For Their Own Good?*, London, National Early Years Network.

Louv, R. (2006) *Last Child in the Woods: Saving our Children from Nature Deficit Disorder*, New York, Workman.

Massey, S. (2005) *The Benefits of Forest School Experience for Children in their Early Years*, Worcestershire LEA, available online at <http://www.worcestershire.gov.uk/cms/pdf/Worcs%20Forest%20School%20Research%20Academic%20Journal.pdf> [Accessed 12 April 2010].

Maynard, T. (2003) 'Forest School Swansea Port Talbot: An Evaluation', University of Wales Swansea, unpublished, available online at <http://www.swan.ac.uk/staff/academic/HumanSciences/maynardtrisha/> [Accessed 1 September 2009].

Maynard, T. (2007) 'Forest Schools in Great Britain: An initial exploration', *Contemporary Issues in Early Childhood*, **8**(4): 320–31, available online at <http://www.wwwords.co.uk/rss/abstract.asp?j=ciecandaid=3133> [Accessed 1 September 2009].

Moyles, J. (2005) *The Excellence of Play*, Maidenhead, McGraw-Hill.

Murray, R. (2004) *Forest Schools Project Evaluation: A Study in Wales*, London, New Economics Foundation, available online at <http://www.neweconomics.org/gen/uploads/bheolf55nxgesmexvhdh0v4529072004140937.pdf> [Accessed 1 September 2009].

Murray, R. and O'Brien, E. (2005) *Such Enthusiasm – A Joy to See: An Evaluation of Forest School in England*, Forest Research, available online at <http://www.forestresearch.gov.uk/pdf/ForestSchoolEnglandReport.pdf/$FILE/ForestSchoolEnglandReport.pdf> [Accessed 1 September 2009].

National Office for Statistics (2010) *Fall in Number of Children Injured or Killed on Roads*, available online at <http://www.statistics.gov.uk/CCI/nugget.asp?ID=2197andPos=4andColRank=2andRank=1000> [Accessed 12 April 2010].

Ofsted (2006) *Inclusion: Does it Matter Where Children are Taught?*, available online at <http://www.ofsted.gov.uk/Ofsted-home/Publications-and-research/Browse-all-by/Education/Inclusion/Special-educational-needs/Inclusion-does-it-matter-where-pupils-are-taught/(language)/eng-GB> [Accessed 12 April 2010].

Prout, A. and James, A. (1997) 'A new paradigm for the sociology of childhood? Provenance, promise and problems', in A. James and A. Prout (eds) *Constructing and Reconstructing Childhood*, Basingstoke, Falmer.

Rogoff, B. (1990) *Apprenticeship in Thinking*, Oxford, Oxford University Press.

Rose, J. (2009) *Independent Review of the Primary Curriculum*, London, DCSF.

Skinner, B.F. (1953) *Science and Human Behaviour*, New York, Simon & Schuster.

Waters, M. (2006) '*Towards a World Class Primary Curriculum*', available online at <http://www.devon.gov.uk/daph-mick-waters.pdf> [Accessed 2 November 2009].

Weare, K. (2000) *Promoting Mental, Emotional and Social Health: A Whole School Approach*, London, Routledge.

Weare, K. (2004) *Developing the Emotionally Literate School*, London, Paul Chapman.

Welsh Assembly Government (2009) *Foundation Phase Outdoor Learning Experiences 2009*, available online at <http://wales.gov.uk/docs/dcells/publications/090916foundationolereporten.pdf> [Accessed 5 April 2010].

Wenger, E. (1998) *Communities of Practice: Learning, Meaning and Identity*, Cambridge, Cambridge University Press.

Index